AOP in .NET

AOP in .NET

PRACTICAL ASPECT-ORIENTED PROGRAMMING

MATTHEW D. GROVES

MANNING
SHELTER ISLAND

Manning Publications Co.　　　　Development editors: Frank Pohlmann, Cynthia Kane
20 Baldwin Road　　　　　　　　Technical proofreader: Javier Lozano
PO Box 261　　　　　　　　　　　　　　Copyeditor: Nancy Kotary
Shelter Island, NY 11964　　　　　　　　Proofreader: Elizabeth Martin
　　　　　　　　　　　　　　　　　Typesetter: Dottie Marsico
　　　　　　　　　　　　　Cover designer: Marija Tudor

ISBN 9781617291142
Printed in the United States of America
1 2 3 4 5 6 7 8 9 10 – MAL – 18 17 16 15 14 13

To my children Matthew and Emma

I will never grow tired of your yelling, "Daddy, Daddy!"
and tackling me when you hear the creak of my office door.

brief contents

contents

foreword

Like many great advances in our industry, the explicit concept of aspect-oriented programming (AOP) was developed at what is now known as PARC, a Xerox Company. Soon after, in 2001, the AspectJ extensions brought AOP to Java. Aspects have enjoyed a long history in the Java community, but for many .NET developers, aspects are still considered new and exotic. Even so, many .NET developers have been using them without knowing it.

Aspects provide a means of separating cross-cutting concerns from your core implementation code into separate modules. Rather than having every method contain logging code, for example, a logging aspect can be applied to methods external to the method implementation. It's a powerful technique to help employ the principle of separation of concerns within code.

In *AOP in .NET*, Matthew D. Groves deftly shines a light on the many ways developers can take advantage of aspects in .NET. He begins with an approachable introduction to AOP and builds on that with an example of an application written without aspects, which is then cleaned up with aspects. Subsequent chapters dig deeper into the various types of aspects and how to apply them using PostSharp and Castle DynamicProxy.

Each chapter builds on the previous one in a distinct, understandable style, each with sample code that clarifies the concepts covered in the chapter. Great care was obviously put into the code samples.

One example in particular shows how aspects are not limited to intermediate language (IL) rewriting and method interception. He challenges this implicit assumption by showing an aspect that wraps an HTTP request boundary in ASP.NET through a custom `HttpModule` implementation. It's an example that might not, at first glance, be thought of as an aspect. But on reflection, it obviously meets the definition. Aspects are not limited to compile-time interception. This drives home the point that many developers have been using aspects of one form or another for a long time without realizing it.

One subject near and dear to me is unit testing and this book contains an entire chapter covering the implications of unit testing and how to unit test aspects. It's clear this book is not just meant to educate the reader on a subject, but to help the reader integrate the techniques and technologies with real-world practices.

AOP in .NET is a great resource for those interested in learning how aspects can help maintain separation of concerns in a code base. I encourage you to take a look.

PHIL HAACK
DEVELOPER, GITHUB

A few years ago I was working on a team of consultants embedded in an organization (that shall remain unnamed). Our job was to create a system that would help increase a key source of revenue. This organization's IT department had many problems: political, technical, organizational, and financial. As consultants, we, naturally, wanted to overhaul everything immediately to solve these problems, but the reality of consulting is that we had to take very slow, very small steps toward the goal. In the meantime, we had to work around the technical and organizational problems in order to help solve the financial ones, and that's how I first learned about aspect-oriented programming (AOP).

We were creating a website for the public to submit registration information and pay fees. One of the constraints we faced when writing this system was the enterprise database. We had to access the enterprise data via an unreliable and error-prone service that was meant to act as this organization's SOA (service-oriented architecture). There were some good ideas in this service, but the implementation was poor: sometimes as many as half the requests to this system would result in an exception, seemingly at random. After considerable testing and tinkering, we discovered that simply retrying the identical request once or twice would result in a successful request. Because of this, we didn't want to use this buggy, unproven SOA service, but at that point we didn't have a choice.

We needed to create a reliable website that would be able to function with an unreliable layer of data persistence and enterprise services. What we built was a piece of code that would begin a transaction, try a request, catch exceptions of a certain type, and retry the request until it succeeded, or roll it back if it didn't. If it didn't succeed, it would log the exception type, the exception message, and some related information about the request. With this log, we hoped to first, build evidence that we could use to prove how unreliable this SOA service was, and second, be able to match exceptions with any customer-reported technical issues. What we built was a critical transaction helper class that was used over and over every time we needed to use the SOA service.

This leads me to one of the organizational problems: the QA department was responsible for testing our application, but QA was notorious for being overworked and/or unreliable. This meant that they might not get around to reporting a bug that they found in our project until possibly two weeks later, or more. If one of us on the team accidentally forgot to use our transaction helper class when accessing the SOA service (or when someone new to the team was unaware of this helper class), then we might not find out for weeks, even if QA was (un)lucky enough to get one of the random exceptions.

I was pulling my hair out: surely there was a way to refactor this nonfunctional requirement so we didn't have to worry about forgetting it. Plus, it was getting tangled up with the rest of our code, making it harder to read and maintain.

By chance, I was attending a .NET conference in Ohio, and Michael Kramer, an acquaintance of mine, was giving an introductory talk on AOP using PostSharp. He showed basic 101-level examples, similar to the ones you'll see early in this book. The idea of being able to write a piece of code that would be in class A yet run somewhere else (say, before and after the methods in class B) was astounding to me, and I mentally checked out of the rest of the conference and immediately started thinking of ways to apply AOP to the transaction helper class problem.

Fast-forward to now, and I'm still using AOP to solve similar problems (although I left that organization and the consulting business altogether). I started speaking at software conferences about AOP, started blogging about AOP, and became something of a community advocate for AOP. I was often asked if I could recommend a book on the topic for .NET developers, and I really couldn't. I eventually decided that this book had to be written. So that's what you have here, a book on a topic about which I am very passionate—not only because it's a powerful and useful tool when used properly, but because it helped me out in a very tough situation.

acknowledgments

There are so many people who have influenced my career and experience, and thus this book. Everyone on Twitter whom I follow, everyone I've worked with, all the attendees and speakers that I meet at user groups and conferences. Even if it's a small thing like teaching me a keyboard shortcut, I owe you a debt of gratitude.

I'd like to specifically acknowledge:

Nick Chase, Frank Pohlmann, Cynthia Kane, Michael Stephens, Bert Bates, Elizabeth Martin, Mary Piergies, and everyone else at Manning. Thank you for your guidance and help, and for getting this ship into the water.

Seth Petry-Johnson, Jonathan Hammond, Jesse Riley, David Giard, Charles Husemann, Brady Gaster, Chris Farrell, Jim Christopher, Steve Horn, H. Alan Stevens, Jason Follas, Brian Watson, Richard Dudley, Jay Harris, James Bender, Steve Fischer, John Dages, Brian Prince. I could fill a book with all the great people I've met on my career's journey. If I forgot to include you, I'm sorry; I owe you lunch.

Dan Allen, for giving me my first programming job.

Michael Kramer, for that fateful day when he unwittingly unleashed AOP into my life.

Everyone I've worked with at OSU, Quick Solutions, and Telligent.

Xiaoran Wang, for the tremendous diagrams (explaining tangling, scattering, and weaving) that he was kind enough to let me use in this book.

Vince Fabro for being an inspiring, patient leader in tough times, and Jonathan Mitchem for making our time in the foxholes more educational and entertaining than I ever expected.

Jason Gilmore, for your guidance and all you do for the developer community.

Ben Maddox, whose honesty and integrity are like gold.

Mark Greenway, for being an amazingly smart and helpful guy, and naming the guy on the book cover the "Archduke of Programmerland."

Gael Fraiteur and Britt King, for working so hard on your product and for encouraging and supporting me. Donald Belcham, Dustin Davis, Joe Kuemerle, Chad England, the rest of the PostSharp MVPs, and all community advocates for aspect-oriented programming.

Craig McKeachie, for giving me really good advice.

Bill Sempf, for being an inspiration and a mentor.

Phil Haack, for being gracious enough to write the foreword, not to mention his long list of incredible contributions to the .NET community.

Jim Holmes, a selfless (albeit poorly dressed) legend who spreads joy and awesomeness wherever he treads.

Jon Plante, for playing video games with me during a terribly difficult time in my life. I have been, and always shall be, your friend.

Javier Lozano, for his careful technical review of the final manuscript and source code shortly before the start of production.

My reviewers, who read the manuscript several times during its development and provided invaluable feedback: Aaron Colcord, Heather Campbell, Jeremy Baker, Jonathan Clark, Koen Handekyn, Maarten Balliauw, Margriet Bruggeman, Mark Bellhouse, Mark Greenway, Mick Wilson, Nikander Bruggeman, Paul Stack, Phil Haack, Pim Van Oerle, Stuart Grassie, and Toby Moore.

My entire family, specifically, my parents Kevin and Mary, for always encouraging me, even when my greatest aspiration as a seven-year-old was to be a garbage collector (ironic, considering that I now write managed code). If you don't make it through the first chapter without being bored to tears, I completely understand, and I love you anyway. And Dad, thanks for teaching me BASIC on a TRS-80 all those years ago.

And of course, my wife Ali, who encourages me, puts my needs above her own, and has given me the gifts that keep on giving: our children. I love you.

about this book

Aspect-oriented programming (AOP) is a concept that is too often surrounded by dense language and academic terminology, which can make it difficult for a working developer—who is already short on time and struggling to meet deadlines—to understand, apply, and get value from AOP quickly. It's unfortunate, because at its core, AOP is much less difficult than it sounds and can provide immediate benefits to real-world projects.

My goal has been to write the book that I wish I had read years ago and to show that AOP is much easier done than said. To that end, this book is somewhat informal in tone and short on theory, and it contains lots of code samples, with which I hope you follow along.

As much as I want this book to take a generalized approach to AOP, in order to show you real aspects I have to use real tools. I have chosen PostSharp (specifically, the free version, PostSharp Express edition) as the primary framework that I will be using most often. Castle DynamicProxy examples are also used frequently. I also discuss some of the advanced features of the paid version of PostSharp, and other tools and frameworks will be used and discussed in the course of the book, as well as in appendix A.

Roadmap

Chapter 1 introduces AOP. It covers some of the features and terms that are used in AOP. You will also write a "Hello, World" aspect.

Chapter 2 is a complete project tutorial. You will start a new project, implement features, add cross-cutting concerns, and then refactor it using AOP.

Chapters 3, 4, and 5 cover different types of aspects in more detail, with real-world examples for each.

Chapter 6 discusses the impact that AOP has on unit testing. You'll learn how to write unit tests for aspects and write unit tests for code on which aspects are used.

Chapter 7 discusses the implementation details of how AOP tools work. You have a choice of weaving style that will dictate both the capabilities and the trade-offs involved in the two major categories of AOP tools.

Chapter 8 covers some of the architectural concerns involved in using AOP, as well as the architectural abilties that it can give you.

Chapter 9 explores what happens when you need to use multiple aspects on the same piece of code. This chapter's real-world example also provides a capstone example that shows many of the concepts from chapters 1 through 8 working in concert.

Appendix A describes the ecosystem of .NET AOP tools, including both compile-time and runtime tools. Appendix B covers NuGet basics.

Who should read this book?

This book is primarily for developers and architects looking to reduce repetition and boilerplate in their projects. Generally speaking, the type of developer who will get the most out of this book is a developer faced with large projects that can have a lot of repetition and boilerplate. Small or tiny projects can still benefit from AOP—just not as much.

This book assumes that you have a working knowledge of C# and .NET. I also assume some familiarity with design patterns, architecture, and inversion of control. The nature of cross-cutting concerns means that AOP is involved with multiple areas of focus, including UI, databases, caching tools, threading frameworks, and so on. When possible, I try to give as much context as I reasonably can without going too far into a rabbit-hole of subject matter that has been covered more completely by other books.

Code conventions and downloads

This book includes many examples involving AOP. Most often, these examples are in C#, but sometimes they use other languages such as HTML, XAML, or plain XML. Source code in listings, or in text, is in a `fixed-width font like this` to separate it from ordinary text. Whenever C# class names, method names, variables, and other elements are mentioned in text, they will also be displayed in a fixed-width font. Code annotations accompany many of the code listings, highlighting important concepts.

Some of the examples are long. Often they have been reformatted with indentation and line breaks to fit in the space allotted in this book. The full source code is available for you on GitHub (https://github.com/mgroves/AOPinNET) and from the publisher's website at www.manning.com/AOPin.NET. The instructions to use the samples in this book are mentioned briefly in the chapters, and more details about NuGet are available in appendix B.

Author Online

The purchase of *AOP in .NET* includes free access to a private web forum run by Manning Publications where you can make comments about the book, ask technical questions, and receive help from the author and other users. To access the forum and subscribe to it, visit http://manning.com/AOPin.NET. This page provides information on how to get on the forum once you are registered, what kind of help is available, and the rules of conduct on the forum.

Manning's commitment to our readers is to provide a venue where a meaningful dialogue between individual readers and between readers and the author can take place. It is not a commitment to any specific amount of participation on the part of the author, whose contribution to the forum remains voluntary (and unpaid). Let your voice be heard, and keep the author on his toes!

The Author Online forum and the archives of previous discussions will be accessible from the publisher's website as long as the book is in print.

About the author

MATTHEW D. GROVES is a guy who loves to code. It doesn't matter if it's "enterprisey" C# apps, cool jQuery stuff, contributing to OSS, or rolling up his sleeves to dig into some PHP. He has been coding professionally ever since he wrote a QuickBASIC point-of-sale app for his parents' pizza shop back in the 1990s. He currently works from home in Columbus, Ohio, on the Telligent product team. He loves spending time with his wife and two children, watching the Cincinnati Reds, and getting involved in the developer community. He also teaches at Capital University in Columbus, Ohio.

You can find Matthew's blog at http://crosscuttingconcerns.com. Trade insults, horse jokes, and funny cat pictures with him on Twitter at http://twitter.com/mgroves.

About the cover illustration

The figure on the cover of *AOP in .NET* is captioned a "Farmer from Kastela, Dalmatia, Croatia." The illustration is taken from the reproduction published in 2006 of a 19th-century collection of costumes and ethnographic descriptions entitled *Dalmatia* by Professor Frane Carrara (1812-1854), an archaeologist and historian, and the first director of the Museum of Antiquity in Split, Croatia. The illustrations were obtained from a helpful librarian at the Ethnographic Museum (formerly the Museum of Antiquity), itself situated in the Roman core of the medieval center of Split: the ruins of Emperor Diocletian's retirement palace from around AD 304. The book includes finely colored illustrations of figures from different regions of Croatia, accompanied by descriptions of the costumes and of everyday life.

Once an ancient Greek port, a stopover point for Roman soldiers and a summer place for Croatian kings, Kastela is today a popular tourist resort on the Adriatic coast. Along its long sandy beaches there are terraces and lookouts, tennis courts and other sports grounds, and hotels and villas, surrounded by the lush greenery of pine and tamaris trees. The man on the cover, clearly a prosperous farmer from the region, is wearing black woolen trousers and a red vest over a white linen shirt. On his shoulders is a fur cape, and a red belt, red cap, and red socks complete the outfit; in his hand he holds a satchel. The rich and colorful embroidery on his costume is typical for this region of Croatia.

Dress codes have changed since the 19th century and the diversity by region, so rich at the time, has faded away. It is now hard to tell apart the inhabitants of different continents, let alone different towns or regions. Perhaps we have traded cultural diversity for a more varied personal life—certainly for a more varied and fast-paced technological life.

At a time when it is hard to tell one computer book from another, Manning celebrates the inventiveness and initiative of the computer business with book covers based on the rich diversity of regional life of two centuries ago, brought back to life by illustrations from collections such as this one.

Part 1

Getting started with AOP

Aspect-oriented programming sounds complicated, but it really isn't. It helps you spend less time copying and pasting the same boilerplate code, reducing repetition, and gives you more time to add value to your project.

Chapter 1 introduces you to AOP, its history and what problems it was created to solve. You'll write a "Hello, World" aspect using PostSharp as your first project.

Chapter 2 is a crash course in using AOP. You'll code the business logic for Acme Car Rental Company, add cross-cutting concerns without AOP, and then explore refactoring it to use AOP.

Introducing AOP

This chapter covers

- A brief history of AOP
- What problems AOP was created to solve
- Writing a very simple aspect using PostSharp

In this first chapter, I'll start in an obvious place—introducing you to aspect-oriented programming (AOP), where it came from, and what problems it'll help you solve.

We'll look at several tools as you progress through this book, but I will focus on PostSharp and Castle DynamicProxy. These aren't the only tools available to .NET developers, but they're popular ones that have stood the test of time. The concepts and code you use in this book should still be applicable if you use a different tool (see appendix A for notes on the ecosystem of AOP tools in .NET).

We'll use PostSharp in this chapter, but before you start typing out real code, we'll look at features central to the software concept of AOP itself. I'll talk about cross-cutting concerns, what a nonfunctional requirement is (and contrast it with a functional requirement), and what nonfunctional requirements have to do with AOP.

Finally, I'll walk you through a basic "Hello, World!" example using AOP in .NET. I'll break apart that example, identifying the individual puzzle pieces and explaining how they fit together into something called an aspect.

1.1   *What is AOP?*

AOP is a relatively young concept in computer science. Like many advancements in modern computing—including the mouse, IPV6, the graphical user interface (GUI), and Ethernet—AOP was created at Xerox PARC (now known as PARC, a Xerox company).

Gregor Kiczales lead a team of researchers who first described AOP in 1997. He and his team were concerned about the use of repetition and boilerplate that were often necessary and costly in large object-oriented code bases. Common examples of such boilerplate can be seen with logging, caching, and transacting.

In the resulting research paper, "Aspect-Oriented Programming," Kiczales and his team describe problems that object-oriented programming (OOP) techniques were unable to capture and solve in a clear way. What they observed was that these cross-cutting concerns ended up scattered throughout the code. This tangled code becomes increasingly difficult to develop and modify. They analyzed all of the technical reasons why this tangling pattern occurs and why it's difficult to avoid, even with the proper use of design patterns.

The paper describes a solution that is complementary to OOP—that is, "aspects" that encapsulate the cross-cutting concerns and allow them to be reused. It suggests several implementations of this solution, which ultimately led to the creation of AspectJ, the leading AOP tool still in use today (for Java).

One of my goals with this book is to avoid some of the complex language and academic terminology associated with AOP. If you're interested in diving deeper into the complex research, the "Aspect-Oriented Programming" white paper (http://mng.bz/xWIb) is definitely worth a read.

I don't want to give you the idea that using AOP is more complicated than it really is. Instead, I want to focus on solving problems in your .NET projects with AOP. Next, we'll go through the main features of AOP that were outlined in the original paper, but I'll try to avoid a dense academic approach.

1.1.1   *Features*

Like many developer tools and software concepts, AOP has unique terms and wording to describe its features, the individual pieces that are put together to make the complete picture.

This is usually the part of AOP that makes people's eyes glaze over and suddenly remember that hilarious YouTube cat video they've been meaning to watch (again). But hang in there, and I'll do my best to make these terms approachable. I'm not going to cover every detail of the exact terminology; I want to keep things simple and practical for now.

AOP'S PURPOSE: CROSS-CUTTING CONCERNS

One of the main drivers leading to the invention of AOP was the presence of cross-cutting concerns in OOP. Cross-cutting concerns are pieces of functionality that are used across multiple parts of a system. They cut across, as opposed to standing alone.

This term is perhaps the softest in AOP terminology because it's more of an architectural concept than a technical one. Cross-cutting concerns and nonfunctional requirements have a lot of overlap: a nonfunctional requirement will often cut across many parts of your application.

Logging is a common example. Logging could be used in the user interface (UI) layer, the business logic, the persistence layer, and so on. Even within an individual layer, logging could be used across many classes and services, crossing all the normal boundaries.

> **Functional and nonfunctional requirements**
>
> Functional requirements are the value-adding requirements of your project—the business logic, the UI, the persistence (database).
>
> Nonfunctional requirements are secondary, yet essential elements of a project. Examples include logging, security, performance, and data transactions.

Cross-cutting concerns exist regardless of whether you use AOP. Consider a method that does X. If you want to perform logging (C), then the method has to perform X and C. If you need logging for methods Y and Z, you'd have to put C into each of those methods, too. C is the cross-cutting concern.

Although cross-cutting concern is a conceptual term that's defined by a sentence or two, the *advice* is the concrete code that does the work.

AN ASPECT'S JOB: THE ADVICE

The advice is the code that performs the cross-cutting concern. For a cross-cutting concern such as logging, the code could be a call to the log4net library or NLog. It could be a simple one-line statement—such as `Log.Write ("information")`—or a bunch of logic to examine and log arguments, timestamps, performance metrics, and so on.

Advice is the "what" of AOP. Now you need the "where."

AN ASPECT'S MAP: A POINTCUT

Pointcuts are the where. Before defining a pointcut, I need to define a *join point*. A join point is a place that can be defined between logical steps of the execution of your program. Imagine your program as a low-level flowchart, as shown in figure 1.1.

Any gap in that flowchart could be described as a join point, as in figure 1.2.

Now that you know what a join point is, I can define a *pointcut*. A pointcut is a set of join points (or an expression that describes a set of join points). An example of a join point is "before I call `svc.SaveName()`"; an example of a pointcut is "before I call any method." Pointcuts can be simple, such as "before every method in a class," or complex, such as "before every method in a class in the namespace `MyServices` except for private methods and method `DeleteName`."

Consider the snippet of pseudocode in this listing.

Listing 1.1 A simple program that calls service methods in sequence

```
nameService.SaveName();                    ◁——— nameService is of type NameService.
nameService.GetListOfNames();
addressService.SaveAddress();              ◁——— addressService is of type AddressService.
```

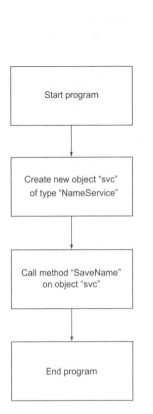

Figure 1.1   A low-level flowchart of a program that uses a single service

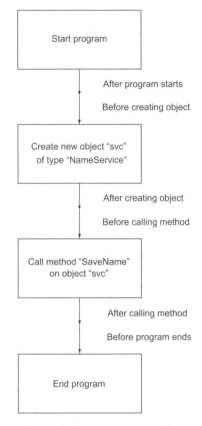

Figure 1.2   The same low-level flowchart with possible join points identified

Let's create a simple flowchart (figure 1.3) of the previous code, identifying only the exit join points in that short snippet.

Suppose I want to insert advice (some piece of code) only on the exit join points of NameService objects. My pointcut could be expressed in English as "exiting a method of NameService."

How to express that pointcut in code (if it can be expressed at all) is dependent on the AOP tool you're using. In reality, just because I can define a join point in English doesn't mean I can reach it with a tool. Some join points are far too low level and not generally practical.

Once you've identified the what (advice) and the where (join points/pointcuts), you can define an aspect. The aspect works through a process known as *weaving*.

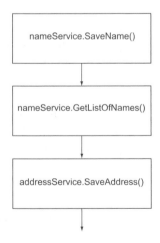

Figure 1.3   Flowchart representation—imagine exit join points after each step

HOW AOP WORKS: WEAVING

When cross-cutting concerns are coded without AOP, the code often goes inside a method, intermixed with the core logic of the method. This approach is known as *tangling*, because the core logic code and the cross-cutting concern code are tangled together (like spaghetti).

When the cross-cutting concern code is used in multiple methods and multiple classes (using copy and paste, for instance), this approach is called *scattering*, because the code gets scattered throughout your application.

In figure 1.4, the core business logic code is shown in green, and the logging code is shown in red. (In the printed book, the lighter gray in the figures represents green; the darker color represents red.) This figure represents a code base that is not using any aspects: the cross-cutting concern code is in the same classes as the core business logic.

When you refactor to use AOP, you move all the red code (advice) into a new class, and all that should remain in the original class is the green code that performs the business logic. Then you tell the AOP tool to apply the aspect (red class) to the business class (green class) by specifying a pointcut. The AOP tool performs this combinational step with a process called weaving, as shown in figure 1.5.

In the previous figure, the combined code looks like the original code, mixing green and red into one class. (This appearance is close to the truth, but in reality there may be additional work that the AOP tool inserts to do its job.) You won't see any of the combined code in your source code files. The code you do see—the classes you work with, write, and maintain—has a nice organized separation.

The way that AOP tools perform weaving differs from tool to tool. I'll talk more about this concept in chapter 7, and you can learn more details about specific AOP tools in appendix A.

```
class BusinessModule1 {                      class BusinessModule2 {
    ... core data members                        ... core data members
    ... logging members                          ... logging members


    public Method1 () {                          public Method1 () {
        ... log start                                ... log start
        ... core operation      tangling            ... core operation
        ... log end                                  ... log end

    }                                            }

                            scattering

    public Method2 () {                          public Method2 () {
        ... log start                                ... log start
        ... core operation  logging    logging      ... core operation
        ... log end                                  ... log end

    }                                            }

}                                            }
```

Figure 1.4 Tangling and scattering. In the printed volume, X represents red code and Y, the green code.

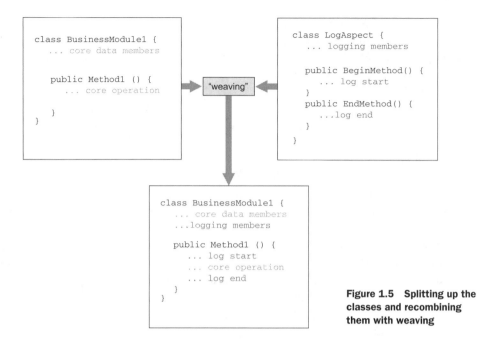

Figure 1.5   **Splitting up the classes and recombining them with weaving**

1.1.2   *Benefits*

The main benefit to using AOP is clean code that's easier to read, less prone to bugs, and easier to maintain.

Making code easier to read is important because it allows new team members to get comfortable and up to speed quickly. Additionally, your future self will thank you. Have you ever looked at a piece of code you wrote a month ago and been baffled by it? AOP allows you to move tangled code into its own classes and leave behind more declarative, clearer code.

AOP helps you make your code less expensive to maintain. Certainly, making your code more readable will make maintenance easier, but that's only part of the story. If a piece of boilerplate code that handles threading (for instance) is used and reused in your application, then any fixes or changes to that code must be made everywhere. Refactoring that code into its own encapsulated aspect makes it quicker to change all the code in one place.

CLEAN UP SPAGHETTI CODE

You may have heard the myth that if you put a frog in a pot of boiling water, it'll jump right out, but if you put the frog in a pan of cold water and slowly turn up the heat, it won't notice that it's being cooked until it's too late. Even though this is only a myth, its allegorical point rings true for many things. If you're asked to add a lot of cross-cutting concerns to an already large code base, you might balk at adding the code only one method at a time. Just like a frog thrown into a pot of boiling water, you'll jump out immediately and look for cooler water to swim in.

But when you start a new project or add features to a small project, the heat of adding cross-cutting concerns to a few places might not be so sudden.

When I add a first cross-cutting concern to my young project, it takes only a few lines and repeats only a couple of times. No big deal. I'll just copy and paste it when I need it, and I'll clean it up later.

The temptation to "just get it working" is strong. I'll literally copy and paste that code to another part of my application and make (usually minor) changes so that the pasted code works. Call it copy-and-paste programming or copy-and-paste inheritance.

This scattered or tangled code has even been classified as an antipattern. This particular antipattern has been called shotgun surgery. Code other than the main business logic gets mixed in via copy/paste over and over with other code, much like a burst from a shotgun shell spreads out all over a target. Avoiding this pattern is the point of the Single Responsibility Principle: a class should have only one reason to change. Although surgery with a shotgun may accomplish one task (like removing an appendix), it will cause many other problems. Surgery should be done with a more precise tool, such as a laser or a scalpel.

> **Antipatterns**
>
> An antipattern is a pattern that's been identified in software engineering, such as any pattern you might find in the Gang of Four *Design Patterns* book (the full title is *Design Patterns: Elements of Reusable Object-Oriented Software*, but because of its four authors, it's often called the "Gang of Four book"). Unlike those *good* patterns, an antipattern is a pattern that often leads to bugs, expensive maintenance, and headaches.

This copy-and-paste strategy may help you get something done fast, but in the long term you end up with messy, expensive spaghetti code. Hence the well-known rule of thumb: Don't Repeat Yourself (DRY).

All these things can add up to a boiled frog. I don't want you to get boiled. Instead of a tedious spiral into spaghetti code, let's move beyond copy and paste and use good design patterns.

REDUCE REPETITION

When you move beyond simple copy and paste, you start using techniques such as dependency injection and/or the decorator pattern to handle cross-cutting concerns. This is good. You're writing loosely coupled code and making things easier to test. But when it comes to cross-cutting concerns, when you're using dependency injection (DI), you may still end up with tangling/scattering. If you take it to the next level and use the decorator pattern, you may still end up with a lot of pseudocode.

Imagine that you've refactored a cross-cutting concern such as transaction management (begin/commit/rollback) to a separate service. It might look like the pseudocode in the following.

Listing 1.2   Example of refactoring using DI instead of AOP

```
public class InvoiceService {
    ITransactionManagementService _transaction;
    IInvoiceData _invoicedb;
    InvoiceService(IInvoiceData invoicedb,
        ITransactionManagementService transaction)
    {
        _invoicedb = invoicedb;
        _transaction = transaction;
    }

    void CreateInvoice(ShoppingCart cart) {
        _transaction.Start();
        _invoicedb.CreateNewInvoice();
        foreach(item in cart)
            _invoicedb.AddItem(item);
        _invoicedb.ProcessSalesTax();
        _transaction.Commit();
    }
}
```

Two services are required to instantiate this class; one of them is for a cross-cutting concern.

Even though we're using DI, the use of the dependencies is tangled.

CreateInvoice has to manage the start and end of a transaction itself and its core invoice concerns.

In this example, the InvoiceService isn't dependent on a specific transaction management service implementation. It will use whatever service is passed to it via the interface: the exact implementation is a detail left to another service. (This is a form of dependency inversion called DI). This approach is better than hard-coding transaction code into every method. But I would argue that although the transaction management code is loosely coupled, it's still tangled up with the InvoiceService code: you still have to put _transaction.Start() and _transaction.Commit() among the rest of your code. This approach also makes unit testing a little more tedious: the more dependencies, the more stubs/fakes you need to use.

If you're familiar with DI, you may also be familiar with the use of the decorator pattern. Suppose the InvoiceService class has an interface, such as IInvoiceService. We could then define a decorator to handle all the transactions. It would implement the same interface, and it would take the real InvoiceService as a dependency through its constructor, as shown next.

Listing 1.3   Use of the decorator pattern in pseudocode

```
public class TransactionDecorator : IInvoiceData {
    IInvoiceData _realService;
    ITransactionManagementService _transaction;
    public TransactionDecorator(IInvoiceData svc,
        ITransactionManagementService _trans) {
        _realService = svc;
        _transaction = trans;
    }
    public void CreateInvoice(ShoppingCart cart) {
        _transaction.Start();
        _realService.CreateInvoice(cart);
        _transaction.End();
    }
}
```

Decorator implements the same interface.

Depends on the service it's decorating

Depends on a transaction implementation

Transaction Start now lives in the decorator.

Transaction End also lives in the decorator.

The decorated method is called.

This decorator (and all the dependencies) are configured with an Inversion of Control (IoC) tool (for example, StructureMap) to be used instead of an InvoiceService instance directly. Now we're following the open/closed principle by extending InvoiceService to add transaction management without modifying the Invoice-Service class. This is a great starting point, and sometimes this approach might be sufficient for a small project to handle cross-cutting concerns.

But consider the weakness of this approach, particularly as your project grows. Cross-cutting concerns are things such as logging and transaction management that are potentially used in many different classes. With this decorator, we've cleaned up only one class: InvoiceService. If there's another class, such as SalesRepService, we need to write another decorator for it. And if there's a third class, such as PaymentService? You guessed it: another decorator class. If you have 100 service classes that all need transaction management, you need 100 decorators. Talk about repetition!

At some point between decorator 3 and decorator 100 (only you can decide how much repetition is too much), it becomes practical to ditch decorators for cross-cutting concerns and move to using a single aspect. An aspect will look similar to a decorator, but with an AOP tool it becomes more general purpose. Let's write an aspect class and use an attribute to indicate where the aspect should be used, as in the next example (which is still pseudocode).

Listing 1.4   Using AOP instead of DI for cross-cutting concerns

```
public class InvoiceService {
    IInvoiceData _invoicedb;                        Still only one service
    InvoiceService(IInvoiceData invoicedb) {        is being passed in.
        _invoicedb = invoicedb;
    }
                                                    CreateInvoice doesn't
    [TransactionAspect]                             contain any
    void CreateInvoice(ShoppingCart cart) {         transaction code.
        _invoicedb.CreateNewInvoice();
        foreach (item in cart)
        _invoicedb.AddItem(item);
    }
}

public class TransactionAspect {
    ITransactionManagementService _transaction;
    TransactionAspect(ITransactionManagementService transaction) {
        _transaction = transaction;
    }
                                                    The transaction Start
    void OnEntry() {                                is moved to OnEntry
        _transaction.Start();                       in an aspect.
    }
                                                    The transaction End
    void OnSuccess() {                              is moved to OnExit in
        _transaction.Commit();                      an aspect.

    }
}
```

Note that AOP has at no point completely replaced DI (nor should it). InvoiceService is still using DI to get the IInvoiceData instance, which is critical to performing the business logic and isn't a cross-cutting concern. But ITransactionManagementService is no longer a dependency of InvoiceService: it's been moved to an aspect. You don't have any more tangling because CreateInvoice no longer has any transaction code.

ENCAPSULATION

Instead of 100 decorators, you have only one aspect. With that one aspect, you've encapsulated the cross-cutting concern into one class.

Let's continue with the example and build out the project some more. Next is a pseudocode class that doesn't follow the Single Responsibility Principle (SRP) due to a cross-cutting concern.

Listing 1.5 Pseudocode example of an extremely simple AddressBookService

```
public class AddressBookService {
    public string GetPhoneNumber(string name) {
        if(name is null) throw new ArgumentException("name");
        var entry = PhoneNumberDatabase.GetEntryByName(name);
        return entry.PhoneNumber;
    }
}
```

This class looks easy enough to read and maintain, but it's doing two things: it's getting the phone number based on the name passed in, and it's checking to make sure that the name argument isn't invalid. Even though checking the argument for validity is related to the service method, it's still secondary functionality that could be separated and reused.

The following is what the pseudocode might look like with that concern separated using AOP.

Listing 1.6 Pseudocode example with argument checking split out using AOP

```
public class AddressBookService {
    [CheckForNullArgumentsAspect]              ◁—— Aspect is applied as an attribute.
    public string GetPhoneNumber(string name) {
        var entry = PhoneNumberDatabase.GetEntryByName(name);
        return entry.PhoneNumber;
    }
}
public class CheckForNullArgumentsAspect {     ◁—— Aspect class
    public void OnEntry(MethodInformation method)
    {
        foreach(arg in method.Arguments)
            if(arg is null) throw ArgumentException(arg.name)
    }
}
```

One new addition to this example is a MethodInformation parameter for OnEntry, which supplies some information about the method so that the arguments can be checked for nulls.

I can't overstate how trivial this example is, but with the code separated (as in the next example), the `CheckForNullArgumentsAspect` code can be reused on other methods for which you want to ensure that the arguments are valid.

Listing 1.7 Encapsulated and reusable code

```
public class AddressBookService {
    [CheckForNullArgumentAspect]
    public string GetPhoneNumber(string name) { ... }
}

public class InvoiceService {
    [CheckForNullArgumentAspect]
    public Invoice GetInvoiceByName(string name) { ... }
    [CheckForNullArgumentAspect]
    public void CreateInvoice(ShoppingCart cart) { ... }
}

public class PaymentSevice {
    [CheckForNullArgumentAspect]
    public Payment FindPaymentByInvoice(string invoiceId) { ... }
}
```

Let's look at the previous listing with maintenance in mind. If we want to change something with `Invoices`, we need to change only `InvoiceService`. If we want to change something with the null checking, we need to change only `CheckForNull-ArgumentAspect`. Each of the classes involved has only one reason to change. We're now less likely to cause a bug or a regression when making a change.

If any of this seems familiar to you, it's perhaps because you've already been using similar techniques in .NET that aren't labelled as aspects.

1.1.3 *AOP in your daily life*

"Are you telling me I could've had another acronym on my resume all this time?" As a .NET developer, you might do several common things every day that are part of AOP, such as:

- ASP.NET Forms Authentication
- An implementation of ASP.NET's `IHttpModule`
- ASP.NET MVC Authentication
- ASP.NET MVC implementations of `IActionFilter`

ASP.NET has an `IHttpModule` that you can implement and set up in web.config. When you do this, each module will run for every page request to your web application. Inside an `IHttpModule` implementation, you can define event handlers that run at the beginning or at the end of requests (`BeginRequest` and `EndRequest`, respectively). When you do this, you're creating a *boundary* aspect: code that's running at the boundaries of a page request.

If you've used out-of-the-box forms authentication, then you've already been implementing such an approach. ASP.NET Forms Authentication uses the `Forms-AuthenticationModule` behind the scenes, which is itself an implementation

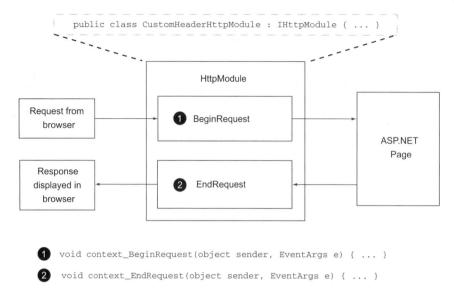

```
public class CustomHeaderHttpModule : IHttpModule { ... }
```

1 void context_BeginRequest(object sender, EventArgs e) { ... }

2 void context_EndRequest(object sender, EventArgs e) { ... }

Figure 1.6   The HttpModule lifecycle in relation to the request->ASP.NET page->response

of IHttpModule (see figure 1.6). Instead of putting code on every page to check authentication, you (wisely) use this module to encapsulate the authentication. If the authentication changes, you change only the configuration, not every single page. If you create a new page, you don't have to worry about forgetting to add authentication code to it.

The same is true for ASP.NET MVC applications. You have the ability to create Attribute classes that implement IActionFilter. These attributes can be applied to actions, and they run code before and after the action executes (OnActionExecuting and OnActionExecuted, respectively). If you use the default AccountController that comes standard with a new ASP.NET MVC project, you've probably seen the [Authorize] attribute in action. AuthorizeAttribute is a built-in implementation of an IActionFilter (figure 1.7) that handles forms authentication for you so you don't have to put authentication code in all of your controller action methods.

ASP.NET developers aren't the only ones who may have seen and used AOP without realizing it. These are examples of AOP used within the .NET framework—they don't have anything explicitly called an aspect. If you've seen these examples before, you already have an idea of how AOP can help you.

Now that you're familiar with the benefits and features of AOP, let's write some real code. Warm up Visual Studio. You're about to write your first aspect.

1.2   *Hello, World*

We'll get to more useful examples in later chapters; for now, let's get your first aspect out of the way to give you a taste of what's in store. As we write this aspect, I'll point out

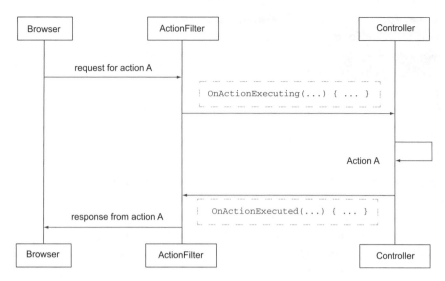

Figure 1.7   The ASP.NET MVC ActionFilter lifecycle

some of the AOP features (advice, pointcut, and so on) along the way. Don't worry if you don't fully understand what's going on yet. Follow along just to get your feet wet.

I'll be using Visual Studio and PostSharp. Both Visual Studio 2010 and Visual Studio 2012 should work fine. Visual Studio Express (which is a free download) should work, too. I'm also using NuGet, which is a great package manager tool for .NET that integrates with Visual Studio. If NuGet is not part of your arsenal, you should definitely download it from NuGet.org and install it. It will make your life as a .NET developer much easier. Appendix B outlines the basics of NuGet, but you can read more about it at NuGet.org.

Start by selecting File->New Project->Console Application. Call it whatever you want, but I'm calling mine HelloWorld. You should be looking at an empty console project such as the following:

```
class Program {
    static void Main(string[] args) {
    }
}
```

Next, install PostSharp with NuGet. NuGet can work from a PowerShell command line within Visual Studio called the Package Manager Console. To install PostSharp via the Package Manager Console, use the `Install-Package` command (it should look like the following example):

```
PM> Install-Package postsharp
Successfully installed 'PostSharp 2.1.6.17'.
Successfully added 'PostSharp 2.1.6.17' to HelloWorld.
```

Alternatively, you can do it via the Visual Studio UI by first right-clicking References in Solution Explorer, as shown in figure 1.8.

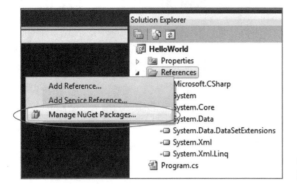

**Figure 1.8   Starting
NuGet with the UI**

Select Online, search for PostSharp, and click Install (see figure 1.9).

You may get a PostSharp message that asks you about licensing. Accept the free trial and continue, but rest assured that even when that trial expires, you'll still be able to use all the PostSharp examples in this book with the free PostSharp Express Edition (unless otherwise noted). Additionally, the Express Edition is free for commercial use, so you can use it at your job, too. (You still need a license, but it's a free license.) Now that PostSharp is installed, you can close out of the NuGet dialog. In Solution Explorer under References, you should see a new PostSharp reference added to your project.

Now you're ready to start writing your first aspect. Create a class with one simple method that writes only to `Console`. Mine looks like the following:

```
public class MyClass {
    public void MyMethod() {
        Console.WriteLine("Hello, world!");
    }
}
```

Instantiate a `MyClass` object inside the `Main` method, and call the method. The following code shows how the `Program` class should look now:

```
class Program {
    static void Main(string[] args) {
        var myObject = new MyClass();
        myObject.MyMethod();
    }
}
```

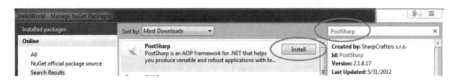

Figure 1.9   Search for PostSharp and install with NuGet UI

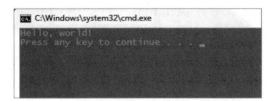

Figure 1.10 Console output of "Hello, world!"

Execute that program now (F5 or Ctrl+F5 in Visual Studio), and your output should look like figure 1.10.

We're not pushing the limits of innovation just yet, but hang in there. Before we create an aspect, let's specify what cross-cutting concern this aspect will be taking care of. Let's keep it simple and define our requirement as "log something before and after the Hello, world! message is written." We could cram an extra couple of Console.WriteLine statements into MyMethod, but instead, let's steer away from modifying MyClass and write something that can be reused with other classes.

Create a new class that inherits from OnMethodBoundaryAspect, which is a base class in the PostSharp.Aspects namespace, something like the following:

```
[Serializable]
public class MyAspect : OnMethodBoundaryAspect {

}
```

PostSharp requires aspect classes to be Serializable (because PostSharp instantiates aspects at compile time, so they can be persisted between compile time and run time. This will be covered in more detail in chapter 7).

Congratulations! You've just written an aspect, even though it doesn't do anything yet. Like the name of the base class implies, this aspect allows you to insert code on the boundaries of methods.

Remember join points? Every method has boundary join points: before the method starts, when the method ends, when the method throws an exception, and when the method ends without exception (in PostSharp, these are OnEntry, OnExit, OnException, and OnSuccess, respectively).

Let's make an aspect that inserts code before and after a method is called. Start by overriding the OnEntry method. Inside that method, write something to Console, such as the following:

```
[Serializable]
public class MyAspect : OnMethodBoundaryAspect {
    public override void OnEntry(MethodExecutionArgs args) {
        Console.WriteLine("Before the method");
    }
}
```

Notice the MethodExecutionArgs parameter. It's there to give information and context about the method being bounded. We won't use it in this simple example, but argument objects like that are almost always used in a real aspect.

Think back to the advice feature of an aspect. In this case, the advice is just one line of code: `Console.WriteLine("Before the method");`. Create another override, but this time override `OnExit`, as the following code shows:

```
[Serializable]
public class MyAspect : OnMethodBoundaryAspect {
    public override void OnEntry(MethodExecutionArgs args) {
        Console.WriteLine("Before the method");
    }
    public override void OnExit(MethodExecutionArgs args) {
        Console.WriteLine("After the method");
    }
}
```

Once again, the advice is just another `Console.WriteLine` statement.

Now you've written an aspect that will write to `Console` before and after a method. But which method? We've only partially specified the where or the pointcut. We know that the join points are *before* and *after* a method. But which method(s)?

The most basic way to tell PostSharp which method (or methods) to apply this aspect to is to use the aspect as an attribute on the method. For instance, to put it on the boundaries of the "Hello, world" method from earlier, use `MyAspect` as an attribute, as in the following example.

```
public class MyClass {
    [MyAspect]
    public void MyMethod() {
        Console.WriteLine("Hello, world!");
    }
}
```

Now, run the application again (F5 or Ctrl+F5). Right after the program is compiled, PostSharp will take over and perform the weaving. PostSharp is a *post compiler* AOP tool, so it will modify your program after it has been compiled but before it has been executed.

When your program is executed, you should see output like that in figure 1.11.

Attributes
In reality, you aren't required to put attributes on every piece of code when using PostSharp. In chapter 8, I cover the ability of PostSharp to multicast attributes. In the meantime, I'll continue to use individual attributes just to keep things simple.

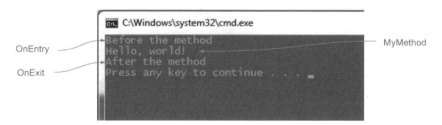

Figure 1.11 Output with `MyAspect` applied

That's it! You've now written an aspect and told PostSharp where to use it, and Post-Sharp has performed the weaving.

This example may not seem that impressive, but notice that you were able to put code around the `MyMethod` method without making any changes to `MyMethod` itself. Yeah, you did have to add that `[MyAspect]` attribute, but you'll see in later chapters more efficient and/or centralized ways of applying PostSharp aspects by multicasting attributes. Also, using attributes isn't the only way to use AOP: tools such as Castle DynamicProxy use an IoC tool, and I'll examine that tool in later chapters as well. You're well on your way to mastering AOP in .NET.

1.3 Summary

AOP isn't as complicated as it might sound. It might take some getting used to, because you may have to adjust the way you think about cross-cutting concerns. But there will be plenty more examples in this book to help you get started.

AOP is an inspiring, powerful tool that's fun to use. I'm in awe of the implementations of the various tools such as PostSharp and Castle DynamicProxy, both written by people far smarter than I. These are tools that I like and that I'll use in this book, but if you aren't totally comfortable with them, you can check out some of the other AOP tools for .NET (see appendix A).

Whatever tool you decide to use, AOP will help you do your job more effectively. You'll spend less time copying and pasting the same boilerplate code or fixing the same bug in that boilerplate 100 times. In abstract terms, this helps you adhere to the single responsibility principle and use the open/closed principle effectively, without repetition. In real-world terms, it will allow you to spend more time adding value and less time doing mindless, tedious work. It will get you to happy hour faster; whether happy hour is a literal happy hour at your local pub, or your son's baseball game, AOP is going to help you get there in a better frame of mind—and on time.

Acme Car Rental

This chapter covers

- Creating requirements for a fictional project
- Writing code from scratch to satisfy the requirements
- Taking a pass to refactor messy code, without any AOP
- Taking a different pass to refactor, this time using AOP

In this chapter, you'll be coding the business logic for a new application for the (fictional) Acme Car Rental Company. You'll be given the requirements; you can then follow along as I gradually add code to conform to those requirements.

I'll start from scratch and not use any AOP. The business requirements are the most important, so we'll do those first. Once the business logic is working, we'll add code to cover the nonfunctional requirements. Once we've fulfilled the requirements, we'll look at possible ways to clean up and refactor the code, again without using any AOP to refactor the cross-cutting concerns.

After this first pass, you'll turn to the long tail of an application's life. Software is rarely static for long: new features are requested and new bugs are discovered. A piece of software is rarely in development longer than it's in production, which means that most of the software's life is the maintenance phase. An application that's hard or expensive to maintain leads to either high costs or low quality (or both) and eventually spirals into a big ball of mud.

Then, we'll take one more pass at refactoring the code, this time with PostSharp. We'll isolate the individual cross-cutting concerns into their own classes. Once we've refactored, we'll examine some of the benefits of using AOP, particularly with regard to adding more features (such as more business logic). At the end of this chapter, you should have a good idea of how to use AOP and understand its benefits.

2.1   *Start a new project*

You're a developer/architect at Acme Car Rental, and you've recently joined a team that's starting a new project called the customer loyalty program (a.k.a. Acme Rewards). The goal of this program is to reward customers for their repeat business and, it is hoped, to increase sales. For certain rentals, the customers will get points, which can be redeemed for future rentals or other items.

We'll assume a basic three-layer application structure, as shown in figure 2.1. You will start by writing the core business logic layer which contains all of the rules that apply to the loyalty program. The persistence layer keeps track of the loyalty points. The business logic layer is used by all of the UIs available: the website, the mobile application, and the desktop programs that the clerks use (and we leave the door open to other UIs in the future).

In this chapter, we'll mainly look at the business logic (the middle layer). We can assume that the persistence logic is already done (or that the decision of which persistence technology to use is being postponed and we're instead using stubs or a transient in-memory database like SQLite for now). We'll also assume that the UI will be implemented once the business logic is in place.

I highly encourage you to follow along on your own with this chapter; the best way to learn is to work hands-on with the code yourself.

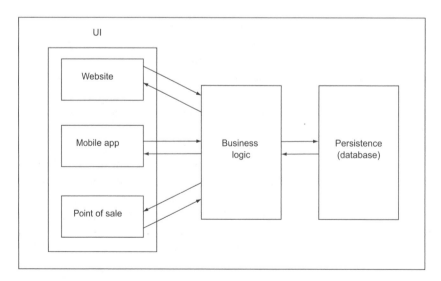

Figure 2.1   Three-layer system architecture

To follow along, you'll need the tools I mentioned in the first chapter's "Hello, World" example: Visual Studio (the free Express edition will work), NuGet, and PostSharp (installed via NuGet; again, the free Express edition will work fine). All of the code is available for download from Manning's website (http://www.manning.com/AOPin.NET) or on GitHub (my GitHub name is mgroves) if you want to follow along without all those tiresome keystrokes.

A note on tools

Any version of Visual Studio 2010 or 2012 should be sufficient to follow along. Post-Sharp has additional features to help you identify what aspects have been applied and where. Those extensions won't work with Express editions, but they aren't necessary to complete the examples in this book. Visual Studio 2008 could work, if you're determined to use it, although without NuGet it will be more difficult.

If you aren't familiar with NuGet, see appendix B. NuGet's support for Visual Studio 2010 Express editions seems to be limited to the Web Developer edition. But all Visual Studio 2012 Express editions support NuGet.

2.1.1 Business requirements

The project manager works with you and the stakeholders (such as sales and/or marketing) to identify the business requirements of the loyalty program (illustrated in figure 2.2). You've identified two main sets of requirements: accruing and redeeming rewards.

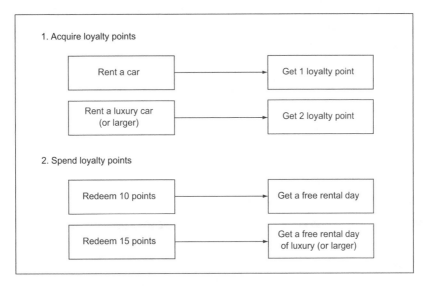

Figure 2.2 Loyalty program rules

Customers accrue at least one point for every qualifying car they rent per each day they rent it. Luxury cars and larger vehicles are worth two points per rental day. The points are added to a customer's account after he has paid and returned the rental vehicle.

Once a customer has accrued 10 points, he can start spending those points on rewards. Ten points are worth a free day of car rental and 15 points earns the customer a free day's rental of a luxury car or larger vehicle rental.

That's all the business requirements for now, but you've dealt with sales and marketing before: there's sure to be something that they'll want to change or add in the future.

2.1.2   *Necessary nonfunctional requirements*

Before you give an estimate of time and cost to your project manager, you have your own technical concerns that must be addressed.

First, you see the need for some sort of logging. Customers could get angry if their points are tallied incorrectly, so you want to make sure you have a record of everything that your business logic is doing (particularly at first).

Second, because this business code will be used by multiple UI applications (web, mobile, desktop), you want to make sure that you're careful about the data that gets passed to your code. Your team may or may not end up writing the integration code in those UIs, so you need to be sure to write defensive code that checks for edge cases and arguments that don't make sense.

Again, because this code will be used by multiple UI applications over varying types of connections (slow cell phone connections, web browsers in remote countries, and so on), you need to put in transactions and retry logic to make sure that data integrity is maintained and users have a pleasant experience.

Finally, because you can't plan for everything, and you may not even know what type of persistence is going to be used at this point, you'll need to have some way to handle exceptions (and probably log them).

2.2   *Life without AOP*

You submit your estimate to the project manager, and all the necessary approvals and paperwork have been signed. You're now ready to get started.

Let's begin. Open Visual Studio and select File->New Project. Use the Class Library template, as shown in figure 2.3. Put the project wherever you want and call the project what you wish—I'm calling it AcmeCarRental.

Delete the Class1.cs file. Now you have a blank slate.

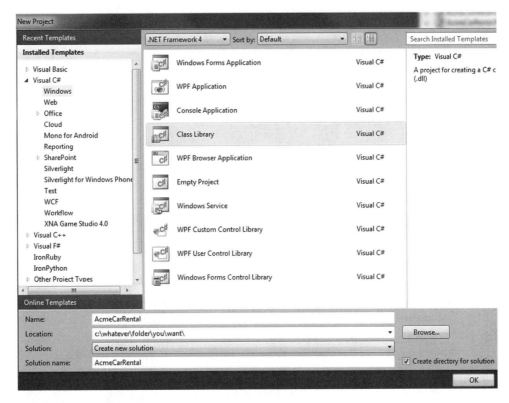

Figure 2.3   Start new project

2.2.1   *Write the business logic*

Let's start by creating an interface for accruing loyalty points. ILoyaltyAccrual-Service seems like as good as name as any.

```
public interface ILoyaltyAccrualService {
    void Accrue(RentalAgreement agreement);
}
```

The RentalAgreement is an entity that's already common to the Acme Car Rental domain, so it would likely be in a different assembly, but for demonstration purposes, we'll create one in an Entities folder.

```
public class RentalAgreement {
    public Guid Id { get; set; }
    public Customer Customer { get; set; }
    public Vehicle Vehicle { get; set; }
    public DateTime StartDate { get; set; }
    public DateTime EndDate { get; set; }
}
```

Two more entities in that RentalAgreement can be added to the Entities folder: Customer and Vehicle. There's also a Size enumeration, for convenience.

```
public class Customer {
    public Guid Id { get; set; }
    public string Name { get; set; }
    public string DriversLicense { get; set; }
    public DateTime DateOfBirth { get; set; }
    }

public class Vehicle {
    public Guid Id { get; set; }
    public string Make { get; set; }
    public string Model { get; set; }
    public Size Size { get; set; }
    public string Vin { get; set; }
    }

public enum Size {
    Compact = 0, Midsize, FullSize, Luxury, Truck, SUV
}
```

With that out of the way, let's go back and look at the ILoyaltyAccrualService interface. This interface has an Accrue method that interacts with these entities. Software at Acme will be calling the Accrue method with these entities. Let's write an implementation of the accrual service (see listing 2.1). It will depend on a data service to persist the data. The Accrue method will contain the business logic to figure out the number of days in the agreement, determine how many points each of those days are worth, and store the calculated number of total points in the database.

The ILoyaltyDataService has only two methods, AddPoints and SubtractPoints.

Listing 2.1 An implementation of the accrual service

```
public class LoyaltyAccrualService : ILoyaltyAccrualService {
    readonly ILoyaltyDataService _loyaltyDataService;

    public LoyaltyAccrualService(ILoyaltyDataService service) {
        _loyaltyDataService = service;
    }

    public void Accrue(RentalAgreement agreement) {
        var rentalTimeSpan =
            (agreement.EndDate.Subtract(agreement.StartDate));
        var numberOfDays = (int) Math.Floor(rentalTimeSpan.TotalDays);
        var pointsPerDay = 1;
        if (agreement.Vehicle.Size >= Size.Luxury)
            pointsPerDay = 2;
        var points = numberOfDays*pointsPerDay;
        _loyaltyDataService.AddPoints(agreement.Customer.Id, points);
    }
}
```

The service must be passed in to this object when the object is instantiated.

This method contains the logic and rules of the loyalty program.

Calls a persistence service method to store the accrued points

That database interface, ILoyaltyDataService, represents the data layer that will get passed in to the constructor via DI. Again, we're focused on only the business logic for now, so its implementation (FakeLoyaltyDataService) isn't going to do any database manipulation:

```
public class FakeLoyaltyDataService : ILoyaltyDataService {
    public void AddPoints(Guid customerId, int points) {
        Console.WriteLine("Adding {0} points for customer '{1}'",
            points, customerId);
    }
}
```

And you're finished with the accrual portion of the business logic. Hooray!

Now, on to what the customer cares about: redeeming loyalty points for free stuff. Let's create another interface, ILoyaltyRedemptionService:

```
public interface ILoyaltyRedemptionService {
    void Redeem(Invoice invoice, int numberOfDays);
}
```

The Invoice class also belongs in the common entities folder, and looks like the following:

```
public class Invoice {
    public Guid Id { get; set; }
    public Customer Customer { get; set; }
    public Vehicle Vehicle { get; set; }
    public decimal CostPerDay { get; set; }
    public decimal Discount { get; set; }
}
```

The Redeem implementation subtracts the points from the customer's account based on the vehicle he's getting (and the number of free days he's redeeming) and populates the discount amount in the invoice. It also uses the ILoyaltyDataService to subtract the calculated points from the database, as the following code shows:

```
public class LoyaltyRedemptionService : ILoyaltyRedemptionService {
    readonly ILoyaltyDataService _loyaltyDataService;

    public LoyaltyRedemptionService(ILoyaltyDataService service) {
        _loyaltyDataService = service;
    }

    public void Redeem(Invoice invoice, int numberOfDays) {
        var pointsPerDay = 10;
        if (invoice.Vehicle.Size >= Size.Luxury)
            pointsPerDay = 15;
        var points = numberOfDays*pointsPerDay;
        _loyaltyDataService.SubtractPoints(invoice.Customer.Id, points);
        invoice.Discount = numberOfDays*invoice.CostPerDay;
    }
}
```

The following is the fake SubtractPoints implementation, which is similar to the fake AddPoints implementation. A corresponding method signature is also added to the ILoyaltyDataService interface:

```
public void SubtractPoints(Guid customerId, int points) {
    Console.WriteLine("Subtracting {0} points for customer '{1}'",
        points, customerId);
}
```

Our completed business logic is ready for a trial run.

2.2.2   *Testing the business logic*

I created a simple `Console` UI project to simulate the use of the business logic, as the following shows.

Listing 2.2   A simple `Console` application to test the business logic

```
class Program {
    static void Main(string[] args) {
        SimulateAddingPoints();

        Console.WriteLine();
        Console.WriteLine(" ***");
        Console.WriteLine();

        SimulateRemovingPoints();

        Console.WriteLine();
        Console.WriteLine();
    }

    static void SimulateAddingPoints() {
        var dataService = new FakeLoyaltyDataService();
        var service = new LoyaltyAccrualService(dataService);
        var rentalAgreement = new RentalAgreement {
            Customer = new Customer {
                Id = Guid.NewGuid(),
                Name = "Matthew D. Groves",
                DateOfBirth = new DateTime(1980, 2, 10),
                DriversLicense = "RR123456"
            },
            Vehicle = new Vehicle {
                Id = Guid.NewGuid(),
                Make = "Honda",
                Model = "Accord",
                Size = Size.Compact,
                Vin = "1HABC123"
            },
            StartDate = DateTime.Now.AddDays(-3),
            EndDate = DateTime.Now
        };
        service.Accrue(rentalAgreement);
    }

    static void SimulateRemovingPoints() {
        var dataService = new FakeLoyaltyDataService();
        var service = new LoyaltyRedemptionService(dataService);
        var invoice = new Invoice {
            Customer = new Customer {
                Id = Guid.NewGuid(),
```

This is a basic windows console application.

We'll simulate addition (accrual) of points.

We'll simulate subtraction (redemption) of points.

We aren't concerned with the database right now, so we're using a fake data service.

The accrual method requires a Rental Agreement object to apply the business logic to, so I've created one that will earn three points.

We'll send the Rental Agreement to the accrual service method.

Again, a fake data service is being used.

The redemption service requires an invoice to which to apply the loyalty discount.

```
            Name = "Jacob Watson",
            DateOfBirth = new DateTime(1977, 4, 15),
            DriversLicense = "RR009911"
        },
        Vehicle = new Vehicle {
            Id = Guid.NewGuid(),
            Make = "Cadillac",
            Model = "Sedan",
            Size = Size.Luxury,
            Vin = "2BDI"
        },
        CostPerDay = 29.95m,
        Id = Guid.NewGuid()
    };
    service.Redeem(invoice, 3);
    }
}
```

The redemption service also needs a number of days to redeem points for; I've chosen three.

Figure 2.4 shows the console output; the fake data services write to the screen instead of to the database.

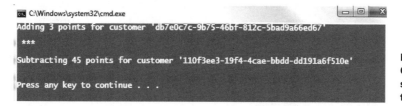

Figure 2.4 Console output simulating writes to the database

The business logic is now complete. Our code is clean and separated. It's easy to read and it's going to be easy to maintain. This service will get marketing pumped up, and it's sure to increase your bonus once sales go through the roof.

But wait a minute: this code can't go into production as is. There are all kinds of things that could go wrong that we need to prepare for. Let's get cracking on those nonfunctional requirements.

2.2.3 Add logging

Being able to audit loyalty transactions isn't a requirement (yet), but to be on the safe side, it's a good idea to log every request, at least for quality assurance (QA) purposes. In production, you may want to limit or eliminate logging, but for now let's put some simple logging in place to help developers reproduce any bugs that QA finds.

I won't use a real logging framework. There are many good ones for .NET, such as NLog and log4net, and I encourage you to check those out. The point of this book isn't to learn a logging tool, so let's log to `Console` (or `Debug` or `Trace`, if you prefer) for now.

When logging the accrual of points, we should log information about the customer, the vehicle, and the dates. Let's log that the `Accrue` method is being used (with a timestamp) first. Then, logging the IDs of the customer and the vehicle should be enough to go on for now. Let's also log when the accrual ends, along with a time-stamp, as shown next.

Listing 2.3   Accrue code, now with logging

```
public void Accrue(RentalAgreement agreement) {          ◁───  This is the same Accrue
                                                               method as before, with
    // logging                                                 some logging added.
    Console.WriteLine("Accrue: {0}", DateTime.Now);
    Console.WriteLine("Customer: {0}", agreement.Customer.Id);   ◁──  Write key
    Console.WriteLine("Vehicle: {0}", agreement.Vehicle.Id);          information to
                                                                      the log:
                                                                      customer ID
    var rentalTimeSpan =                                              and vehicle ID.
        (agreement.EndDate.Subtract(agreement.StartDate));
    var numberOfDays = (int) Math.Floor(rentalTimeSpan.TotalDays);
    var pointsPerDay = 1;
    if (agreement.Vehicle.Size >= Size.Luxury)
        pointsPerDay = 2;
    var points = numberOfDays*pointsPerDay;
    _loyaltyDataService.AddPoints(agreement.Customer.Id, points);


    // logging
    Console.WriteLine("Accrue complete: {0}", DateTime.Now);
}
```

Write in the log (the Console again) that the Accrue method is being used (and when).

Close the book by writing one more log message that the Accrual is complete.

Add similar logging code to the Redeem implementation.

Listing 2.4   Redeem code, now with logging

```
public void Redeem(Invoice invoice, int numberOfDays) {  ◁──  This is the same
                                                               Redeem code as before,
    // logging                                                 with logging added.
    Console.WriteLine("Redeem: {0}", DateTime.Now);
    Console.WriteLine("Invoice: {0}", invoice.Id);             ◁──  Log key
                                                                    information,
    var pointsPerDay = 10;                                          in this case
    if (invoice.Vehicle.Size >= Size.Luxury)                        the invoice ID
        pointsPerDay = 15;
    var points = numberOfDays*pointsPerDay;
    _loyaltyDataService.SubtractPoints(invoice.Customer.Id, points);
    invoice.Discount = numberOfDays*invoice.CostPerDay;


    // logging
    Console.WriteLine("Redeem complete: {0}", DateTime.Now);
}
```

Similar to Accrue, except now logging when a Redeem call has started.

Close the book with one final log message that the Redeem call has ended.

And there you have it. That wasn't so bad—just a few extra lines of code in each imple-mentation.

2.2.4 Introducing defensive programming

Because this core loyalty business logic has no control over the data that gets passed in as parameters, we may have to check for worst-case scenarios. For a simple example, what if a null reference is passed in for the RentalAgreement parameter? That's not a problem that our logic can cope with, so an exception should be thrown. We hope the code calling our API can cope with that exception. If not, then at least we're alerting the UI developers and/or QA that something has gone wrong. This philosophy is known as *defensive programming*. Like defensive driving, it's meant to reduce the risk of dangerous (or in the case of programming, invalid) scenarios by anticipating invalid contexts or mistakes in other parts of the application.

In the following listing, you'll put defensive programming in place to check for the invalid scenario of a null RentalAgreement being passed in.

Listing 2.5 Accrue with defensive programming

```
public void Accrue(RentalAgreement agreement) {
    // defensive programming
    if(agreement == null) throw new ArgumentNullException("agreement");

    // logging
    Console.WriteLine("Accrue: {0}", DateTime.Now);
    Console.WriteLine("Customer: {0}", agreement.Customer.Id);
    Console.WriteLine("Vehicle: {0}", agreement.Vehicle.Id);

    var rentalTimeSpan =
        (agreement.EndDate.Subtract(agreement.StartDate));
    var numberOfDays = (int) Math.Floor(rentalTimeSpan.TotalDays);
    var pointsPerDay = 1;
    if (agreement.Vehicle.Size >= Size.Luxury)
        pointsPerDay = 2;
    var points = numberOfDays*pointsPerDay;
    _loyaltyDataService.AddPoints(agreement.Customer.Id, points);

    // logging
    Console.WriteLine("Accrue complete: {0}", DateTime.Now);
}
```

This is the same Accrue code as in the last section, with defensive programing added.

We hope that a null agreement is never passed in, but if it is, we throw this exception early.

We could check numerous other things about the properties of RentalAgreement as well, but for now that's good enough.

With the Redeem implementation, there are similar issues. The numberOfDays parameter shouldn't be less than 1. Renting a car for zero days? That's an invalid argument.

The Invoice argument could be null as well, so let's also check for that, as shown next.

Listing 2.6 Redeem with defensive programming

```
public void Redeem(Invoice invoice, int numberOfDays) {
    // defensive programming
```

The same Redeem method as in the last section, with defensive programming added

A null Invoice
passed in will
cause an
exception to
be thrown.

```
if(invoice == null) throw new ArgumentNullException("invoice");
if(numberOfDays <= 0)
    throw new ArgumentException("","numberOfDays");

// logging
Console.WriteLine("Redeem: {0}", DateTime.Now);
Console.WriteLine("Invoice: {0}", invoice.Id);

var pointsPerDay = 10;
if (invoice.Vehicle.Size >= Size.Luxury)
    pointsPerDay = 15;
var points = numberOfDays*pointsPerDay;
_loyaltyDataService.SubtractPoints(invoice.Customer.Id, points);
invoice.Discount = numberOfDays*invoice.CostPerDay;

// logging
Console.WriteLine("Redeem complete: {0}", DateTime.Now);
}
```

It makes sense to
redeem a
positive amount
of days, so throw
an exception
otherwise.

Now our code is starting to get more defensive. If something goes wrong outside the control of this core logic, we aren't going to let it affect us.

With logging and defensive programming in place, the Accrue and Redeem methods are starting to get a little long, and a bit repetitive as well. But let's soldier on for now and look at transactions and retries.

2.2.5   *Working with transactions and retries*

Transactions are necessary if we're using more than one data layer operation in order to make them atomic. That is, we want all the data layer calls to succeed (commit), or for none of them to succeed (rollback). This business logic class might not be the best place for this operation, particularly because we're unsure about exactly what persistence technology will be used. But hypothetically, it could be put in this layer.

Let's assume for now that the underlying data layer will use some technology that's compatible with .NET's built-in ambient transaction class: TransactionScope (you'll need to add a System.Transactions reference). Combining with a try/catch block, we can add transaction code to the Accrue implementation, as shown next.

Listing 2.7   Accrue with a transaction

Same method
as last section,
but we
continue to
build on it by
using a
transaction.

```
public void Accrue(RentalAgreement agreement) {
    // defensive programming
    if(agreement == null) throw new ArgumentNullException("agreement");

    // logging
    Console.WriteLine("Accrue: {0}", DateTime.Now);
    Console.WriteLine("Customer: {0}", agreement.Customer.Id);
    Console.WriteLine("Vehicle: {0}", agreement.Vehicle.Id);

    using (var scope = new TransactionScope()) {
        try {
            var rentalTime =
                (agreement.EndDate.Subtract(agreement.StartDate));
```

Instantiating a
new Transaction
scope begins the
transaction.

```
        var numberOfDays = (int) Math.Floor(rentalTime.TotalDays);
        var pointsPerDay = 1;
        if (agreement.Vehicle.Size >= Size.Luxury)
            pointsPerDay = 2;
        var points = numberOfDays*pointsPerDay;
        _dataService.AddPoints(agreement.Customer.Id, points);

        scope.Complete();                        ◁─┐ Calling Complete() signals that
    }                                              │ the transaction was successful.
    catch {
        throw;                        ◁──────┐ A transaction without calling Complete()
    }                                        │ means it will be rolled back.
}
// logging
Console.WriteLine("Accrue complete: {0}", DateTime.Now);
}
```

If there's an exception, then `scope.Complete()` will never be reached, and when scope is disposed, the transaction will be rolled back. For now, we're only rethrowing the exception. Similarly, we can use `TransactionScope` in the `Redeem` method, as shown here.

Listing 2.8 Redeem with a transaction

```
public void Redeem(Invoice invoice, int numberOfDays) {          ◁─┐
    // defensive programming
    if(invoice == null) throw new ArgumentNullException("invoice");
    if(numberOfDays <= 0)
        throw new ArgumentException("","numberOfDays");       Again, the same
                                                             Redeem method
    // logging                                            that we continue to
    Console.WriteLine("Redeem: {0}", DateTime.Now);        build on by adding
    Console.WriteLine("Invoice: {0}", invoice.Id);          a transaction.

    using (var scope = new TransactionScope()) {
        try {
            var pointsPerDay = 10;
            if (invoice.Vehicle.Size >= Size.Luxury)
                pointsPerDay = 15;
            var points = numberOfDays*pointsPerDay;
            _dataService.SubtractPoints(invoice.Customer.Id, points);
            invoice.Discount = numberOfDays*invoice.CostPerDay;

            scope.Complete();                     ◁─┐ Calling Complete() signals that
        }                                           │ the transaction was successful.
        catch {
            throw;                        ◁──┐ A transaction without calling Complete()
        }                                    │ means it will be rolled back.
    }

    // logging
    Console.WriteLine("Redeem complete: {0}", DateTime.Now);
}
```

Instantiating a new Transaction scope begins the transaction.

This code is starting to get long and ugly. The original business logic is now a couple of indentations deep, surrounded by a bunch of code to take care of the cross-cutting concerns: logging, defensive programming, and the use of a transaction.

But we're not even done. Let's assume that the underlying data persistence layer is prone to occasional high traffic and that some requests will thus fail (for example, throwing a timeout exception). If that's the case, then performing a couple of retries will keep our program running smoothly (albeit a little slower during those high-traffic times). Let's put a loop around the transaction. Every time the transaction rolls back, we'll increment the retry count. Once the retry count hits a limit, we'll let it go, as shown here.

Listing 2.9 Accrue with transaction and retries

```
public void Accrue(RentalAgreement agreement) {
    // defensive programming
    if(agreement == null) throw new ArgumentNullException("agreement");

    // logging
    Console.WriteLine("Accrue: {0}", DateTime.Now);
    Console.WriteLine("Customer: {0}", agreement.Customer.Id);
    Console.WriteLine("Vehicle: {0}", agreement.Vehicle.Id);

    using (var scope = new TransactionScope()) {        Retry the
        var retries = 3;                                transaction up
        var succeeded = false;                          to three times
        while (!succeeded) {              Keep looping until success
            try {
                var rentalTime =
                    (agreement.EndDate.Subtract(agreement.StartDate));
                var days = (int) Math.Floor(rentalTime.TotalDays);
                var pointsPerDay = 1;
                if (agreement.Vehicle.Size >= Size.Luxury)
                    pointsPerDay = 2;
                var points = days * pointsPerDay;
                _dataService.AddPoints(agreement.Customer.Id, points);

                scope.Complete();               The complete logging
                succeeded = true;               had to be moved
                                                inside the try block.
                // logging
                Console.WriteLine("Accrue complete: {0}", DateTime.Now);
            }
            catch {
                if(retries >=0)         Don't rethrow the
                    retries--;          exception until you run
                else                    out of retry attempts.
                    throw;
            }
        }
    }
}
```

After the transaction is complete, set succeeded to true to make this the last loop iteration.

Notice that the Accrue complete logging had to be moved inside the try block as well. Add similar code for redemption, as shown in the following listing.

Listing 2.10 Redeem with transaction and retries

```
public void Redeem(Invoice invoice, int numberOfDays) {
    // defensive programming
    if(invoice == null) throw new ArgumentNullException("invoice");
    if(numberOfDays <= 0)
        throw new ArgumentException("","numberOfDays");

    // logging
    Console.WriteLine("Redeem: {0}", DateTime.Now);
    Console.WriteLine("Invoice: {0}", invoice.Id);

    // start new transaction
    using (var scope = new TransactionScope())
    {
        var retries = 3;
        var succeeded = false;
        while (!succeeded) {
            try {
                var pointsPerDay = 10;
                if (invoice.Vehicle.Size >= Size.Luxury)
                    pointsPerDay = 15;
                var pts = numberOfDays * pointsPerDay;
                _dataService.SubtractPoints(invoice.Customer.Id, pts);
                invoice.Discount = numberOfDays*invoice.CostPerDay;

                // complete transaction
                scope.Complete();
                succeeded = true;

                // logging
                Console.WriteLine("Redeem complete: {0}", DateTime.Now);
            }
            catch {
                // don't rethrow until the
                // retry limit is reached
                if (retries >= 0)
                    retries--;
                else
                    throw;
            }
        }
    }
}
```

Annotations:
- Retry the transaction up to three times
- Keep looping until success
- After the transaction is complete, set succeeded to true to make this the last loop iteration.
- The logging had to be moved inside the try block as well.
- Don't rethrow the exception until you run out of retry attempts.

Wow! Yet another indentation of the original business logic, and more clutter to go with it. Now the cross-cutting concerns are taking up roughly half of the lines of code in both of these methods.

But we're still not done. We need to talk some more about handling exceptions.

2.2.6 Handling exceptions

Wait, *more* exception handling? Wasn't that first try/catch block enough? Maybe. But if some condition occurs that a retry won't fix (perhaps a server goes completely offline), then after the retry limit is reached, the exception will be rethrown. And if that's the case, then you'll need to handle that exception some other way (before it crashes your program).

So let's add one more try/catch block immediately after the defensive programming that envelopes everything else, as the following listing shows.

Listing 2.11   Accrue with exception handling

```
public void Accrue(RentalAgreement agreement)
{
    // defensive programming
    if(agreement == null) throw new ArgumentNullException("agreement");

    // logging
    Console.WriteLine("Accrue: {0}", DateTime.Now);
    Console.WriteLine("Customer: {0}", agreement.Customer.Id);
    Console.WriteLine("Vehicle: {0}", agreement.Vehicle.Id);

    try                                    ⟵┐  One more try statement
    {                                         │  to surround everything in
        // start new transaction              │  the transaction (including
        using (var scope = new TransactionScope())  │  the transaction)
        {
            var retries = 3;
            var succeeded = false;
            while (!succeeded)
            {
                try
                {
                    var rentalTime =
                        (agreement.EndDate.Subtract(
                            agreement.StartDate));
                    var days =
                        (int) Math.Floor(rentalTime.TotalDays);
                    var pointsPerDay = 1;
                    if (agreement.Vehicle.Size >= Size.Luxury)
                        pointsPerDay = 2;
                    var points = days * pointsPerDay;
                    _dataService.AddPoints(
                        agreement.Customer.Id, points);

                    scope.Complete();
                    succeeded = true;

                    // logging
                    Console.WriteLine("Accrue complete: {0}",
                        DateTime.Now);
                }
                catch
                {
                    // don't re-throw until the
                    // retry limit is reached
                    if(retries >=0)
                        retries--;
                    else
                        throw;
```

```
                    }
                }
            }
        }
        catch (Exception ex)
        {
            if (!ExceptionHandler.Handle(ex))
                throw;
        }
    }
}
```

> A matching catch statement

> If the exception can't be handled, continue to throw it

We might be able to recover from certain exceptions. In the case of other exceptions, we may have to log and tell the customer that something went wrong (and suggest trying again later). Let's do the same thing again with the Redeem method.

Listing 2.12   Redeem with exception handling

```
public void Redeem(Invoice invoice, int numberOfDays) {
    // defensive programming
    if(invoice == null) throw new ArgumentNullException("invoice");
    if(numberOfDays <= 0)
        throw new ArgumentException("","numberOfDays");

    // logging
    Console.WriteLine("Redeem: {0}", DateTime.Now);
    Console.WriteLine("Invoice: {0}", invoice.Id);

    try
    {
        // start new transaction
        using (var scope = new TransactionScope())
        {
            // retry up to three times
            var retries = 3;
            var succeeded = false;
            while (!succeeded)
            {
                try
                {
                    var pointsPerDay = 10;
                    if (invoice.Vehicle.Size >= Size.Luxury)
                        pointsPerDay = 15;
                    var points = numberOfDays*pointsPerDay;
                    _dataService.SubtractPoints(
                        invoice.Customer.Id, points);
                    invoice.Discount = numberOfDays*invoice.CostPerDay;

                    // complete transaction
                    scope.Complete();
                    succeeded = true;

                    // logging
                    Console.WriteLine("Redeem complete: {0}",
                        DateTime.Now);
                }
                catch
```

> Surround the transaction and business logic

```
                {
                    // don't re-throw until the
                    // retry limit is reached
                    if (retries >= 0)
                        retries--;
                    else
                        throw;
                }
            }
        }
    }
    catch(Exception ex)
    {
        if (!ExceptionHandler.Handle(ex))
            throw;
    }
}
```

A matching catch statement for the outermost try statement ◁⎯

Use the same ExceptionHandler to see if the exception can be handled. ◁⎯

At this point, we've implemented all the nonfunctional requirements: logging, defensive programming, transactions, retries, and exception handling. Adding all this code to handle these cross-cutting concerns has made the original Accrue and Redeem balloon to huge methods. The code is ready for production (or more likely a QA/staging environment), but yikes, what a mess!

You might be thinking that this approach involves a bit of overkill. Certainly not all of these cross-cutting concerns will always be necessary. And you're right. You might only need one or two of these solutions in most places, and some of the concerns can move to the data layer or the UI layer. The point I'm trying to make with this example is that cross-cutting concerns can clutter your code. They make the code they are cutting across harder to read, maintain, and debug.

2.2.7   *Refactor without AOP*

It's time to clean up this mess. When refactoring, you should always have unit tests in place so you know that your refactoring didn't cause any regressions, but because this example is relatively small and contrived, I've left them as an exercise for the reader. (I've always wanted to write that.) But don't worry: chapter 6 is devoted to the topic of unit testing and aspects.

As you've noticed, there's a lot of duplicated code between the Accrue and Redeem implementations. Certainly, you can factor this code into its own classes/methods. But let's stop and think about how you're going to do that.

One option is to refactor all those nonfunctional concerns into static methods. This isn't a good idea because it couples the business logic too tightly to the nonfunctional concern code. It makes your method look shorter and more readable, but you're still left with the problem that your methods are doing too much.

You can use a DI strategy and expect that all the logging, defensive programming, and other services will be passed in to the constructors of LoyaltyAccrualService and LoyaltyRedemptionService. Those are going to be some big constructors, but let's look at the next listing to see how this strategy might affect the Redeem method.

Listing 2.13 Redemption service refactored with DI

```
public class LoyaltyRedemptionServiceRefactored
                    : ILoyaltyRedemptionService {
    readonly ILoyaltyDataService _dataService;
    readonly IExceptionHandler _exceptionHandler;
    readonly ITransactionManager _transactionManager;

    public LoyaltyRedemptionServiceRefactored(
                ILoyaltyDataService service,
                IExceptionHandler exceptionHandler,
                ITransactionManager transactionManager) {
        _dataService = service;
        _exceptionHandler = exceptionHandler;
        _transactionManager = transactionManager;No
    }

    public void Redeem(Invoice invoice, int numberOfDays) {
        // defensive programming
        if(invoice == null) throw new ArgumentNullException("invoice");
        if(numberOfDays <= 0)
            throw new ArgumentException("","numberOfDays");

        // logging
        Console.WriteLine("Redeem: {0}", DateTime.Now);
        Console.WriteLine("Invoice: {0}", invoice.Id);

        _exceptionHandler.Wrapper(() => {
                _transactionManager.Wrapper(() => {
                    var pointsPerDay = 10;
                    if (invoice.Vehicle.Size >= Size.Luxury)
                        pointsPerDay = 15;
                    var points = numberOfDays*pointsPerDay;
                    _dataService.SubtractPoints(
                        invoice.Customer.Id, points);
                    invoice.Discount =
                        numberOfDays*invoice.CostPerDay;

                    // logging
                    Console.WriteLine("Redeem complete: {0}",
                        DateTime.Now);
                });
        });
    }
}
```

The loyalty data service is still passed in, as it was before.

An exception handler service instance is now also required.

A transaction manager service is now also required.

The transaction manager has a wrapper of its own in which the retry logic and transaction logic live.

The wrapper method takes a lambda as an argument and will wrap the lambda in the try/catch block.

This version is a little better. I've moved the exception handler code and the transaction/retry code into their own services. This design has its benefits. One, it puts those pieces into their own classes so that they can be reused in the Accrue method. Two, it makes the code easier to read by reducing the noise of the cross-cutting concerns. Those concerns can also be mocked out when writing unit tests later. Mocking is a technique used in writing unit tests so that you don't need to worry about testing several things at the same time. That isolates the code under test, which will be briefly discussed in chapter 6. We can make similar changes to the Accrual method as well.

Listing 2.14   Accrual service refactored with DI

```
public class LoyaltyAccrualServiceRefactored : ILoyaltyAccrualService {
    readonly ILoyaltyDataService _dataService;
    readonly IExceptionHandler _exceptionHandler;
    readonly ITransactionManager _transactionManager;

    public LoyaltyAccrualServiceRefactored(
                    ILoyaltyDataService service,
                    IExceptionHandler exceptionHandler,
                    ITransactionManager transactionManager) {
        _dataService = service;
        _exceptionHandler = exceptionHandler;
        _transactionManager = transactionManager;
    }

    public void Accrue(RentalAgreement agreement) {
        // defensive programming
        if(agreement == null)
            throw new ArgumentNullException("agreement");

        // logging
        Console.WriteLine("Accrue: {0}", DateTime.Now);
        Console.WriteLine("Customer: {0}", agreement.Customer.Id);
        Console.WriteLine("Vehicle: {0}", agreement.Vehicle.Id);

        // exception handling
        _exceptionHandler.Wrapper(() => {
            _transactionManager.Wrapper(() => {
                var rentalTime = (agreement.EndDate
                    .Subtract(agreement.StartDate));
                var numberOfDays =
                    (int) Math.Floor(rentalTime.TotalDays);
                var pointsPerDay = 1;
                if (agreement.Vehicle.Size >= Size.Luxury)
                    pointsPerDay = 2;
                var points = numberOfDays*pointsPerDay;
                _dataService.AddPoints(
                    agreement.Customer.Id, points);

                // logging
                Console.WriteLine("Accrue complete: {0}",
                    DateTime.Now);
            });
        });
    }
```

The loyalty data service is still passed in, as it was before.

An exception handler service instance is now required.

A transaction manager service is now also required.

The wrapper method takes a lambda as an argument and will wrap the lambda in the try/catch block.

The transaction manager has a wrapper of its own in which the retry logic and transaction logic live.

Not bad. Now you've reduced that messy code back to *almost* how it looked when you started—with only the business logic. There's that Wrapper stuff in there now, but it doesn't look all that bad, considering the alternative.

But look at that constructor. It seems excessive, doesn't it? Not to mention that when you do unit testing, you'll have to pass in mocks/stubs for each of these dependencies in order to run the test. You might call this a constructor gone wild: methods that have a lot of parameters usually indicate that something is wrong and that refactoring should be done, and constructors are no exception. When you see this sort of thing, it may indicate that the service is doing too much and isn't following the single responsibility principle.

> ### Code smells
>
> A *code smell* is a slang term for often-observed patterns in code that may (but not always) indicate a deeper problem. It's not a bug, per se, but it indicates that you might have a problem with the architecture. It's a heuristic (a rule of thumb). Much like a bad smell in the refrigerator could indicate rotten food hiding in the back, a code smell could indicate a rotten design that should be cleaned up.

We could combine the exception handler and the transaction manager services into one service, as the next listing shows.

Listing 2.15　Combined exception handler and transaction handler

```
public interface ITransactionManager2 {
    void Wrapper(Action method);
}

public class TransactionManager2 : ITransactionManager2 {
    public void Wrapper(Action method) {
        using (var scope = new TransactionScope()) {
            var retries = 3;
            var succeeded = false;
            while (!succeeded) {
                try {
                    method();
                    scope.Complete();
                    succeeded = true;
                }
                catch (Exception ex) {
                    if (retries >= 0)
                        retries--;
                    else {
                        if (!Exceptions.Handle(ex))
                            throw;
                    }
                }
            }
        }
    }
}
```

The Wrapper method expects an Action argument that it will wrap some code around.

This syntax results in the Action argument being executed.

This code isn't too shabby, because things seem pretty cohesive as a single service (though the name could use some work). Combining services isn't always going to work, though.

One other way to deal with too many dependencies being injected is to move all these individual services into an aggregate service or façade service (that is, use the façade pattern to combine all of these little services into one service that orchestrates all the little services). In our case, the TransactionManager and ExceptionHandler services would stay separate, but you'd use a third façade class to orchestrate their use.

THE FACADE PATTERN   Façade is a pattern that's used to provide a simplified interface to a larger or more complex piece of code. For instance, a service class that provides a wide variety of methods and options can be put behind a façade interface that reduces complexity by limiting options or providing a small subset of simplified methods.

Listing 2.16   An aggregate service for orchestrating two services

```
public interface ITransactionFacade {
    void Wrapper(Action action);
}

public class TransactionFacade : ITransactionFacade {
    readonly IExceptionHandler _exceptionHandler;
    readonly ITransactionManager _transactionManager;

    public TransactionFacade(
            IExceptionHandler exceptionHandler,
            ITransactionManager transactionManager) {
        _exceptionHandler = exceptionHandler;
        _transactionManager = transactionManager;
    }

    public void Wrapper(Action action) {
        _exceptionHandler.Wrapper(() => {
            _transactionManager.Wrapper(() => {
                action();
            });
        });
    }
}
```

It also requires a transaction manager service.

This façade service requires an exception service.

This façade provides orchestration of the exception handler wrapper . . .

. . . and the transaction manager wrapper.

This approach reduces the need to have multiple wrappers, reducing the amount of `Wrapper` boilerplate that we need in the `Accrual` service and `Redemption` service methods.

But look at what's still left: defensive programming and logging, both of which depend on the parameters of the method. Factoring those concerns out could be messy and could involve reflection. (In other languages such as PHP, JavaScript, or Ruby, this might not be as difficult.)

Refactoring with the decorator pattern

One other way that you could refactor this code without using AOP and that you might also be familiar with is the decorator or proxy pattern. You'll see in chapter 7 how this pattern can be used to refactor this kind of code. (Spoiler alert: the decorator/proxy pattern is just a simple form of AOP.)

Don't get me wrong: I would prefer to use the refactored code over the original mess, for sure. But if there were a way I could somehow get all the way back to the code I started with—only the business logic—that would be even better. It would be the easiest code to read, and I'd have fewer constructor-injected services to worry about. I wouldn't have to worry about forgetting or accidentally omitting one of these cross-cutting services every time the business logic changes, thus reducing the cost of change.

2.3 *The cost of change*

One constant in software engineering is change. Requirements change. Business rules change. Technology changes.

Any change in business rules or requirements would be challenging to deal with in the original version of the business logic (before we refactored). You'd have to climb through all the loops, `try`/`catches` and `ifs`, in order to find the meat of the business logic. Once you made the change, you'd have to hope that it didn't affect the nonfunctional concerns (otherwise, you might have to copy and paste those changes everywhere).

The refactoring we did with DI and/or the façade pattern is pretty good, but it's more vulnerable to change than you might think. In this section, I want to discuss, however briefly, some of the reasons for change and the costs associated with them because in the next section, we'll refactor the Acme Car Rental code again, except that we'll be using PostSharp to demonstrate that AOP can help reduce the costs associated with change.

2.3.1 *Requirements will change*

Requirements change for any number of reasons. The core assumptions that went into making the requirements could be invalid. The requirements may have been vague in the beginning and get clearer and more concrete only as the software starts taking shape. Your stakeholders could change their minds. What seems like a simple change to them might mean a world of difference in the code (and vice versa).

Even though I know that this axiom—that requirements will change—is true, and even though I've seen it over and over again, I still often make the mistake of coding as if nothing will change. Almost every time I make this mistake, I regret it. Being a good developer means not only accepting that requirements may change but also *expecting* them to change. And even when I do code with change in mind, I often find that I run into the limits of a programming language. Or I find myself lost in architecture land, where I'm continually refactoring back and forth, trying to find a perfect, elegant way of expressing a solution.

2.3.2 *Small versus large projects*

The size of your project matters a great deal. If you're a one-person team writing a piece of simple software (for example, a website with maybe one or two forms and mostly static content), then the cost of change may be low because you have less things that can change. If this is the case, you can relax those architectural muscles a little bit. You aren't cooking a 5-course meal at a 5-star restaurant for 100 tables every night—you're just throwing a bag of popcorn in the microwave for yourself.

The size of a "small" project is something for which I can't give you a concrete measure. But I must warn you that what you thought was going to be a small, trivial project can turn into a complex medium-to-large project quickly. So unless you're entirely certain that you won't need all the benefits of a well-architectured application, it's better to be safe than sorry. Otherwise, you might end up building a pyramid and continuously piling rocks on top of each other with brute force.

2.3.3 *Signature changes*

One of the things that you'll have to look out for is method signature changes. Consider whether you need to change the signature of a method by adding or removing parameters. If you remove a parameter, you have to remove the defensive programming for that parameter; otherwise, your project won't build. If you change a parameter's type, then your defensive programming edge case may also change (from null to 0 or vice versa). And even more dangerously, if you add a parameter, you have to remember to add the defensive programming for that parameter. Unfortunately, your compiler won't help you there—you'll have to remember.

If you look back at the `Accrue` and `Redeem` methods, you can see that a signature change anywhere will immediately affect the defensive programming and logging concerns, as this listing shows.

Listing 2.17 `Accrue` method's defensive programming and logging

```
public void Accrue(RentalAgreement agreement) {
    // defensive programming
    if(agreement == null) throw new ArgumentNullException("agreement");

    // logging
    Console.WriteLine("Accrue: {0}", DateTime.Now);
    Console.WriteLine("Customer: {0}", agreement.Customer.Id);
    Console.WriteLine("Vehicle: {0}", agreement.Vehicle.Id);

    // ... snip ...

    // logging
    Console.WriteLine("Accrue complete: {0}", DateTime.Now);
}
```

If there's another parameter added to this method, you have to remember to add another line of defensive programming. If the parameter's name changes from `agreement` to `rentalAgreement`, then you have to remember to change the `string` being passed to `ArgumentNullException`'s constructor. If the method itself changes names (to `Accrual`, for instance), you'll have to change the logging to reflect the new name. Refactoring tools such as ReSharper, unit tests, and the C# compiler itself will help you out, but they can do only so much. For the rest of it, you have to rely on your own and your team's vigilance.

2.3.4 *Working on a team*

One of the problems with change comes from working on a software team. If you work on software completely by yourself, you may never experience this problem (although you might. Read on).

Suppose there's a new requirement that needs another method on the `ILoyalty-AccrueService` interface. Maybe this task falls to some other team member, and this team member implements the business logic and calls the task complete. Unfortunately, this team member forgot to use the `Wrapper` method of `TransactionFacade`. His code passes unit tests, so it's sent over to QA. If you're working on an Agile project, this might not be a huge issue: QA could catch it and report it back to you within one sprint. In a waterfall project, QA might not discover this bug until months later. Months later, you might not even remember what your intentions were that caused the bug. It's like you're working with a new team member: your past self.

Worst case: it might even pass QA, assuming conditions are such that an exception or retry isn't necessary or noticed. Whoops! Code made it into production without defensive programming, logging, transactions, and so on.

Unfortunately, with DI and/or façade service(s), we can't do much more with the architecture, because the code is still scattered around—just remember to communicate well with your team, pair program, code review. And hope that no one forgets. The bigger the team and the bigger the project, the harder this gets.

2.4 *Refactor with AOP*

Let's try refactoring the code again, this time using AOP. Using NuGet, add PostSharp to your project. You can do this with the `Install-Package postsharp` command in the Package Manager Console. Alternatively, you can use the NuGet UI by right-clicking References and selecting Manage NuGet Packages. Then click Online, search for PostSharp, and click Install (note that I'm using NuGet 2.0 at the time of this writing).

PostSharp has a trial version of its full Professional edition, and there's also a free Express edition (which requires a license, but it's a free license). Either one of these will work, but I won't use any features in this chapter that you can't use with the Express edition.

Now that PostSharp is installed, let's start moving nonfunctional features into their own aspects.

2.4.1 *Start simple and isolate the logging*

Let's start with an easy cross-cutting concern to refactor: logging. Let's log a timestamp when the method is called, and the name of the method. I'll create a class that inherits one of PostSharp's built-in base classes, `OnMethodBoundaryAspect`, which allows us to insert code at the boundaries of a method, as the following listing shows.

Listing 2.18   A method boundary aspect to handle logging

```
[Serializable]
public class LoggingAspect : OnMethodBoundaryAspect {
    public override void OnEntry(MethodExecutionArgs args) {
        Console.WriteLine("{0}: {1}", args.Method.Name, DateTime.Now);
    }

    public override void OnSuccess(MethodExecutionArgs args) {
        Console.WriteLine("{0} complete: {1}",
            args.Method.Name, DateTime.Now);
    }
}
```

Notice that we can get the method name from the `MethodExecutionArgs` argument, so right away we know that this aspect can be reused for redemption, too. `Logging-Aspect` is similar to the "Hello, World" aspect from the previous chapter. Apply the aspect using an attribute, as shown here.

Listing 2.19   Applying the logging aspect to the `Accrue` and `Redeem` methods

```
[LoggingAspect]
 public void Accrue(RentalAgreement agreement) {
     // ... snip ...
}
```
> LoggingAspect being used as an attribute on Accrue

```
[LoggingAspect]
 public void Redeem(Invoice invoice, int numberOfDays) {
     // ... snip ...
}
```
> The same aspect being applied to Redeem

And now you can remove the logging code from each of those methods.

Before we run the console application again to make sure that this is working, you might have noticed that I left something out: the logging of the ID values from the parameters being passed in. With PostSharp, I'm able to examine all of the arguments being passed in, but in order to get the IDs, I have to work a little more (see the following listing). I could apply brute force to it with a couple of `if` statements.

Listing 2.20   Examining and logging argument value

```
public override void OnEntry(MethodExecutionArgs args) {
    Console.WriteLine("{0}: {1}", args.Method.Name, DateTime.Now);

    foreach (var argument in args.Arguments) {
        if (argument.GetType() == typeof(RentalAgreement)) {
            Console.WriteLine("Customer: {0}",
                ((RentalAgreement)argument).Customer.Id);
            Console.WriteLine("Vehicle: {0}",
                ((RentalAgreement)argument).Vehicle.Id);
        }
        if(argument.GetType() == typeof(Invoice))
            Console.WriteLine("Invoice: {0}", ((Invoice)argument).Id);
    }
}
```
> Loop through the arguments using the PostSharp API.

> Check to see whether the argument is a Rental-Agreement.

> Check to see whether the argument is an Invoice.

That's fine for this contrived example, but in a bigger application, you could have dozens or hundreds of different types. If your requirement is to log entity IDs and information, you might want to use a common interface (or base class) on your entities. If you had an `ILoggable` interface with a `string LogInformation()` method and you made both `Invoice` and `RentalAgreement` implement that interface, then you could do something like what's shown here.

Listing 2.21 An alternative way to log certain entities

This code assumes that entities that should be logged implement a hypothetical ILoggable interface that includes a LogInformation() method (at least).

```
public override void OnEntry(MethodExecutionArgs args) {
    Console.WriteLine("{0}: {1}", args.Method.Name, DateTime.Now);

    foreach (var argument in args.Arguments)          ⟵  Again, looping through the
        if(argument != null)                              arguments with PostSharp's API
            if (typeof(ILoggable).IsAssignableFrom(argument.GetType()))
                Console.WriteLine(
                    ((ILoggable)argument).LogInformation());
}
```

Reflection would be another option for general use. But this is a decision that you'll have to make, because it will be related to the specifics of the logging requirements of your project.

The `Redeem` and `Accrue` methods are starting to shrink, because we've moved logging functionality to its own class. Next, let's move defensive programming to its own class.

2.4.2 Refactor defensive programming

To refactor the defensive programming shown in listing 2.22, I'll again use the `OnMethodBoundaryAspect` base class. Let's check to make sure that none of the arguments are null and that none of the `int` arguments are zero or negative.

Listing 2.22 A defensive programming aspect

Use the PostSharp API to get information about the parameters.
Defend against zero/negative integers

```
[Serializable]
public class DefensiveProgramming : OnMethodBoundaryAspect {
    public override void OnEntry(MethodExecutionArgs args) {        We also need
        var parameters = args.Method.GetParameters();              argument
        var arguments = args.Arguments;              ⟵            information to
        for (int i = 0; i < arguments.Count; i++) {                match it with.
            if (arguments[i] == null)           ⟵  Defend against null arguments
                throw new ArgumentNullException(parameters[i].Name);
            if (arguments[i].GetType() == typeof(int)
                && (int)arguments[i] <= 0)
                throw new ArgumentException("", parameters[i].Name);
        }
    }
}
```

Check first to see whether the argument is null. After that, see whether the argument is an integer and whether it's a valid integer (such as a negative number). You can perform these tests by passing in nulls or negative numbers in the console application. (It should crash your console application, but you should see the correct `Argument-NullException` or `ArgumentException` with the parameter name.)

Again, notice that there's nothing in this class that couples directly to any of the parameter types or service classes, meaning that it can be used on both services, as in the following listing.

Listing 2.23   Refactoring to aspects with an attribute

```
[LoggingAspect]
[DefensiveProgramming]
public void Accrue(RentalAgreement agreement) {
     // ... snip ...
}

[LoggingAspect]
[DefensiveProgramming]
public void Redeem(Invoice invoice, int numberOfDays) {
     // ... snip ...
}
```

Defensive programming aspects

The defensive programming aspect that I've written here is probably not the best approach to writing a general-purpose aspect. With C#, you can put attributes directly on each parameter, so you can take that approach instead. In fact, this is what Phil Haack did when he recently created the NullGuard library (available on NuGet and GitHub).

At this point, it's important to point out that attributes in .NET aren't applied in a deterministic way. Although `LoggingAspect` is listed first, that doesn't necessarily mean that it will be applied first, and vice versa. This is why I had to put the null check [`if(argument != null)`] in the logging aspect: in case the logging aspect gets applied first. PostSharp has some features that allow you to specify ordering of aspects, which is covered in chapters 8 and 9.

For the rest of this section, I'm going to assume two things:

- When you use AOP for the first time in your project, you'll probably start with only one aspect, which means that you won't have to worry about ordering/ dependencies at first.
- The aspects in this example will be applied in the order that we want.

With defensive programming and logging out of the way, we're on our way back to the nice, clean business logic that we started with. Next up: let's get that transaction management code into its own class.

2.4.3 *Creating an aspect for transactions and retries*

To refactor transaction management code this time, instead of `OnMethodBoundary-Aspect`, I'll use `MethodInterceptionAspect`, as the next example (listing 2.24) shows. Instead of inserting code at the *boundaries* of a method, this aspect will *intercept* any calls to the method. An interception aspect will run code instead of the method that's being intercepted; a boundary aspect will run code before and after a method executes. I'll explore boundaries and interception more thoroughly in later chapters.

Listing 2.24 A transaction aspect

```
[Serializable]
public class TransactionManagement : MethodInterceptionAspect {
    public override void OnInvoke(MethodInterceptionArgs args) {
        // start new transaction
        using (var scope = new TransactionScope()) {
            // retry up to three times
            var retries = 3;
            var succeeded = false;
            while (!succeeded) {
                try {
                    args.Proceed();

                    // complete transaction
                    scope.Complete();
                    succeeded = true;
                }
                catch {
                    // don't re-throw until the
                    // retry limit is reached
                    if (retries >= 0)
                        retries--;
                    else
                        throw;
                }
            }
        }
    }
}
```

This aspect will run the code in OnInvoke instead of the intercepted method. → (points to `public override void OnInvoke(MethodInterceptionArgs args) {`)

Use the PostSharp API to proceed to the intercepted method here. ← (points to `args.Proceed();`)

That example is largely identical to the code we wrote inside of the service methods, except that I've replaced the business logic code with a call to `args.Proceed()`. The `Proceed()` call means "proceed to the method that was intercepted." Once again, I've moved all of the transaction code into its own class, and it can be applied with an attribute, as in the following listing.

Listing 2.25 Continuing to refactor with aspects

```
[DefensiveProgramming]
[LoggingAspect]
[TransactionManagement]
public void Accrue(RentalAgreement agreement) {
    // ... snip ...
```

```
}

[DefensiveProgramming]
[LoggingAspect]
[TransactionManagement]
public void Redeem(Invoice invoice, int numberOfDays) {
    // ... snip ...
}
```

Make sure to remove that transaction code from `Accrue` and `Redeem`.

In order to demonstrate that the transaction aspect is working, you can put some `Console.WriteLine()`s at the start and end of the `OnInvoke()` function, as figure 2.5 shows.

One more cross-cutting concern to go: exception handling.

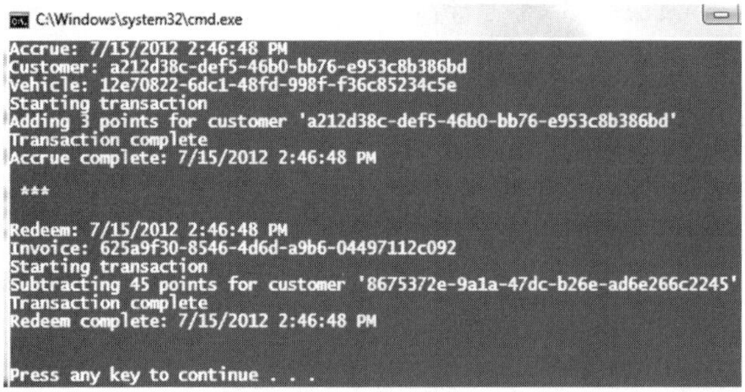

Figure 2.5   Console output with the use of AOP

2.4.4   Put exception handling into its own class

For the exception handling aspect, I could use `OnMethodBoundaryAspect` again, or I could use `OnExceptionAspect`. Either way, it should look similar to the following.

> **Listing 2.26   An aspect to handle exceptions**

```
[Serializable]
public class ExceptionAspect : OnExceptionAspect {
    public override void OnException(MethodExecutionArgs args) {
        if (Exceptions.Handle(args.Exception))
            args.FlowBehavior = FlowBehavior.Continue;
    }
}
```

I'll still use the `Exceptions` static class. There's something new in this aspect: `Flow-Behavior`, which is how you specify what you want to happen once the aspect is done. In the previous example, I set the behavior to `Continue` if the exception was handled. This means that the exception will be swallowed and the program will continue. Otherwise, the default `FlowBehavior` for an `OnExceptionAspect` is `RethrowException`, which means that the aspect will have no effect on the method and the exception will be thrown as normal.

Once more, add this attribute to your services and remove the exception handling code from inside of them. Now all of the cross-cutting concerns have been refactored. Let's take a look at the finished product.

Listing 2.27 All cross-cutting concerns refactored into aspects

```
[DefensiveProgramming]
[ExceptionAspect]
[LoggingAspect]
[TransactionManagement]
public void Accrue(RentalAgreement agreement) {
    var rentalTime =
        (agreement.EndDate.Subtract(
            agreement.StartDate));
    var days = (int) Math.Floor(rentalTime.TotalDays);
    var pointsPerDay = 1;
    if (agreement.Vehicle.Size >= Size.Luxury)
        pointsPerDay = 2;
    var pts = days * pointsPerDay;
    _dataService.AddPoints(agreement.Customer.Id, pts);
}

[DefensiveProgramming]
[ExceptionAspect]
[LoggingAspect]
[TransactionManagement]
public void Redeem(Invoice invoice, int numberOfDays) {
    var pointsPerDay = 10;
    if (invoice.Vehicle.Size >= Size.Luxury)
        pointsPerDay = 15;
    var points = numberOfDays*pointsPerDay;
    _dataService.SubtractPoints(invoice.Customer.Id, points);
    invoice.Discount = numberOfDays*invoice.CostPerDay;
}
```

The Accrue method is back to being only the business logic with which we started.

The Redeem method is also back to only business logic.

Looks good to me. All of the cross-cutting concerns are now in their own classes. The services are back to their initial unspoiled single responsibility state. They're easier to read.

Are they easier to change? If you add or change the names of the methods or the parameters of the methods, then the aspects you wrote can cope with that (particularly defensive programming and logging). The aspects don't care if the business logic changes (for example, if you changed it from 10/15 points to 15/20 points). The business logic doesn't care if you switch from using `Console` to using log4net/NLog. Or if you need to use something else besides `TransactionScope`. Or if you want to change the maximum retries from three to five.

Even more important, if you add a new method to either service (or if you add a new service), you can reuse the aspects that you've already written instead of copying and pasting similar code every time.

Maybe you're looking at that stack of attributes on each method—isn't that just another form of tight coupling and/or repetition that will have to be copied and pasted? Perhaps. For this example, it's not a big deal because our project is so small. In later chapters, you'll learn how to multicast aspects to an entire class, namespace, or assembly with PostSharp.

2.5   *Summary*

The first goal of this chapter was to demonstrate that cross-cutting concerns can muck up your code. Normal OOP and good use of design patterns can help you refactor but in many cases can get you only part of the way and can still leave your business logic tightly coupled to cross-cutting concerns. Even if your code follows principles such as Single Responsibility and DI, often it's not enough and can still leave your code tangled, scattered, or repetitive.

The second goal was to show that the cost of change is tied to how flexible, readable, and modular your code is. Even with good refactoring, you'll find some cross-cutting concerns in traditional OOP that can't be easily decoupled.

The final goal was to show how an AOP tool such as PostSharp is able to get you that last mile of loose coupling among cross-cutting concerns. In the PostSharp-refactored version, each of the cross-cutting concerns had its own class, and the services were reduced to performing business logic and *only* business logic.

This chapter is a crash course in using AOP. If this is your first time writing an aspect (it probably isn't—even if you think it is, keep reading and you'll see that it might not be), then you're well on your way to creating better architected software that's more flexible and easier to change and maintain. In the next chapter, I'm going to expand on the reasons to use AOP, focus on the benefits it provides, and examine in more detail how cross-cutting concerns can wreak havoc in your code.

Part 2

The Fundamentals
of AOP

These four chapters cover common types of aspects provided by third-party frameworks. Chapter 3 focuses on method interception and how to use Castle DynamicProxy as well as PostSharp to intercept methods.

In chapter 4, method interception and method bounding are compared. You'll learn how to write an ASP.NET HttpModule to help detect whether a user is on a mobile device, in order to direct them to your mobile app.

Location interception, covered in chapter 5, is a less common feature of AOP frameworks, but you'll learn all about it using PostSharp. Another tool that will be explored in this chapter is NotifyPropertyWeaver, which uses a more specialized approach.

All code needs to be tested, even when using AOP. Chapter 6 covers unit testing of aspects as well as testing code to which that aspects are applied. We'll use NUnit with Castle DynamicProxy and PostSharp, and discuss dependencies within aspects.

Call this instead: intercepting methods

3

This chapter covers

- What method interception means
- Using Castle DynamicProxy to intercept methods
- Writing a data transaction aspect
- Using PostSharp to intercept methods
- Writing a threading aspect

In chapter one, I talked about join points and pointcuts. I left the definition of these terms fairly broad, defining a join point as any point in between your code and describing a pointcut as a collection of join points. I kept these definitions loose because aspects can theoretically be applied to *any* location in your code that you can describe. You could put an aspect inside of an `if` statement or use it to modify a `for` loop. But you don't need to do that 99% of the time in practical application.

Good frameworks (like PostSharp and Castle DynamicProxy) make it easy to write aspects using predefined join points and give you limited ability to describe pointcuts. However, you'll retain enough flexibility to tackle the vast majority of AOP use cases.

What about that 1%?

Low-level tools are available that let you modify or create code all the way down to the instruction level (IL). These tools include Mono.Cecil, the PostSharp SDK, .NET Reflection, and Reflection.Emit. But these tools aren't the focus of this book. I'm focusing on writing aspects, not on the entire realm of metaprogramming. We'll revisit some of the low-level tools in chapter 7 and appendix A.

In the next few chapters, I cover common types of aspects that these third-party frameworks provide. In this chapter, we'll look at method interception aspects. These are aspects that run code in place of another method, whenever that method is called. Even though I'll be using only two tools in this chapter, method interception is perhaps the most common feature of all AOP frameworks. PostSharp and Castle DynamicProxy make it easy to jump right in and start coding. Once you have a good feel for method interceptors with these frameworks, you should be able to tread water with any framework that includes method interception.

The point of this chapter isn't to teach you everything about these two frameworks but to give you a push in the right direction with one of the most common features in all AOP frameworks. At the end, you'll know how to write simple method interception aspects, and you'll have a couple of practical aspects for data transactions and threading to build upon.

3.1   *Method interception*

A method interception aspect is one that runs a piece of code in place of the method being intercepted. The aspect is executed instead of the method. It's like having a middleman or a gatekeeper between normal execution and a method.

To illustrate this concept, let's look at a simple program that calls a single method. The method returns control to the program when it's done. (Sometimes a method returns a value to the program, but not in this example.) Figure 3.1 shows a normal program flow of a hypothethical Twitter service method used to send a tweet.

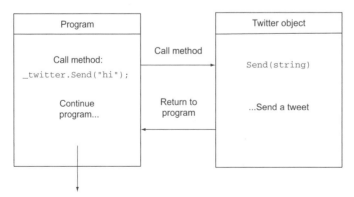

Figure 3.1   Normal flow: calling a method and returning control

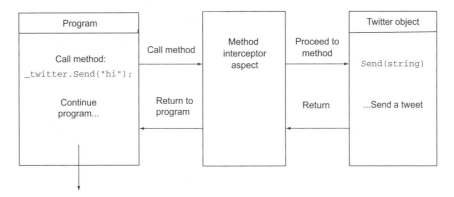

Figure 3.2 Intercepted flow: the method interceptor is a middleman

Intercepting that method to call some other code may sound like a bad idea, like adding a middleman to a transaction: why not just deal directly? But just like middlemen in real life, method interception does serve an important purpose. Figure 3.2 shows a diagram of the same program as before with an added method interceptor.

What could we put in that interceptor? We could log that a tweet is about to be sent. We could validate the string being sent. We could modify the string being sent to the method. We could log that the tweet was sent. If the tweet failed (for example, if Send throws an exception or returns false), we could log that it failed. If it fails, we could try resending the tweet. We could add a variety of behavior without changing one line of code in the Send method itself.

Note that you aren't completely replacing the method. In most cases, the aspect allows execution to continue to the intercepted method. What you're doing is having some other piece of code run before the method executes (and/or after the method returns).

Now that I've defined and illustrated method interception, let's create a method interception aspect in real code. By the end of this section, you'll be able to write a method interception aspect using the PostSharp framework.

3.1.1 PostSharp method interception

Let's try to move the diagrams from the previous section into a real implementation in code. This exercise will help you learn how to write method interception code and give you an introduction to the PostSharp way of writing a method interception aspect. I'll create the basic program in a console application, then add a method interceptor to it.

Start a new project in Visual Studio: select Console Application. I'm calling my project TweetPostSharp. You can add PostSharp easily to your project with NuGet. You can install it with the NuGet UI by searching for PostSharp or install it with NuGet's package manager console.

```
PM> Install-Package PostSharp
Successfully installed 'PostSharp 2.1.7.10'.
Successfully added 'PostSharp 2.1.7.10' to TweetPostSharp.
```

I'll start by creating the `Twitter` service class. This class won't interface with `Twitter`; it'll just write to `Console` for demonstration. I'll also create an instance of it in `Main` and call its `Send` method.

> **Listing 3.1   Calling `Send` method on `TwitterClient` service class**

```
public class TwitterClient {
    public void Send(string msg) {
        Console.WriteLine("Sending: {0}", msg);
    }
}

class Program {
    static void Main(string[] args) {
        var svc = new TwitterClient();
        svc.Send("hi");
    }
}
```

Compile and run, and you should see the modest console output shown in figure 3.3.

So far, so good. We've written code to match the diagram. Now it's time to use PostSharp to create the interceptor aspect. Use the following code to create a class that inherits the `MethodInterceptionAspect` base class:

> **Serializable**
> Make sure to use the `[Serializable]` attribute on aspect classes when using PostSharp. The PostSharp framework needs to instantiate and serialize aspect objects so that they can be deserialized and used after compiling.

```
[Serializable]
public class MyInterceptorAspect : MethodInterceptionAspect
{

}
```

Now that you have an interceptor, you need to indicate what method it should intercept. With PostSharp, you do this by using the aspect class as an attribute (listing 3.2).

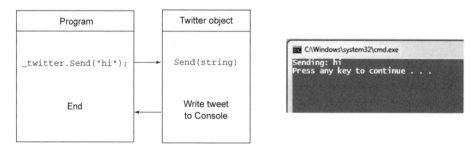

Figure 3.3 Console output simulating a tweet

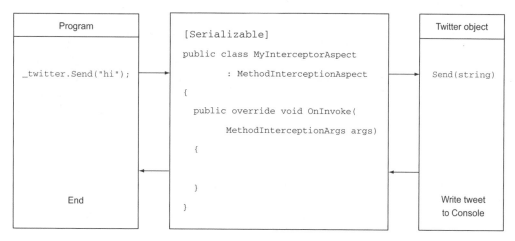

Figure 3.4   Diagram with a real PostSharp method interception aspect

```
public class TwitterClient {
    [MyInterceptorAspect]
    public void Send(string msg) {
        Console.WriteLine("Sending: {0}", msg);
    }
}
```

This service doesn't send a message to Twitter; instead, it's writing to Console for demonstration.

And there you have it: now you're intercepting any calls to Send with MyInterceptor-Aspect, as figure 3.4 illustrates.

But it's not even close to being useful, because there's nothing in MyInterceptor-Aspect yet.

We'll get to some examples of real behavior that you might want to use in an aspect later in this chapter. For now, let's write to Console to demonstrate the basics. To start adding some intercepting behavior with PostSharp, override the base class's OnInvoke method:

```
[Serializable]
public class MyInterceptorAspect : MethodInterceptionAspect {
    public override void OnInvoke(MethodInterceptionArgs args) {

    }
}
```

If you were to run the program at this point, the interceptor would run the code in OnInvoke, but because OnInvoke doesn't do anything, the real Send method that was intercepted won't ever be called. To proceed to the intercepted method, use the args parameter's Invoke method:

```
[Serializable]
public class MyInterceptorAspect : MethodInterceptionAspect {
```

```
public override void OnInvoke(MethodInterceptionArgs args) {
    args.Proceed();                              ◁──┐  Proceed means "Proceed to
}                                                   │  the intercepted method."
```
}

Run the program again and the Send method will be called, writing to console. The program is still not too interesting, because it's not adding any additional behavior yet: it's only a passthrough to the method. Now let's add code to the interceptor:

```
[Serializable]
public class MyInterceptorAspect : MethodInterceptionAspect {
    public override void OnInvoke(MethodInterceptionArgs args) {
        Console.WriteLine("Interceptor 1");      ◁──┐  Writing to console before
        args.Proceed();                             │  "proceeding" to the
        Console.WriteLine("Interceptor 2");         │  intercepted method
    }
}
```

Writing to console after the intercepted method successfully executes (points to `Console.WriteLine("Interceptor 2");`)

Run the application. Figure 3.5 shows the new output that you'll see.

It's not yet an interesting use of interception, but it's a start. You'll see how to use a Post-Sharp interception aspect to make threading easier a couple of sections from now. But first, let's look at another way to write interceptors: using Castle DynamicProxy.

```
C:\Windows\system32\cmd.exe
Sending: hi
Press any key to continue . . .
```

Figure 3.5   Console output with interceptor

3.1.2   *Castle DynamicProxy method interception*

We're going to write the same program and interceptor as in the previous section. This time, you'll use a different tool that has a similar API: Castle DynamicProxy. These tools provide similar capabilities as far as method interception, but they differ in many key ways. We'll explore the details of how AOP tools are implemented (Post-Sharp and DynamicProxy in particular) in chapter 7. For now, because we're only scratching the surface, let's say that PostSharp does its work right after compilation and DynamicProxy does its work during runtime.

You can use the same project if you want, but I'll create a new console project called TweetDynamicProxy. Castle DynamicProxy is part of the Castle.Core library. I'll install it with NuGet, using the package manager console:

```
PM> Install-Package Castle.Core
Successfully installed 'Castle.Core 3.1.0'.
Successfully added 'Castle.Core 3.1.0' to TweetDynamicProxy.
```

I'll use the same Main and TwitterClient code I used in an earlier section.

> **Listing 3.3   Calling the Send method on the TwitterClient service class**

```
public class TwitterClient {
    public void Send(string msg) {
```

```
        Console.WriteLine("Sending: {0}", msg);
    }
}

class Program {
    static void Main(string[] args) {
        var svc = new TwitterClient();
        svc.Send("hi");
    }
}
```

Run it, and you'll see the same output, as shown in figure 3.6.

Figure 3.6 Console output simulating a tweet again

To create an interceptor with Castle DynamicProxy, create a class that implements the
IInterceptor interface (the interface has one method: Intercept):

```
public class MyInterceptorAspect : IInterceptor {
    public void Intercept(IInvocation invocation) {

    }
}
```

Now we need to tell DynamicProxy what code to intercept. With PostSharp, you can
pick a single method, but with Castle DynamicProxy, you apply an interceptor to an
entire object. (DynamicProxy can target individual methods like PostSharp, using
IInterceptorSelector, but it still must create a proxy for an entire class.) Using Castle DynamicProxy, this is a two-step process:

1 Create a ProxyGenerator.
2 Use the ProxyGenerator to apply the interceptor.

Create a ProxyGenerator with normal instantiation. Use that proxy generator to apply
the interceptor and pass it an instance of the TwitterClient object. I'll use the
CreateClassProxy method of the ProxyGenerator's API because it's the fastest way to
demonstrate DynamicProxy, but we'll explore other options later. Make these changes
in the Main method:

```
        static void Main(string[] args)
        {
            var proxyGenerator = new ProxyGenerator();   ⟵  Create a ProxyGenerator to
                                                              act as an object factory
            var svc = proxyGenerator
                .CreateClassProxy<TwitterClient>(         ⟵  CreateClassProxy's first argument is
                    new MyInterceptorAspect());               an instance of the interceptor to use.
            svc.Send("hi");
        }
```

The type specified (TwitterClient) will be the class that is proxied.

There's one more critical step in making this work. The `Send` method must be made into a `virtual` method. If you don't do this, then the interception code won't be executed:

```
public class TwitterClient {
    public virtual void Send(string msg) {
        Console.WriteLine("Sending: {0}", msg);
    }
}
```

Castle DynamicProxy and virtual

The type of object that `CreateClassProxy` returns isn't `TwitterClient`, but it's a type that's generated dynamically with `TwitterClient` as its base class. Therefore, each method that you want to intercept must be `virtual` in order to add additional functionality.

If you've used NHibernate, then you're familiar with its similar requirements. This isn't merely coincidence: NHibernate uses Castle DynamicProxy.

If you find this design annoying or cumbersome, don't panic. I only had to do this because I am intercepting a concrete class (`TwitterClient`). If I had used an interface as well (`ITwitterClient`, for instance), then I could use a `ProxyGenerator` method such as `CreateInterfaceProxyWithTarget` instead, and the members wouldn't have to be virtual. In fact, I'll do this in later examples that use Castle DynamicProxy along with an IoC tool such as `StructureMap`.

Now you're intercepting the method call, but the `MyInterceptorAspect` isn't doing anything—not even calling the intercepted method. Let's at least get this interceptor to act as a passthrough first, and then we can add behavior to it.

To tell the interceptor to proceed to the intercepted method, use the `invocation` parameter's `Proceed` method:

```
public class MyInterceptorAspect : IInterceptor {
    public void Intercept(IInvocation invocation) {
        invocation.Proceed();
    }
}
```

> Like PostSharp, DynamicProxy has a proceed method in its API, which does the same thing: proceeds to the intercepted method.

Now it's at least working as a passthrough. Let's add behavior to the interceptor (see the next listing). Again, you're only writing to `Console` for now. (We'll look at more realistic examples later in this chapter.)

Listing 3.4 Adding code to the interceptor

```
public class MyInterceptorAspect : IInterceptor {
    public void Intercept(IInvocation invocation) {
        Console.WriteLine("Interceptor 1");
        invocation.Proceed();
        Console.WriteLine("Interceptor 2");
    }
}
```

> Like the previous PostSharp example, sandwich a proceed between Console.WriteLine commands

And as figure 3.7 shows, we'll see the same console output that we saw with the PostSharp example (figure 3.5).

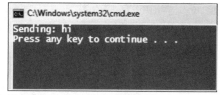

Figure 3.7   Console output with a tweet and interceptors

As before, this isn't a particularly interesting example, but you're on your way to understanding the basics of method interception. PostSharp and Castle DynamicProxy differ in many significant ways, but as far as the basics of method interception, they have similar APIs and capabilities.

Let's leave the Twitter example by the wayside for now and dig into a much more practical example. In the previous section, you learned the basics of writing method interception aspects in two of the most popular AOP frameworks for .NET. Let's put your new expertise to work. In the next section, we'll use more of the Castle Dynamic-Proxy API to write an aspect that can help make data transactions easier.

3.2   Real-world example: data transactions

Transaction management can be an important part of working with databases. If several database operations are related, you often want them all to succeed or you want them all to fail. Any other combination might cause your data to enter an invalid or inconsistent state.

One way this goal can be achieved is with transactions. The basic components of a transaction are:

- *Begin*—Mark where a transaction starts.
- *Perform related operations*—For example, database operations (usually two or more).
- *Commit*—When operations are completed, commit indicates that the transaction is over.
- *Rollback*—If something goes wrong in the operations, roll back instead of committing, and return to the beginning state.
- *Retry (optional)*—Not strictly related to transactions, but after a rollback, a retry can often be attempted.

Transactions can be useful, but they're definitely a cross-cutting concern that can add a lot of boilerplate and noise to your code. Therefore, an aspect can come in handy. Next, we're going to create a transaction aspect using an interceptor aspect with Castle DynamicProxy.

3.2.1   Ensuring data integrity with begin and commit

To start, let's focus on the basic structure of a transacton: begin and commit. For this section, I'll assume that our transaction will always behave, so I won't add any rollback code yet.

As in the previous examples, I'm going to create a console project and add Castle DynamicProxy using NuGet. I'll call this example DataTransactionsCastle.

Before we can demonstrate a transaction, we have to create some code worth transacting with. Let's start by creating a service class. This call will have one method that creates an invoice. This method will take an invoice as a parameter and perform several database operations. The actual database operations aren't important for this example, so to demonstrate the possibilities I'm going to create three methods that behave in three different ways:

- A Save method that always succeeds, to demonstrate the happy path.
- A Save method that succeeds after a retry, to demonstrate how retries work.
- A Save method that always fails, to demonstrate running out of retry attempts.

The following listing shows the code for the three methods. For a failure, you can throw whatever exception you want, but I'll use DataException, which is in the System.Data namespace.

Listing 3.5   Three different transaction scenarios

```
public class InvoiceService {
    public virtual void Save(Invoice invoice) {

    }
    bool _isRetry;
    public virtual void SaveRetry(Invoice invoice) {
        if (!_isRetry) {
            _isRetry = true;
            throw new DataException();
        }
    }

    public virtual void SaveFail(Invoice invoice) {
        throw new DataException();
    }
}
```

No exceptions are thrown here, so this method will always succeed.

Real method(s) would have multiple data operations in them to save an invoice (for example, multiple insert/select queries).

This method will fail the first time through, but will succeed every time after that.

This method will always throw an exception and fail.

Note that I've made all three methods virtual, in anticipation of using Castle DynamicProxy.

In a Main method, I can create an invoice, pass it to the Save method, and then write a success message to console, as shown here.

Listing 3.6   A Main method to try out the Save scenarios

```
static void Main(string[] args) {
    var invoiceService = new InvoiceService();
    var invoice = new Invoice
    {
        InvoiceId = Guid.NewGuid(),
        InvoiceDate = DateTime.Now,
        Items = new List<string> {"Item1", "Item2", "Item3"}
    };
    invoiceService.Save(invoice);
```

```
//invoiceService.SaveRetry(invoice);
//invoiceService.SaveFail(invoice);
Console.WriteLine("Save successful");
}
```

The console output would show the save successful message, as shown in figure 3.8.

If I switch `Save` with `SaveRetry` (see figure 3.9) or `SaveFail` (see figure 3.10), I get an exception from each.

I've split these three possibilities out into their own methods for demonstration; in reality, all three conditions would exist in an individual service method. The first example is what we're all rooting for, but we need to plan for the other scenarios, too.

We could add transaction code directly to the service class, but think back to the Single Responsibility Principle. A class should have only one reason to change. If we add transaction code, then we're making this class do two things. Instead, let's create a separate interceptor to do all the work in a reusable way.

Let's first create an empty interceptor and wire it up to the invoice service instance. I'll call it `TransactionWithRetries` because over time I'll add retry capabilities to it. For now, let's use the interceptor to create a transaction, as in the following listing.

Listing 3.7 Basic transaction interceptor, used with proxy generator

```
public class TransactionWithRetries : IInterceptor {
    public void Intercept(IInvocation invocation)
    {
        var trans = new TransactionScope();
        invocation.Proceed();
        trans.Complete();
    }
}
```

Proceed to the intercepted method; all of its operations will be included in the transaction.

Instantiating TransactionScope starts a new transaction.

When the method succeeds, using Complete will indicate that the transaction can be committed.

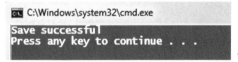

Figure 3.8 Console reporting that the save was successful.

Figure 3.9 SaveRetry fails on the first attempt.

Figure 3.10 SaveFail will always fail.

The first thing I'm doing in the previous code is use a `TransactionScope`, as in chapter 2.

TransactionScope

`TransactionScope` is part of `System.Transactions`, which comes with the .NET framework. If `TransactionScope` is disposed of (such as via a `using` block ending or by calling `Dispose` explicitly) without calling the `Complete` method on it, then `TransactionScope` will consider the operation a failure and will roll back.

`TransactionScope` is a helpful API to manage ambient transactions (ambient meaning that databases that support `TransactionScope` will automatically manage the transaction themselves). This API is supported by a variety of popular databases, including Microsoft SQL.

If you're using a database or some transaction-based system that doesn't support `TransactionScope`, you can still use an interceptor, but you'll have to change the code to use the appropriate supported transaction API (for instance, using the `Begin-Transaction` API to get your database provider's `IDbTransaction` implementation).

If the intercepted method proceeds without exception (and we're all rooting for it to do so), then it will call `Complete()` on the `TransactionScope` and we're done.

To start using this aspect, again make use of a `ProxyGenerator` in `Main`, as the following listing shows.

Listing 3.8   Using `ProxyGenerator` to apply the `TransactionWithRetries` aspect

```
static void Main(string[] args) {
    var proxyGenerator = new ProxyGenerator();
    var invoiceService = proxyGenerator            Wrap an instance of
        .CreateClassProxy<InvoiceService>(          InvoiceService with the
            new TransactionWithRetries());          transaction interceptor
                                                    aspect via ProxyGenerator
    var invoice = new Invoice {
        InvoiceId = Guid.NewGuid(),
        InvoiceDate = DateTime.Now,
        Items = new List<string> {"Item1", "Item2", "Item3"}    Leave one of the
    };                                                          three scenarios
    invoiceService.Save(invoice);                               uncommented
    //invoiceService.SaveRetry(invoice);                        to test it
    //invoiceService.SaveFail(invoice);            Write a message to console to
    Console.WriteLine("Save successful");          indicate that the uncommented
}                                                  method finished successfully
```

Now all of the `Save` methods will be placed inside of transactions. We start a new transaction (begin) by instantiating a new `TransactionScope` object. We end (commit) the transaction by calling its `Complete` method. Now the ideal scenario (represented by `Save`) is covered. What if something goes wrong?

3.2.2   *When transactions go bad: rollback*

Of course, if transactions always succeeded, there would be no need for transactions. The whole point of them is to identify a series of commands that can be rolled back if something goes wrong. So in this section, I'll talk about how to add a rollback to our transaction aspect.

Because we're using .NET's `TransactionScope`, there is no explicit rollback command. The closest equivalent is its `Dispose()` method. If `TransactionScope` is disposed before its `Complete()` method is called, `TransactionScope` will then perform a rollback. Otherwise, it won't. So, as the next listing shows, we must add a `Dispose` call to our transaction interceptor aspect.

> **Listing 3.9   Using `Dispose` to rollback**

```
public class TransactionWithRetries : IInterceptor {
    public void Intercept(IInvocation invocation) {
        var trans = new TransactionScope();
        invocation.Proceed();
        trans.Complete();
        trans.Dispose();
    }
}
```

A new TransactionScope object starts a new ambient transaction.

Using Complete means that the transaction can be safely committed.

Calling Dispose on a TransactionScope commits the transaction immediately if Complete has been called, otherwise it will rollback the transaction immediately.

In C#, we can write this a little more concisely with the `using` syntax (which works only with objects that implement .NET's `IDisposable` interface):

```
public class TransactionWithRetries : IInterceptor {
    public void Intercept(IInvocation invocation) {
        using (var trans = new TransactionScope()) {
            invocation.Proceed();
            trans.Complete();
        }
    }
}
```

The using syntax starts with a new instance of a disposable object

When the using block terminates, Dispose is called on the object specified in the using statement.

If the intercepted method completes without throwing an exception, then `trans.Complete()` will be called and the transaction will be committed. If an exception occurs in the intercepted method, then the `TransactionScope` object will be disposed of before `trans.Complete()` gets a chance to be called (thanks to the `using` syntax and the .NET garbage collector), triggering a rollback.

This aspect continues to cover the ideal scenario (`Save`), and it now also covers the worst-case scenario (`SaveFail`). All we have left to do is cover the last scenario: `SaveRetry`.

3.2.3   *When all else fails, retry*

Let's review the three possibilities: success, retry success, and failure. The interceptor we've written so far covers the possibility of success, certainly. It also covers the possibility of failure, because it won't allow any of the operations to finish unless they all succeed (by using a rollback). But it doesn't cover the possibility of retry success.

This listing shows how we can add a loop to retry.

Listing 3.10   Adding a loop to retry

```
public void Intercept(IInvocation invocation) {
    var retries = 3;                                    ◁—┐  The number of retries
    var succeeded = false;                                   must be specified;
    while (!succeeded)                                       otherwise, you could
      {                                                      be stuck retrying for a
        using (var trans = new TransactionScope())           long time.
        {
            try
            {
                invocation.Proceed();                         When the intercepted
                trans.Complete();                             method succeeds and
                succeeded = true;              ◁—┘            the transaction is
            }                                                 complete, it's safe to
            catch (Exception)                                 assume success.
            {
                if (retries >= 0)
                {
                    Console.WriteLine("Retrying");            Decrement the retry
                    retries--;                    ◁—          count and let the code
                }                                             loop again
                else
                    throw;            ◁—┐
            }                            When you run out of retries, rethrow the
        }                                exception (you could also put logging or
    }                                    other exception handling code here).
}
```

Keep retrying until the method succeeds

At this point, we've added a loop and a retry condition. I've hardcoded this aspect to retry up to three times. We need only one to get the SaveRetry service to succeed this time, as figure 3.11 shows.

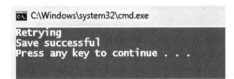

Figure 3.11   Success after one retry

But I think we can do better than hardcoding. Let's move the number of retries to a constructor parameter so that it can be more easily configured, as shown next.

Listing 3.11   Transaction with maximum retries specified in constructor

```
public class TransactionWithRetries : IInterceptor {
    readonly int _maxRetries;                           ◁—┐  Store the maximum retries
    public TransactionWithRetries(int maxRetries) {          as a public property to be
        _maxRetries = maxRetries;                            used when intercepting.
```

```
    }

    public void Intercept(IInvocation invocation) {
        var retries = _maxRetries;
        var succeeded = false;
        while (!succeeded) {
            using (var trans = new TransactionScope()) {
                try {
                    invocation.Proceed();
                    trans.Complete();
                    succeeded = true;
                }
                catch (Exception) {
                    if (retries >= 0) {
                        Console.WriteLine("Retrying");
                        retries--;
                    }
                    else throw;
                }
            }
        }
    }
}
```

> Instead of a hard-coded value, use the value that was passed to the constructor.

To use that interceptor with the proxy generator, add the number of retries as an argument to the constructor:

```
var invoiceService = proxyGenerator
    .CreateClassProxy<InvoiceService>(
        new TransactionWithRetries(3));
```

We can make one more little improvement to this interceptor aspect. Instead of writing only "Retrying" to the console when there's a retry, it would be much more helpful to see "Retrying" and the name of the method. For instance, "Retrying SaveRetry," as figure 3.12 shows.

How do we get the method name? You may have already noticed (via intellisense) that Proceed() isn't the only thing you can do with the invocation parameter to the Intercept method. This parameter also has other interesting contextual information.

For instance, invocation.Method returns a MethodInfo object (from the System .Reflection namespace), representing the method that is being intercepted. Among other things, the MethodInfo class has a Name property, which can give us the method's name. Change the Console.WriteLine statement to the following:

```
Console.WriteLine("Retrying {0}", invocation.Method.Name);
```

Now you'll get the "Retrying SaveRetry" message written to console. Experiment with the other properties available to you on that IInvocation invocation parameter:

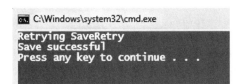

Figure 3.12 Console reporting that there was one retry before successful save

there's a lot of contextual information that you can read and modify with it. You've created a very useful interceptor aspect, and you've barely scratched the surface of the DynamicProxy API.

Let's shift back to PostSharp now and look at a real-world example of a PostSharp interceptor aspect.

3.3   *Real-world example: threading*

When you load a program into memory and start to execute it, it's known as a process. The CPU reads each instruction of the process, one at a time. Sometimes you want more than one thing to be processed. While you're waiting for a slow web service, you may want to keep the user informed of progress via the UI. To do this, you might use threads, which are like miniprocesses.

Web developers don't see as many opportunities to use the threading capabilities of .NET as do desktop or mobile developers. But even for veteran desktop developers, threading can be a painful experience: it's hard to write, hard to debug, hard to read, and hard to test. Yet threading often can't be avoided when writing code to create a responsive desktop experience.

I'm not going to tell you that using aspects will make threading easier to debug and test. You'll probably need another book for that. But we can take a step in the right direction by making threaded code a little easier to write (and to read).

Let's start with a quick refresher on the basics of threading in a .NET application.

3.3.1   *The basics of .NET threading*

You can do threading with .NET in a few different ways. As multicore programming becomes more important and more common, the number of ways to write a multithreaded program increases. Microsoft and other third-party tools provide a number of threading options that are all worth exploring further.

I'm going to focus on the old-fashioned `Thread` class for the example in this section. If you prefer another way of writing threaded code, there's good news: AOP makes it easy to make that change in a modular, encapsulated way instead of in multiple places cross-cutting your code.

Now let's get started writing some threaded code.

Suppose you have a method called `DoWork` that takes a long time to run, and therefore you want to run it in a worker thread, freeing up the UI to update the users on the status of the work or allow them to start other operations. To run `DoWork` in another thread, simply create a `Thread` object and start it:

```
var thread = new Thread(DoWork);
thread.Start();
```

This code may look simple, but the `Thread` class has a lot of other capabilities: checking to see whether a thread is still alive, setting it to be a background thread, thread priority, and so on. And often you'll need other parts of the `System.Threading` API, such as `ManualResetEvent`, `ThreadPool`, `Mutex`, and perhaps the `lock` keyword. Even with other APIs and newer tools, I can't overstate how complex threads can be to use: threads are not something that you should undertake lightly.

For this section, I'm going to focus on a common and relatively simple use case for threads: a graphic UI that triggers worker threads (which may themselves need to update the UI) in order to demonstrate a valuable way to use method interception.

3.3.2   UI threads and worker threads

I'm going to start by creating a simple desktop application that uses threading without any AOP. I'll create a new Windows Forms Application project in Visual Studio. You should get a Form1 class created by default. I'll add one button and one ListBox to make it look something like figure 3.13.

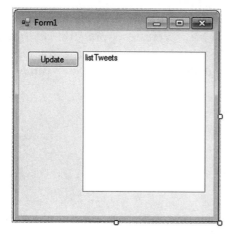

Figure 3.13   A desktop application

I want this form to update the list of tweets via a web service when I click the update button. The following is a service class to get (simulated) tweets:

```
public class TwitterService {
    public string GetTweet() {
        Thread.Sleep(3000);
        return "Tweet from " + DateTime.Now.TimeOfDay;
    }
}
```

> Simulate a slow web service by putting the thread to sleep

Double-click the Update button in the Visual Studio form editor to automatically generate a click event handler. Put a bit of code in that method to update the ListBox of tweets, as shown here.

Listing 3.12   Full Form1 class with button click event handler

```
public partial class Form1 : Form {
    TwitterService _twitter;

    public Form1() {
        InitializeComponent();
```

> This is the code-behind that Form1 uses. It's partial because all the generated layout code is in a separate code-behind file.

```
    }

    protected override void OnLoad(EventArgs e) {
        _twitter = new TwitterService();
    }

    private void btnUpdate_Click(object sender, EventArgs e) {
        var tweet = _twitter.GetTweet();
        listTweets.Items.Add(tweet);
    }
}
```

This method handles the button click event, which is automatically configured for you by Visual Studio.

That works, but if you run it, you'll find that while the GetTweet method is running, nothing else on the UI works. You can't move the window, you can't press the button again, and you can't scroll or click on items in the list, as figure 3.14 illustrates.

I don't want the UI to lock up while it's hitting the web service (maybe I'll want to show a loading animation or allow the user to perform other operations while the list of tweets is loading). In order to do this, I have to create a worker thread to run while the UI thread remains available to handle other operations (clicks, scrolling, etc.). I'll move the tweet update code into its own method and start a thread to run it:

```
private void btnUpdate_Click(object sender, EventArgs e) {
    var thread = new Thread(GetNewTweet);
    thread.Start();
}

void GetNewTweet() {
    var tweet = _twitter.GetTweet();
    listTweets.Items.Add(tweet);
}
```

That looks good. Run it (not in debug mode), and you'll see that the UI remains responsive after you click Update. You can even click Update again to trigger another thread (and so on).

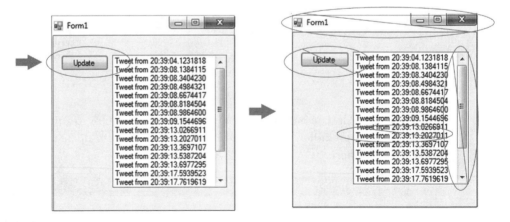

Figure 3.14 Because GetTweet **runs on the UI thread, the other UI controls are unable to accept input while it's running.**

Try it again in debug mode, and you'll get an InvalidOperationException when your code tries to add an item to the list. What gives? In a Windows Forms application, the UI controls aren't thread-safe. Much like a database transaction, if you're manipulating a UI control from multiple threads, you could put it into an inconsistent state. Therefore, manipulating Control objects from a thread other than the UI thread is a bad idea. (You'll always get an exception in debug mode, and you may get all kinds of bad behavior or exceptions when not in debug mode.)

So how do we check whether we're running on the UI thread? And if we're not, how do we run the code on the UI thread? Use the InvokeRequired and Invoke members of Form1, inherited from the Form base class, as shown next.

Listing 3.13   Checking whether Invoke is necessary

```
void GetNewTweet()
{
    var tweet = _twitter.GetTweet();
    if (InvokeRequired)
        this.Invoke(new Action(() => listTweets.Items.Add(tweet)));
    else
        listTweets.Items.Add(tweet);
}
```

> **InvokeRequired and Invoke**
>
> InvokeRequired is the way to ask whether the current thread is on the UI thread. If it is true, then the current thread is *not* on the UI thread. If that's the case, then you must use Invoke to execute code that will be working with Windows Forms controls.
>
> This pattern isn't limited to Windows Forms. The specific way to check the current thread and use the UI thread may vary depending on the type of application you're using. Windows Presentation Foundation (WPF) uses Dispatcher.CheckAccess and Dispatcher.Invoke. Other UI technologies such as Mono for Android, Windows Phone, and Silverlight may also vary.

There's some repetition now, so it might be best to refactor into yet another method, GetNewTweet:

```
void GetNewTweet() {
    var tweet = _twitter.GetTweet();
    if (InvokeRequired)
        this.Invoke(new Action(() => UpdateTweetListBox(tweet)));      ⟵
    else
        UpdateTweetListBox(tweet);      ⟵
}
void UpdateTweetListBox(string tweet) {      ⟵
    listTweets.Items.Add(tweet);
}
```

There are other syntaxes that you can use with Invoke; I'm creating an Action object with a lambda.

Replace the repeated code with another call to UpdateTweetListBox

Code to add an item to the list is refactored into this method.

Now run the program again (in debug mode), and it won't cause an Invalid-OperationException. Great, except that now the code has gotten quite long and messy, even for a ridiculously simple example (imagine a more complex form with multiple threaded operations). Don't say I didn't warn you: threading is messy.

But I also promised to show you a way to make threading easier to read and write. Let's imagine a much shorter, clearer, declarative way to write the Form1 code. It would be nice if our code looked more like the following.

Listing 3.14   Wouldn't it be nice if threading were more like this?

```
private void btnUpdate_Click(object sender, EventArgs e) {      ◁  No more Thread
    GetNewTweet();                                                 object in the
}                                                                  click handler

[WorkerThread]                                                 ◁  An attribute declaring
void GetNewTweet() {                                               this method for a
    var tweet = _twitter.GetTweet();                               worker thread
    UpdateTweetListBox(tweet);
}

[UIThread]                                                     ◁  An attribute
void UpdateTweetListBox(string tweet) {                           declaring this
    listTweets.Items.Add(tweet);                                  method for a UI
}
```

There are three main changes in the previous listing. First, in the click event handler (btnUpdate_Click), we're no longer creating a Thread object: we're only calling the method directly. Much clearer to read without any noise about starting a new thread.

Second, the GetNewTweet() method has an attribute that declares that it will be run on a worker thread. Notice that the code inside the method doesn't have any Invoke-Required or Invoke noise. It's easier to read, and we know exactly what it's doing.

Finally, the UpdateTweetListBox() method remains the same, except that it has an attribute declaring that it will be running on the UI thread.

This hypothetical code is shorter, more declarative, and contains no threading details. Putting code on a worker thread becomes as easy as using an attribute. Not only is it declarative, but if we want to change the threading details (to use the .NET 4 Task class, for instance), that needs to be done in only one place.

But this isn't a hypothetical situation: we can do this type of declarative threading with AOP by writing two small interceptor aspects.

3.3.3   *Declarative threading with AOP*

We need two interceptor aspects to achieve declarative threading: one aspect to intercept a method call and put it on a worker thread, and another aspect to intercept a method call and make sure that it runs on the UI thread.

Start by adding PostSharp to your project with NuGet via the NuGet UI or command line (Install-Package PostSharp).

Create a `WorkerThread` aspect class that uses `MethodInterceptionAspect` as a base class and overrides `OnInvoke`:

```
[Serializable]
public class WorkerThread : MethodInterceptionAspect
{
    public override void OnInvoke(MethodInterceptionArgs args)
    {

    }
}
```

The goal is to move the intercepted method on to a new thread. To do this, I'm going to proceed to the intercepted method by using `args.Proceed()`, but I'm going to do it on a new thread:

```
[Serializable]
public class WorkerThread : MethodInterceptionAspect
{
    public override void OnInvoke(MethodInterceptionArgs args)
    {
        var thread = new Thread(args.Proceed);      ◁── Notice the parentheses.
        thread.Start();                                 args.Proceed is being
    }                                                   passed to the Thread
}                                                       constructor.
```

This aspect gets us most of the way there, but if the worker thread needs to update the UI, we'll run into problems again if we don't check `InvokeRequired`. That's why we'll create a companion `UIThread` interceptor aspect. Create a `UIThread` aspect that also uses `MethodInterceptionAspect`:

```
[Serializable]
public class UIThread : MethodInterceptionAspect
{
    public override void OnInvoke(MethodInterceptionArgs args)
    {

    }
}
```

The goal of this aspect is to check whether an `Invoke` is required and to use `Invoke` if it is. But wait a minute: how can I use the `InvokeRequired` property and the `Invoke` method in this class, which is separate from `Form1`? Fortunately, PostSharp provides a way. We can get to the instance object of the method that we're intercepting by using the `args` parameter: `args.Instance`. It returns `object`, so we have to cast it to type `Form` before using `InvokeRequired` and `Invoke` (as shown next).

Listing 3.15 `UIThread` interceptor aspect

```
[Serializable]
public class UIThread : MethodInterceptionAspect
{
```

<table>
<tr>
<td>

This cast is valid only when intercepting a method that is assignable to the Form class (FormI is).

</td>
<td>

```
public override void OnInvoke(MethodInterceptionArgs args)
{
    var form = (Form) args.Instance;
    if (form.InvokeRequired)
        form.Invoke(new Action(args.Proceed));
    else
        args.Proceed();
}
```

</td>
<td>

Take note of the parentheses: args.Proceed is being passed as a parameter to an Action object, which is called by the Invoke code.

</td>
</tr>
</table>

The args parameter (of type MethodInterceptionArgs) contains a lot of other information about the intercepted method: its context, arguments being passed in, and so on. Like the Castle DynamicProxy IInvocation API, I encourage you to explore all the available properties and methods.

Using these two aspects, we can now realize the "wouldn't it be nice" example (repeated here).

Listing 3.16 Declarative threading is now a reality

```
private void btnUpdate_Click(object sender, EventArgs e)
{
    GetNewTweet();
}

[WorkerThread]                          WorkerThread is an
void GetNewTweet()                      aspect class that we
{                                       created.
    var tweet = _twitter.GetTweet();
    UpdateTweetListBox(tweet);
}

[UIThread]                              UIThread is another
void UpdateTweetListBox(string tweet)   aspect class.
{
    listTweets.Items.Add(tweet);
}
```

Not only have we reduced the readability issues and made threads easier (almost fun!) to use, but we've also decoupled threading details from the class and encapsulated them into their own classes. So we could switch to using the Task class by changing only the WorkerThread aspect class, as this listing shows.

Listing 3.17 Changing from `Thread` to `Task`

```
[Serializable]
public class WorkerThread : MethodInterceptionAspect {
    public override void OnInvoke(MethodInterceptionArgs args) {
        var task = new Task(args.Proceed);
        task.Start();
    }
}
```

But ultimately, the point isn't to demonstrate the threading tools themselves (as I've alluded to, threading can be complicated, and there are a multitude of ways to deal with it). Instead, I want to demonstrate that the threading code can often get tangled and scattered throughout the rest of your UI code as a cross-cutting concern and that using an aspect can separate that cross-cutting concern into its own class.

3.4 *Summary*

This chapter covered one of the most common types of aspects: method interception aspects. Method interception aspects are like middlemen between code that's calling a method and the method itself. They give you the opportunity to add or modify method behavior without modifying the method and thus the ability to encapsulate cross-cutting concerns into their own classes, not only for improved organization but also for improved reuse.

PostSharp, Castle DynamicProxy, and other similar tools make it easy to write method interception aspects. Their APIs allow you to proceed to the intercepted method when you want to. Their APIs are also able to give you contextual information about the method being intercepted, including information about the method (for example, the method's name), the class that the method is in, and much more.

I encourage you to work through the two real-world aspects presented in this chapter on your own. Experiment with the tools and their APIs. We'll look at other Post-Sharp features throughout the rest of book. In the next chapter I'll discuss a different kind of aspect: boundary aspects.

Before and after:
boundary aspects

This chapter covers

- What boundaries mean
- Using PostSharp to bound methods
- Writing an ASP.NET HttpModule to help detect
  mobile users
- The differences (and similarities) of method
  interception and method bounding
- Writing a caching aspect with PostSharp

In chapter 3, I covered one of the most common types of method aspects you can write: method interception. These aspects contain code that runs *instead* of the code that it intercepts.

Another type of aspect you might use is a *boundary aspect*, which contains code that runs around the code that it's bounding. (Most commonly, these aspects are methods, but other types of boundaries exist, including page requests, ASP.NET MVC controller actions, and entire programs.)

I'll be using PostSharp to demonstrate a boundary aspect at the method level. I'll also use something that might be familiar already—an ASP.NET HttpModule—to demonstrate a boundary aspect at the page level.

The point of this chapter isn't to teach you everything about PostSharp and ASP.NET's HttpModule but to show you what's meant by the term boundary and how boundary aspects work in general. At the end of this chapter, you'll know how to write boundary aspects, you'll have a couple of practical aspects for caching, and mobile browser detection.

4.1 Boundary aspects

A boundary in the most general sense is an arbitrary line of division between two entities. A boundary between states (a border), for example, is a somewhat arbitrary distinction between two geographical areas. You can travel between the states, but first you must cross the border. When you're finished visiting, you can go back to the other state, but you must once again cross a border.

You'll find lots of boundaries when writing code, too. You might start in a Main method and make a call to another method. Although we don't often think about it, there is a border crossing when a program enters that method body. It's more like a boundary between two U.S. states: as we drive, we see a sign that says "Welcome to Ohio," but it's not like someone's manning a gate to check your passport. When that method's code is finished running, the flow of the program returns to the Main method. Again, it's a boundary that we don't often think about.

With AOP, we get the ability to put code at those boundaries which represent a place and/or a condition where it might be useful to put reusable code. Let's look at how to put code at the boundaries of a method with PostSharp.

4.1.1 PostSharp method bounding

Start a new project in Visual Studio. A Console Application project will be good for this example. I'm calling my project BaseballStatsPostSharp.

If you've been following all of the examples in the book to this point, you probably know what's coming next: NuGet. Install PostSharp with the NuGet UI or the package manager Console. Here's a quick refresher:

```
PM> Install-Package PostSharp
Successfully installed 'PostSharp 2.1.7.10'.
Successfully added 'PostSharp 2.1.7.10' to BaseballStatsPostSharp.
```

I'll start by creating a service that will get Major League Baseball statistics. This service won't interface with real statistics services (like www.baseball-reference.com); it'll just return hard-coded data for demonstration. I'll also create an instance of it in Main and call the service's GetPlayerBattingAverage method, as shown in the next listing.

Listing 4.1 Calling a `GetBattingAverage` method on a service class

```
public class BaseballStats {
    public decimal GetBattingAverage(string playerName) {
        if (playerName == "Joey Votto")
            return 0.309M;
        if (playerName == "Brandon Phillips")
            return 0.300M;
        return 0.000M;
    }
}

class Program {
    static void Main(string[] args) {
        var stats = new BaseballStats();
        var player = "Joey Votto";
        var battingAvg = stats.GetBattingAverage(player);
        Console.WriteLine("{0}'s batting average: {1}",
            player, battingAvg);
    }
}
```

Because we're not calling a real statistics service, feel free to use your own favorite players.

Boundary between the program not running and the program starting

Boundary between the program ending and the program not running

Boundaries between Main and GetBattingAverage

Compile and run, and you should see Console output like that in figure 4.1.

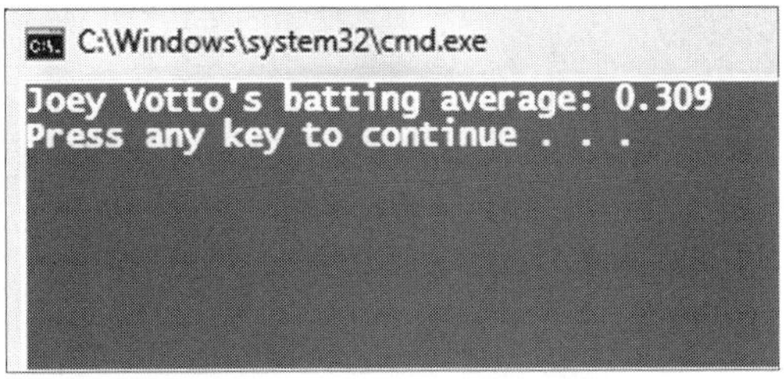

Simple stuff, but take a second to think about all of the boundaries that exist in this example. Because this is a Console application, you can imagine that there's a boundary immediately after the program starts and before the program ends. Another boundary would be between `Main` and `Get-BattingAverage`. A boundary exists when `Main` calls `GetBattingAverage`, and a boundary exists when `GetBattingAverage` returns a value to `Main`.

Figure 4.1 Console reporting results

Let's create a PostSharp aspect class that will let us put code into those boundaries. Create a class that inherits the `OnMethodBoundaryAspect` base class (don't forget to mark it as serializable):

```
[Serializable]
public class MyBoundaryAspect : OnMethodBoundaryAspect
{

}
```

Now you've got a method boundary aspect. Next, indicate what method should be bounded. With PostSharp, you can do this by using the aspect class as an attribute. Let's put it on the `GetBattingAverage` method, as in the following listing.

Listing 4.2   Using an attribute to indicate which method to bound

```
public class BaseballStats
{
    [MyBoundaryAspect]
    public decimal GetBattingAverage(string playerName)
    {
        if (playerName == "Joey Votto")
            return 0.309M;
        if (playerName == "Brandon Phillips")
            return 0.300M;
        return 0.000M;
    }
}
```

Now all of the calls to GetBattingAverage are bounded with MyBoundaryAspect. Of course, MyBoundaryAspect contains no useful code … yet. Let's add some behavior by overriding the OnEntry and OnSuccess methods:

```
[Serializable]
public class MyBoundaryAspect : OnMethodBoundaryAspect {
    public override void OnEntry(MethodExecutionArgs args)
    {
    }

    public override void OnSuccess(MethodExecutionArgs args)
    {
    }
}
```

If you run the program now, the code in OnEntry will run before the code in Get-BattingAverage, and the code in OnSuccess will run after the code in GetBatting-Average. This result still isn't interesting, so let's add some code to those methods:

```
[Serializable]
public class MyBoundaryAspect : OnMethodBoundaryAspect {
    public override void OnEntry(MethodExecutionArgs args)
    {
        Console.WriteLine("Before the method");
    }

    public override void OnSuccess(MethodExecutionArgs args)
    {
        Console.WriteLine("After the method");
    }
}
```

Writing to the Console in the entry boundary, which runs before the method executes

Writing to the Console in the success boundary, which runs after the method completes

Compile and run the application; figure 4.2 shows the new output that you'll see.

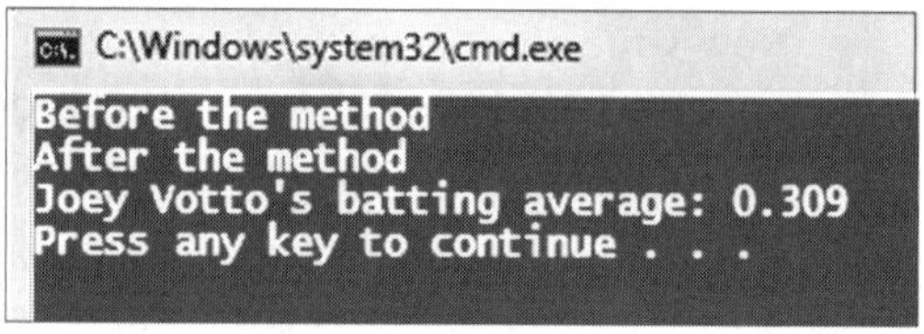

The method is called, the before boundary code runs, the method runs, and the after boundary code runs. After the program

```
C:\Windows\system32\cmd.exe
Before the method
After the method
Joey Votto's batting average: 0.309
Press any key to continue . . .
```

Figure 4.2   Console out with method boundary aspect

execution returns to Main, the Console displays the batting average returned from the method.

This should look somewhat familiar because we used an OnMethodBoundaryAspect in the first chapter's "Hello, World" example, and this example isn't much different. Later in this chapter, we'll look at a more practical use of a PostSharp method boundary aspect when we write an aspect to help with caching.

Before we get to that, I'll discuss some of the differences between the method boundary aspect covered here and the method interception aspects you saw in the previous chapter.

4.1.2 *Method boundaries versus method interception*

Now that you've seen both method interception and method boundary aspects, you might be wondering about any differences between the two. Differences exist, but they're subtle, and single-minded developers could probably use one without ever using the other if they were so inclined. The differences I'll discuss in this section are

- Shared state between aspect methods
- Clarity/intent of code

Figure 4.3 shows a side-by-side comparison of the basic structure of a PostSharp's MethodInterceptionAspect and its equivalent OnMethodBoundary aspect.

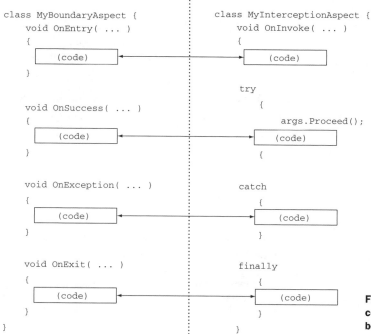

Figure 4.3 Side-by-side comparison of a method boundary and a method interception

Conceptually, you can convert a boundary aspect into an intercept aspect (and vice versa) by copying the code from the areas in the boxes on the left to the areas in the boxes on the right.

But if it's that simple, what's the point of having two different types of method aspects? Well, the answer is that it's usually *not* that simple.

SHARED STATE BETWEEN ASPECT METHODS

Let's look at shared state first. The interception aspect has only one method (OnInvoke), so sharing state isn't a concern—any variables that you use in the beginning of the method you can continue to use in the rest of the method. With a boundary method, it's not as simple. A variable that you declare in OnEntry won't be available in OnSuccess because they're separate methods.

But with PostSharp, you'll have some workarounds for sharing state between the boundary methods. First, you could use a field of the class itself, as in this listing.

> **Listing 4.3   Using a class member for shared state**

```
[Serializable]
public class MyBoundaryAspect : OnMethodBoundaryAspect {
    string _sharedState;

    public override void OnEntry(MethodExecutionArgs args) {
        _sharedState = "AOP rules";
    }

    public override void OnSuccess(MethodExecutionArgs args) {

    }
}
```

A private string member that you can use to share information between methods.

Before the bounded method runs, set the string to a value

After the bounded method runs, the value of _sharedState is still "AOP rules".

This approach does have a major drawback, though. In PostSharp, by default, each bounded method in the class uses the same instance of the aspect class. This aspect is called a *statically scoped aspect*, which means that even if you create multiple instances of a class, a method that's bounded by PostSharp will have only one aspect instance that corresponds to that class. If your aspect implements the IInstanceScopedAspect interface, then it becomes an *instance-scoped aspect*. The default behavior adds less overhead in the code after it's been weaved together but introduces a bit of complexity that may not be completely obvious.

To demonstrate this issue, I'll create another simple Console application that creates two objects of the same type and calls the same method on both of those objects, as shown in the next listing. The method will have an aspect applied to it.

> **Listing 4.4   A Console application showing the pitfalls of using an aspect field in PostSharp**

```
class Program {
    static void Main(string[] args) {
        var demo = new SharedStateDemo();
        var demo2 = new SharedStateDemo();
```

Demo and demo2 are two different instances of the same type.

```
        demo.MyMethod();
        demo2.MyMethod();
    }
}

public class SharedStateDemo {
    [SharedStateDemoAspect]
    public void MyMethod() { }
}
```

◁─┐ **Main is calling the same method on two different instances.**

◁─┐ **This attribute indicates an aspect to be applied to this method.**

MyMethod doesn't do anything, but there's an attribute (OnMethodBoundaryAspect) on it. PostSharp will create only one instance of SharedStateDemoAspect regardless of how many instances of SharedStateDemo you create.

Now let's put a field into the SharedStateDemoAspect class. Set it to be a new Guid in the aspect's constructor.

GUID

GUID is short for globally unique identifier. GUIDs are 128-bit values that are used for unique identification and are often represented in an 8-4-4-4-12 format of hexadecimal digits. Guid.NewGuid() generates a Guid that's unique (not in a mathematical sense, but in a practical and statistical sense) and is therefore good for demonstrating that the same instance is being used.

The pronunciation of GUID is one of some light-hearted controversy: GUID as in squid and GUID as in GOO-id are the two major camps.

Then, in the OnSuccess boundary, write out that Guid to Console:

```
[Serializable]
public class SharedStateDemoAspect : OnMethodBoundaryAspect {
    Guid _sharedState;

    public SharedStateDemoAspect() {
        _sharedState = Guid.NewGuid();
    }

    public override void OnSuccess(MethodExecutionArgs args) {
        Console.WriteLine("_sharedState is '{0}'", _sharedState);
    }
}
```

Notice that I've added an explicit constructor to this aspect. When the aspect is first constructed, it will create a Guid and store it in an aspect field called _sharedState.

All the aspect does is print the value of the Guid when the method is finished. If PostSharp created two SharedStateDemoAspect objects to go along with the two SharedStateDemo objects, then we'd expect to see two different Guids printed to Console. But that's not what happens, as figure 4.4 shows.

This output shows that the constructor was run only once and that all of the MyMethod's are sharing the same SharedStateDemoAspect object. Now, if you created

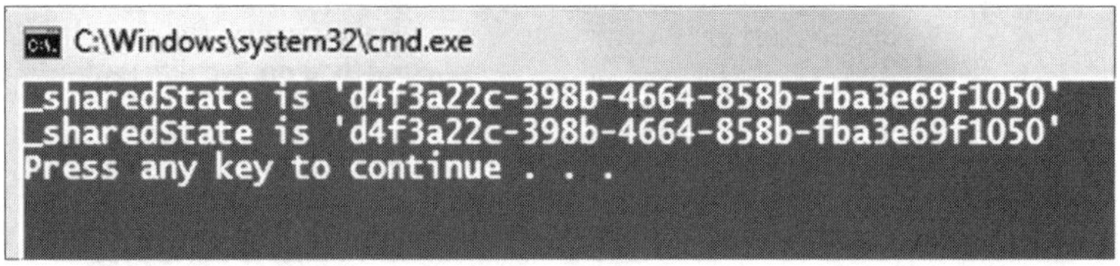

Figure 4.4   Output of the shared state demo

another method (for example, `MyMethod2`), then PostSharp would create another instance for that method.

To summarize: an aspect field isn't necessarily a safe way to communicate between methods of the aspect because it's not thread-safe. Other methods could be making changes to those fields. For this reason, PostSharp provides an API to help share state called `args.MethodExecutionTag`. It's a property of the `args` object that's passed in to each boundary method. This object is unique to each specific time the method is called.

Let's move the `Guid.NewGuid` out of a constructor and into `OnEntry`. And instead of writing out the field to Console in `OnSuccess`, I'll write out `args.Method-ExecutionTag`. The end result looks like the following.

Listing 4.5   Using `MethodExecutionTag` to share state

```
[Serializable]
public class SharedStateDemoAspect : OnMethodBoundaryAspect {
    public override void OnEntry(MethodExecutionArgs args) {
        args.MethodExecutionTag = Guid.NewGuid();
    }

    public override void OnSuccess(MethodExecutionArgs args) {
        Console.WriteLine("_sharedState is '{0}'",
            args.MethodExecutionTag);
    }
}
```

The body of OnSuccess now gets the value from MethodExecutionTag instead of a field.

MethodExecutionTag is of type object, so you can assign anything to it.

Run the code with those changes made and, as figure 4.5 shows, you'll see unique `Guid`s printed to Console.

PostSharp gives us this workaround, but it's not entirely ideal. `MethodExecution-Tag` is of the type `object`, which is fine for storing and printing something as simple as

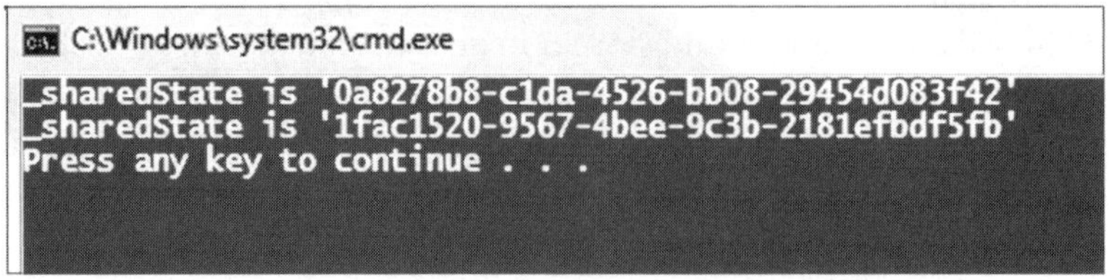

Figure 4.5   Output using `MethodExecutionTag` for shared state

a `Guid`, but if you need more complex shared state, you now have to take the extra step of casting the value of `args.MethodExecutionTag` before you use it. If you have a shared state that consists of multiple objects, you may have to go so far as to create a custom class to store them in the `MethodExecutionTag` property.

Keep in mind that none of these problems exist for a method interception aspect, because `OnInvoke` is the only method, and you can use all of the shared state within that method. The data transaction aspect from the previous chapter is an example of an aspect that uses a lot of shared state—the number of retries, the `TransactionScope` object, and the `succeeded` flag would all potentially have to be shared.

If you're writing an aspect that uses a complex shared state, or a lot of shared state, you might be better off using a method interception aspect instead of a method boundary aspect. If that's the case, why even bother with a method boundary aspect in the first place?

CLARITY/INTENT OF CODE

A method interception aspect certainly has the advantage when it comes to shared state. But what if the shared state is minimal or a shared state isn't necessary? What if you need to run some code at only a single boundary? In these cases, a method boundary aspect might have the upper hand.

Let's write an aspect that runs whenever a method finishes execution (regardless of whether it has succeeded). To do this in a PostSharp method boundary aspect, override the `OnExit` method (as in the next listing). The `OnExit` method is different from `OnSuccess`, which runs only if the bounded method completes without throwing an exception. `OnExit` runs every time the method finishes executing: exception or not.

> **Listing 4.6 A boundary aspect that overrides only `OnExit`**

```
[Serializable]
public class MyBoundaryAspect : OnMethodBoundaryAspect {
    public override void OnExit(MethodExecutionArgs args) {
        Console.WriteLine("{0} execution complete",
            args.Method.Name);
    }
}
```

Even though it's an aspect that doesn't do much, compare it to the following to listing, which you'd write if you were using a method interception aspect instead.

> **Listing 4.7 An equivalent interception aspect**

```
[Serializable]
public class MyInterceptionAspect : MethodInterceptionAspect {
    public override void OnInvoke(MethodInterceptionArgs args) {
        try {
            args.Proceed();                    ⟵——  In the boundary aspect, this proceed was
        }                                             implicit; the code is running around a
                                                      method, not instead of a method.
```

```
finally
{
    Console.WriteLine("{0} execution complete",
        args.Method.Name);
}
```

◁─ In C#, the finally
keyword indicates a
block of code that will
be run regardless of
what happened in the
try block.

```
    }
}
```

Still a trivial example, but it required seven additional lines of code. In this contrived example, it's not much more difficult to read the interception code, but imagine that this aspect was doing something other than writing to Console. It might not be clear at first glance that everything this interception aspect does takes place entirely within the finally block. In fact, unlike the boundary aspect, in which OnExit can be quickly scanned and parsed by yourself and your team members, a developer must examine the body of OnInvoke more closely to see what's occurring. Because the method is being intercepted, any number of things could be happening.

The method boundary aspect hides the details of try/catch/finally and Proceed(). You don't need to write that code, and you don't need to read that code.

Ultimately, although you may be tempted to always use method interception, don't dismiss method bounding if it's available in the AOP tool you decide to use. It can lead to improved clarity and brevity of code.

> ### Performance and memory considerations
>
> Other key differences between method boundary aspects and method interception aspects are performance and memory considerations. These considerations will vary based on the tool you're using.
>
> In PostSharp, when you use a MethodInterceptionAspect, all the arguments are copied from the stack to the heap every time (via boxing). When you use an OnMethodBoundaryAspect, PostSharp detects arguments that aren't used and will write optimized code that won't box them up. If you're writing an aspect that doesn't use the method arguments, using an OnMethodBoundaryAspect will use less memory, which can be important if you're using the aspect in many places. (Note that this optimization feature isn't included in the free version of PostSharp.)

Method boundaries aren't the only types of boundaries that are useful when you're using AOP. In the next section, we'll look at ASP.NET HttpModules, which are useful for putting boundaries around web pages.

4.1.3   *ASP.NET HttpModule bounding*

With standard ASP.NET Web Forms, each file in the project represents a web page to which browsers can make requests. Each page has a layout file (for example, Default.aspx) that contains a combination of HTML (for example, <p>Paragraph</p>),

ASP.NET controls (for example, `<asp:Button ID="myButton" runat="server" />`), and possibly code (for example, C# or VB.NET). These files almost always have a corresponding code behind file (for example, Default.aspx.cs for C#) that contains a class where you can put code to handle the requests made to that page.

If you want to follow along, create a new ASP.NET web application in Visual Studio. I'll call my project AspNetHttpModuleDemo. Add a new Web Form file (without Master Page) called Demo.aspx to the project. You can leave Demo.aspx.cs alone, but go ahead and modify the Demo.aspx HTML to add text that's something like:

```
<%@ Page ... %>                                    Full Page declaration omitted:
                                                   this is generated by Visual Studio.
<!DOCTYPE html>

<html xmlns="http://www.w3.org/1999/xhtml">        The DOCTYPE you see may vary, but
                                                   it isn't important for this demo.
<head runat="server">

    <title>Demo page</title>                       I added text to the default blank
                                                   title that Visual Studio creates.
</head>

<body>

    <p>This is the demo page!</p>                   I replaced the default
                                                   <form /> with a
</body>                                             paragraph of text.

</html>
```

Compile your web application and run it on the web server of your choice. (I'm using Visual Studio's built-in ASP.NET Development Server, also known as Cassini, but IIS and IIS Express should also work fine.) You should see something like figure 4.6 in your browser.

Each request to an ASP.NET page such as Demo.aspx has a complex life cycle, which won't be covered in detail in this book. But one part of the life cycle worth noting is the use of an HttpModule, which allows you to put code at the boundaries of all ASP.NET pages. To create an `HttpModule`, create a class that implements the `IHttpModule` interface (which is in the `System.Web` namespace):

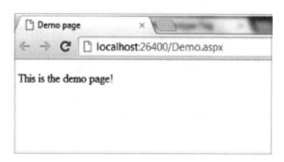

Figure 4.6   Demo.aspx in a browser

```
public class MyHttpModule : IHttpModule
{
    public void Init(HttpApplication context)        Init runs when an
    {                                                instance is created by
    }                                                the HttpApplication.
```

```
public void Dispose()
{
}
}
```

Dispose is necessary to dispose of
any resources such as streams or
database connections.

Each module must be configured to run in the ASP.NET Web.config file. Depending
on the web server you're using (IIS6, IIS7+, Cassini, IIS Express, and so on), the
Web.config may vary. I like to cover all my bases, so I put the configuration in both
`<system.web />` and `<system.webServer />` sections, as shown here.

Listing 4.8 Configuring MyHttpModule in Web.config

```
<?xml version="1.0"?>

<configuration>
  <system.web>
    <compilation debug="true" targetFramework="4.0" />
    <httpModules>
      <add name="MyModule"
           type="AspNetHttpModuleDemo.MyHttpModule" />
    </httpModules>
  </system.web>
  <system.webServer>
      <validation validateIntegratedModeConfiguration="false"/>
      <modules>
        <add name="MyModule"
             type="AspNetHttpModuleDemo.MyHttpModule" />
      </modules>
  </system.webServer>
</configuration>
```

The HttpModules
area is where you
add each
HttpModule.

The
system.webServer
area is where IIS7
looks.

The modules area
is where you add
each HttpModule.

The system.web area where the
IIS6 and ASP.NET Development
Server (Cassini) looks.

Each module needs
an arbitrary name
and the
corresponding type
(full namespace
and class name).

Again, each module
needs an arbitrary
name and the
corresponding type
(full namespace
and class name).

ASP.NET configuration

I want to stress that I'm writing the Web.config in this way to make it easier for all
readers to follow along. In your environment, you might use only IIS6/Cassini or only
IIS7 and therefore you might not need to duplicate configuration. Additionally, configuring HttpModules can be considerably more complex, depending on the nature of
your site, your modules, and whether you have subfolder areas that have their own
web.config files— none of which are covered in this book.

ASP.NET uses multiple worker processes to handle incoming requests. For each worker
process, an instance of HttpApplication is created. Each HttpApplication will create
a new instance of each HttpModule and run the Init command on those modules.
Our Init code isn't doing anything yet, so in the following listing, I've set up some
boundaries using event handlers.

Listing 4.9 Event handlers in `MyHttpModule`

```
public class MyHttpModule : IHttpModule {
    public void Init(HttpApplication context) {
        context.BeginRequest += context_BeginRequest;
        context.EndRequest += context_EndRequest;
    }

    void context_BeginRequest(object sender, EventArgs e)
    {
    }


    void context_EndRequest(object sender, EventArgs e)
    {
    }

    public void Dispose() { }
}
```

The Http-Application parameter has a lot of properties and events.

I'm using a couple of events to set up event handlers for begin/end request events.

The code in here will be run before any page handles a request.

The code in here will be run after all other page life cycle events are done.

Figure 4.7   Demo.aspx page as viewed in a browser

Although the syntax is significantly different, this feels a lot like the method boundary aspect you saw earlier in the chapter. But we still don't have anything meaningful taking place. After you create this class, modify the Web.config file and request the web page in a browser; it should look the same (figure 4.7) as it did when the project was created (figure 4.6).

Let's put some code in those empty methods and see what happens. In the following listing I'll add plain text to the response at the beginning and at the end.

Listing 4.10 Writing text to the response at the beginning and end of a page

```
void context_BeginRequest(object sender, EventArgs e) {
    var app = (HttpApplication) sender;
    app.Response.Write("Before the page");
}

void context_EndRequest(object sender, EventArgs e) {
    var app = (HttpApplication)sender;
    app.Response.Write("After the page");
}
```

A cast is required to use HttpApplication

Now when you view a page in your browser (after you recompile), you'll see something like figure 4.8.

Because you have the `HttpApplication` object available in the boundary methods, you have a lot of flexibility and potential in what you can accomplish. When you examine the properties and events of `HttpApplication`, you'll see that you can do a

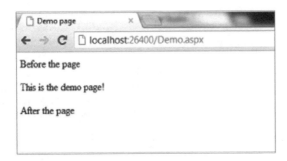

**Figure 4.8 Demo.aspx with
HttpModule viewed in a browser**

lot more than just write text to the response. In the next section, we'll look at a more practical example of using an HttpModule to help enhance the experience of a mobile user.

4.2 *Real-world example: detecting mobile users*

It doesn't seem like too long ago that a mobile web page often meant a stripped-down or severely limited version of the full desktop web page. Tiny screens and slow speeds made this approach a necessity. In recent years, smartphones and improved cellular networks have pushed that delineation much further back.

With the increase in smartphone marketshare came an increase in mobile users, which means that it's important to be able to provide a good experience to both traditional desktop browsers and mobile browsers.

These days, on many mobile devices, use of the standard desktop layout rendering can be adequate for normal use, due to larger screens, better resolutions, and faster connections. But users of mobile devices such as phones and tablets are still different than users of desktop or laptop computers in many ways.

An operation that can be quite easy with a mouse or keyboard can be much more difficult with touch and touch keyboards. Operations that can be done with hotkey combinations or a series of clicks and drags become challenging on a mobile device. Unless a stylus is available (currently uncommon among smartphone users), the precision of screen touches isn't as accurate as a mouse cursor. Clicking a small link or button can be a source of frustration. Typing can also be more arduous. Even though display resolution keeps improving, the smaller size of phone screens still means that you can't show as much readable information on a single mobile screen as you can a desktop screen. For these reasons, many website developers still like to have a native mobile application, alternative mobile site, or at least a mobile theme to improve the mobile user's experience, as they (hopefully) maintain the same level of functionality.

Cellular networks continue to improve, but it's not yet a certainty that a mobile user will have a good, fast connection at all times. A user on a road trip with a spotty connection might be more concerned about getting information quickly than about getting the full rich experience of a high-bandwidth site.

For these reasons, it's still important to be able to recognize mobile users and present them with alternatives or options to best enhance their experience. In this section, we'll look at using AOP to detect mobile users and giving them the option of installing a native application.

4.2.1 Offer a link to an application

Offering a link to your mobile application (or apps) on your home page can be a good way to let your users know that a native application is available for them to use on their device. But keep in mind that not every user always uses the front door. They could be going directly to a page of content via a link that a friend sent, or they could be clicking on a result from a search engine. You could put a link to your mobile application on every page. But now you're taking up screen space for something that only part of your users will be interested in (maybe they don't have a smartphone, aren't using the smartphone, or aren't interested in installing an application).

I think a nice way to deal with this is to show the mobile user an interstitial or splash screen—a web page that is displayed in between the source of the link and the page being linked to. Interstitials have been used for ads, warning messages, and so on. Two examples of interstitials are shown in figure 4.9. For our purposes, we'd like to show incoming users an interstitial to let them know that there's a native application available that they can use instead.

Let's create our own interstitial using an ASP.NET `HttpModule`. My example won't look nearly as nice, but it will have the same functionality. I'm going to create an `HttpModule` that will detect if the user is a mobile user, as shown in figure 4.10. If so, I'm going to redirect them to the interstitial page to give them the option of downloading the native application (via App Store or Google Play) or continuing on to browse the site as normal with the mobile web browser.

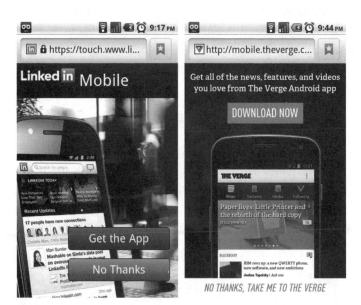

Figure 4.9   Examples of a mobile interstitial when visiting LinkedIn or the Verge

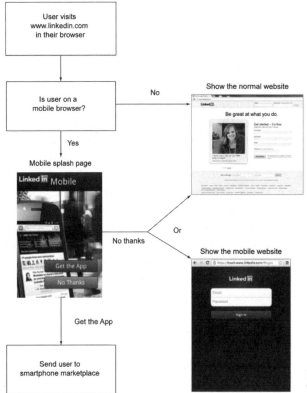

Figure 4.10   Routing a mobile user to their preferred experience

And finally, I don't want to annoy a mobile user by showing this interstitial for every request, so I'll use a cookie to make sure that it's being shown only every so often.

CREATE AN HTTPMODULE

Start by creating an ASP.NET project in Visual Studio. I'm going to use a plain ASP.NET application, not an MVC project. Name it what you want: I'm calling mine MobileBrowserAspNet. The default application template creates a Default.aspx and an About.aspx page, which are sufficient for this example. Because we're using an `HttpModule`, any additional pages that you'll add automatically pick up the same functionality (which is one of the key benefits of this approach: it's modular and reusable). Create a class that implements `IHttpModule`. A bare-bones example would look like this:

```
public class MobileInterstitialModule : IHttpModule {
    public void Init(HttpApplication context)
    {
    }

    public void Dispose()
    {
    }
}
```

We won't need to put anything in the Dispose method for this example because we won't be using any resources that require disposal (for example, a FileStream or Sql-Connection—some resource that's not already handled by .NET's garbage collector).

ASP.NET HttpModules run on every HTTP request to the site. The HttpApplication context parameter passed to Init provides some events that will be invoked for certain boundaries. For the interstitial, we'll be interested in subscribing to the Begin-Request boundary event, as in this listing.

Listing 4.11　Subscribing to the `BeginRequest` boundary event

```
public void Init(HttpApplication context) {
    context.BeginRequest += context_BeginRequest;
}

void context_BeginRequest(object sender, EventArgs e) {

}
```

The code in context_BeginRequest will be run before the page executes, so this is where we check to see whether the user is a mobile user.

CHECK FOR MOBILE USER

Let's start by creating a MobileDetect class. Let's assume that you have native applications available for the big 3 smartphone platforms: Android, iOS (Apple), and Windows Phone. You can approach browser detection in several ways, but I'll keep it simple for now and look to see if the UserAgent contains certain keywords. The following listing isn't a particularly sophisticated method but is fine for our purposes.

Listing 4.12　A class to detect mobile users

```
public class MobileDetect {
    readonly HttpRequest _httpRequest;
    public MobileDetect(HttpContext httpContext) {
        _httpRequest = httpContext.Request;
    }
    public bool IsMobile() {
        return _httpRequest.Browser.IsMobileDevice &&
            (IsAndroid() || IsApple() || IsWindowsPhone());
    }
    public bool IsWindowsPhone() {
        return _httpRequest.UserAgent.Contains("Windows Phone OS");
    }
    public bool IsApple() {
        return _httpRequest.UserAgent.Contains("iPhone")
            || _httpRequest.UserAgent.Contains("iPad");
    }
    public bool IsAndroid() {
        return _httpRequest.UserAgent.Contains("Android");
    }
}
```

Annotations:
- **This class needs an HttpRequest object to examine the user's browser information.**
- **This method should tell us if the user is using one of the big 3 smartphones.**
- **This method examines the UserAgent to see if a Windows Phone is being used.**
- **This method checks to see if an Apple device is being used.**
- **This method checks if a device running the Android OS is being used.**

Now that we have that class available, let's use it to check the incoming request.

REDIRECT TO A MOBILE SPLASH SCREEN

In the next listing, I use `MobileDetect` within the `context_BeginRequest` event handler. If `MobileDetect` says that the incoming request is from a smartphone, it will redirect the user to the splash screen page (which I've called MobileInterstitial.aspx).

Listing 4.13   Detecting a mobile browser

Get a MobileDetect object using the current HttpContext.

The return URL will be sent in the querystring, so it must be encoded as such.

If users decline to download the application, they need to be directed back to the page they were trying to get to in the first place.

Redirect to the splash screen interstitial and pass along the return URL in case it's needed.

```
void context_BeginRequest(object sender, EventArgs e)
{
    var httpContext = HttpContext.Current;
    var mobileDetect = new MobileDetect(httpContext);
    if(mobileDetect.IsMobile())
    {
        var url = httpContext.Request.RawUrl;
        var encodedUrl = HttpUtility.UrlEncode(url);
        httpContext.Response.Redirect(
            "MobileInterstitial.aspx?returnUrl=" + encodedUrl);
    }
}
```

At this point, users are redirected to the interstitial page. But we also need to communicate the page that the user is trying to get to, in case they tap the No Thanks option, so that's why the original URL is being sent to the MobileInterstitial page as the `returnUrl` querystring value.

Create a MobileInterstitial.aspx page. The design of my example in figure 4.11 isn't beautiful, but it's functional: some text and two buttons.

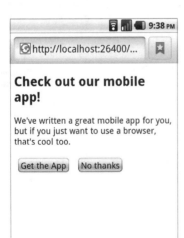

Figure 4.11   Display an interstitial to the mobile user

MobileInterstitial.aspx will have some HTML markup: just two buttons, as shown in this listing. Make sure that the buttons are in a `form`.

Listing 4.14 Basic splash screen with two buttons

```
<html xmlns="http://www.w3.org/1999/xhtml">
<head runat="server">
    <title>Mobile Interstitial</title>
    <meta name="viewport"
        content="user-scalable=no, width=device-width" />
</head>
<body>
    <h2>Check out our mobile app!</h2>
    <p>We've written a great mobile app for you,
        but if you just want to use a browser, that's cool too.</p>
    <form id="form1" runat="server">
        <asp:Button ID="btnDownload" Text="Get the App"
                    runat="server" />
        <asp:Button ID="btnNoThanks" Text="No thanks"
                    runat="server"/>
    </form>
</body>
</html>
```

> This button directs users to their native application store/marketplace.

> This button sends users to the page they originally requested.

To make the buttons do something, I need to write code in the code-behind page (MobileInterstitial.aspx). The `btnDownload_Click` and `btnNoThanks_Click` methods are wired to the click events in `Page_Load` (see listing 4.15).

The `"no thanks"` click event will redirect the browser to the originally requested page. Recall that this information was passed to this page via querystring (`return-Url`), so we can use `Request.QueryString` to get that information and send users on their way.

The `"get the app"` click event will need to redirect the user to the appropriate mobile download portal (the iPhone App Store, for instance). We can get more use out of the `MobileDetect` class to determine where to send the user. Each phone will be able to interpret the URL and send the user to the correct place. For instance, if users are on an Android, they'll be directed to your application in Google Play.

Listing 4.15 Handling the button clicks in code-behind

```
public partial class MobileInterstitial : System.Web.UI.Page {
    protected void Page_Load(object sender, EventArgs e) {
        btnDownload.Click += btnDownload_Click;
        btnNoThanks.Click += btnNoThanks_Click;
    }
    void btnNoThanks_Click(object sender, EventArgs e) {
```

> An event handler for the download button click

> An event handler for the original page

```
                var returnUrl = Request.QueryString["returnUrl"];
                Response.Redirect(HttpUtility.UrlDecode(returnUrl));
            }

        void btnDownload_Click(object sender, EventArgs e) {

            var mobileDetect = new MobileDetect(Context);

            if (mobileDetect.IsAndroid())

                Response.Redirect(

                    "market://search?q=pname:com.myappname.android");

            if (mobileDetect.IsApple())

                Response.Redirect("http://itunes.com/apps/appname");

            if (mobileDetect.IsWindowsPhone())

                Response.Redirect(

                    "http://windowsphone.com/s?appid={my-app-id-guid}");


            }

        }
```

Decode it so that it's a valid URL that the user can be returned to →

Retrieve the returnUrl from the querystring

Using the same MobileDetect class that's used in the HttpModule

The URL format to go to the Google Play store for a specific application →

The URL to use to go to the Apple App Store for a specific application

The URL format to use with the Windows Phone Marketplace

And there you have it. Now every page on your site requested by smartphone users will first present them with a splash screen asking if they want to download the mobile application instead.

But we're not done. Note that I said every page will get a splash screen. That's a problem, because the splash screen itself is also a page. Sounds like an infinite loop. Also, when the user clicks "no thanks" and is redirected back, then the HttpModule runs again, which we don't want it to do. Let's add some checks to the HttpModule to avoid these situations.

ADDING CHECKS

First, check to see if the interstitial itself is being requested. If this is the case, then we can stop execution and return; otherwise, we'll be in an infinite redirect loop. Next, if your users choose not to download the native application, then we need to check for that condition so that we don't send them right back to the interstitial again and again. I'll write two methods to check for each of these conditions, respectively, in context_BeginRequest. The following listing shows the OnMobileInterstitial and ComingFromMobileInterstitial methods.

Listing 4.16   Adding checks to avoid redirect loops

```
    void context_BeginRequest(object sender, EventArgs e) {
        if (OnMobileInterstitial())
            return;
        if (ComingFromMobileInterstitial())
            return;
        var httpContext = HttpContext.Current;
        var mobileDetect = new MobileDetect(httpContext);
        if (mobileDetect.IsMobile())
        {
```

If we're coming from the splash page, then don't proceed. →

If the page being bounded by this HttpModule is the splash page, then don't proceed.

```
                var url = httpContext.Request.RawUrl;
                var encodedUrl = HttpUtility.UrlEncode(url);
                httpContext.Response.Redirect(
                    "MobileInterstitial.aspx?returnUrl=" + encodedUrl);
            }
        }

        bool ComingFromMobileInterstitial() {
            var httpRequest = HttpContext.Current.Request;
            if (httpRequest.UrlReferrer == null)
                return false;
            return httpRequest.UrlReferrer.AbsoluteUri
                .Contains("MobileInterstitial.aspx");
        }

        bool OnMobileInterstitial() {
            var httpRequest = HttpContext.Current.Request;
            return httpRequest.RawUrl
                .Contains("MobileInterstitial.aspx");
        }
```

> The referrer could be null, so put in some defensive programming here to check.

> If the referrer is the splash page (MobileInterstitial.aspx), then return true.

> If the page being bounded is itself the splash page, then return true.

Now the user won't be stuck in loops. But I think we can do better. Suppose a user doesn't want to use the native application and wants to view your site in a normal mobile browser. As it stands now, every time such users want to view a page, they'll be shown the splash screen first, which could get annoying.

4.2.2   *Don't be a pest*

Instead of showing the splash screen for every request, it'd be much better to show the splash screen only once. If users say no thanks, we won't bother them again. One way to do this is to set a cookie when a user clicks "no thanks." Open up MobileInterstitial.aspx.cs again and set a cookie in the "Nothanks" click event:

> **Set the cookie to expire after two minutes**

> **Add the cookie to the response**

```
void btnNoThanks_Click(object sender, EventArgs e) {
    var cookie = new HttpCookie("NoThanks", "set");
    cookie.Expires = DateTime.Now.AddMinutes(2);
    Response.Cookies.Add(cookie);

    var returnUrl = Request.QueryString["returnUrl"];
    Response.Redirect(HttpUtility.UrlDecode(returnUrl));
}
```

> Create a cookie called "NoThanks", the value of which ("set") is arbitrary

I set the cookie to expire after two minutes so that users can see the splash screen up to once every two minutes (if you are following along, you have to wait only two minutes to see this in action). In reality, you might want to set a much longer expiration period (one month, six months, one year) or set it to never expire. To give users more flexibility, you could add a checkbox to the splash screen saying Don't Ask Me Again that determines whether to set an expiration on the cookie.

Now that you've set a cookie, you need to check for that cookie back in the Http-Module. In this listing, I've added a cookie check to context_BeginRequest.

Listing 4.17   Checking for a cookie

```
void context_BeginRequest(object sender, EventArgs e) {
    if (IsNoThanksCookieSet())
        return;
    if (OnMobileInterstitial())
        return;
    if (ComingFromMobileInterstitial())
        return;

    var mobileDetect = new MobileDetect(httpContext);
    if (mobileDetect.IsMobile())
    {
        var url = httpContext.Request.RawUrl;
        var encodedUrl = HttpUtility.UrlEncode(url);
        httpContext.Response.Redirect(
            "MobileInterstitial.aspx?returnUrl=" + encodedUrl);
    }
}

bool IsNoThanksCookieSet() {
    return HttpContext.Current.Request.Cookies["NoThanks"] != null;
}
```

⟵ **If the cookie is set, then stop execution of the HttpModule**

HttpModule used on every page?

Depending on the web server you're using, `HttpModules` could literally affect every page that's requested, including CSS files, image files, text files, and PDF files. You don't want an interstitial that runs on CSS files.

With IIS7, you can configure the module in the Web.config file with `pre-Condition="managedHandler"`, which means that the `HttpModule` will be executed only on files that run managed code (for example, it will provide boundaries for ASPX files but not for CSS files).

If you're using IIS6, it might or might not be configured to allow static files such as CSS files to be processed by ASP.NET. If you can't change the configuration as you wish, then you can add some code to check on this. For example, see if `http-Context.Request.Url.AbsolutePath` contains a .aspx extension.

`HttpModules` can be an excellent way to use AOP to address cross-cutting concerns in your web application. They have powerful and flexible capabilities that are baked right into the ASP.NET framework but are too often overlooked and forgotten.

Now that you've seen a real-world example of a boundary aspect for pages, let's shift back to PostSharp for a real-world use of method boundaries. This time, we'll look at method boundaries to help with caching.

4.3   *Real-world example: caching*

When you're designing and writing code, try to avoid or optimize any process that runs slowly. If a single web page is making a ton of database calls, for instance, often those calls can be consolidated or eliminated to improve performance.

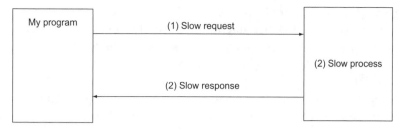

Figure 4.12   You might be victim of slow request transit, slow processes, slow response transit, or all of the above

But sometimes the speed of a process can't be improved. Some processes are more complex and take a lot of time to run. Sometimes you're dependent on external processes (a database, a web service, etc.) over which you have little or no control, as figure 4.12 shows.

But there's good news: if you're in a situation in which you're waiting on information from a slow process, and that information doesn't change often, you might be able to use caching to reduce waiting time. Caching is particularly beneficial to multiuser systems, in which the (unlucky) first user makes a request that's dependent on a slow process. The cache will then take the results of that slow process and store them locally, where it can be retrieved quickly (see figure 4.13). When another request is made, the cache will check to see whether the information has already been retrieved. If so, then it will get only that information and bypass the slow process.

Caching can be a cross-cutting concern. For every method in which you want to use caching, follow these steps:

- Check to see whether the value is already in the cache
- If it is, return the value
- If it's not, run the process as normal
- Get the results of the process and put it in the cache so it can be used next time

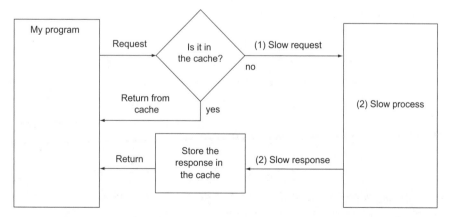

Figure 4.13   How a cache helps with a slow process or slow transit

These steps could lead to a lot of boilerplate code in use in many different parts of the code base, which is a sign that AOP might be a good idea. Let's look at an example of caching (ASP.NET's Cache object) and write an aspect to help use it more effectively.

4.3.1 *ASP.NET Cache*

Many caching tools are available for many different types of programs (Microsoft's Caching Application Block, NCache from Alachisoft, Windows Azure AppFabric for cloud caching). But I want to focus on how AOP can help with caching, not the caching technology itself. Therefore, I'm going to use a cache that's most readily available to .NET developers: the ASP.NET Cache.

The cache is like a dictionary object that's available to you to use in ASP.NET code. In ASP.NET Web Forms, Cache is inherited from the Page base class. In ASP.NET MVC, it's available through HttpContext, which is inherited from the Controller base class. Failing all else, you can get it via HttpContext.Current.Cache.

The Cache object has a simple API, as you'll see in the following snippet. You can use it as a dictionary to add and retrieve values from it. If you try to retrieve a value that hasn't been saved, it will return null.

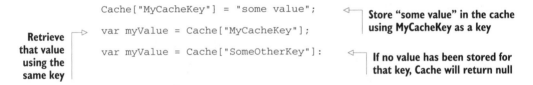

```
Cache["MyCacheKey"] = "some value";            ⊲──┐   Store "some value" in the cache
                                                   │   using MyCacheKey as a key
Retrieve  ⊳  var myValue = Cache["MyCacheKey"];
that value
using the    var myValue = Cache["SomeOtherKey"]:   ⊲──┐   If no value has been stored for
same key                                               │   that key, Cache will return null
```

Cache has other helpful methods such as Add and Insert, which give you the ability to specify whether a cache value will expire. You can also use the Remove method to immediately remove a value from Cache. I'm not going to spend much time on this API, because it's well documented and it's not the main focus of this AOP example.

Cache expiration

A cache value is often set to expire after a certain period of time. For instance, if you store a value using "MyCacheKey" and set it to expire after two hours, then two hours later, if you try to retrieve that value using "MyCacheKey", you'll get a null result.

ASP.NET Cache has several available expiration settings:

- *Absolute expiration*—The value will expire at a given DateTime.
- *Sliding expiration*—The value will expire at a given amount of time after it was last used.
- *Never*—The value will always remain unless the application ends or the cache decides that it needs the memory to store something else.

By default, values you add to the ASP.NET cache never expire.

In the next section, we'll put the ASP.NET Cache to work for a single page of an ASP.NET application, in which caching might come in handy.

4.3.2 An application that could benefit from caching

In the car marketplace, consumers and dealers look to several third-party sources to provide independent information on the market value of used cars (Kelley Blue Book, for instance). In this section, you're not going to write an entire real-world application—you'll write only a small part of one. You'll write a web page to retrieve car values from a hypothetical third-party web service.

To get started, create a new ASP.NET web application project in Visual Studio. Add PostSharp by using NuGet. What we're going to build is something that looks like figure 4.14.

First, create a "Web Form using Master Page" called CarValue.aspx, as listing 4.18 shows. Add HTML and ASP.NET controls to the page to let users specify information about a car. We need three DropDownLists, a submit Button, a Literal to display the value, and a BulletedList to display the contents of the cache (for demonstration purposes only).

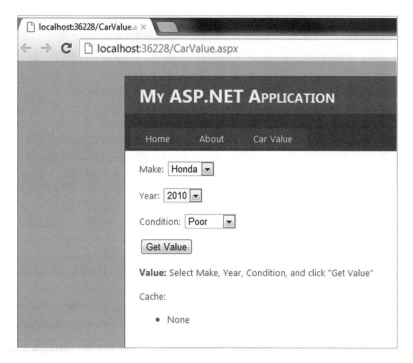

Figure 4.14   A page with a form to look up a car's market value

Listing 4.18   CarValue.aspx HTML and ASP.NET controls

```
<asp:Content ID="HeaderContent" ContentPlaceHolderID="HeadContent"
              runat="server">
    <title>Car Value</title>
</asp:Content>

<asp:Content ID="BodyContent" ContentPlaceHolderID="MainContent"
              runat="server">

    <p>Make: <asp:DropDownList ID="makeDropDown" runat="server" /></p>

    <p>Year: <asp:DropDownList ID="yearDropDown" runat="server" /></p>

    <p>Condition:

        <asp:DropDownList ID="conditionDropDown" runat="server" /></p>


    <asp:Button ID="getValueButton" Text="Get Value" runat="server" />

    <p>

        <strong>Value:</strong>

        <asp:Literal ID="valueLiteral" runat="server">

            Select Make, Year, Condition, and click "Get Value"

        </asp:Literal>

    </p>

    <p>Cache:</p>

    <asp:BulletedList ID="cachedItemsList" runat="server" />

</asp:Content>
```

A drop-down box for the user to select a Make

The user can select the model Year.

The car's condition is selected here.

This button issues the request to get the car's value.

The result of the request is displayed in this Literal.

We'll show the entire contents of Cache on the page for illustration purposes.

In the code-behind class, we need to do several things to make this form work. We need to add items to each of the drop-down boxes to give the user a choice of inputs. These values may normally be retrieved from a database or other data source, but I'll hard-code them, as shown in this listing.

Listing 4.19   Add items to each drop-down list

```
public partial class CarValue : System.Web.UI.Page {
    protected void Page_Load(object sender, EventArgs e) {
        if (!IsPostBack)
            PopulateDropDowns();
    }

    void PopulateDropDowns() {
        makeDropDown.Items.AddRange(new[] {
            new ListItem("Honda", "0"),
            new ListItem("Toyota", "1"),
            new ListItem("Ford", "2")
        });
```

Populate the drop-downs only if this page is being rendered for the first time.

Add a selection of car "makes" to the drop-down list, each with corresponding ID numbers.

```
yearDropDown.Items.AddRange(new[] {
    new ListItem("2010"),
    new ListItem("2011"),
    new ListItem("2012")
});
conditionDropDown.Items.AddRange(new[] {
    new ListItem("Poor", "0"),
    new ListItem("Average", "1"),
    new ListItem("Mint", "2")
});
    }
}
```

⟵ A range of model years for the user to select.

⟵ Three different car conditions, which the third-party service also asks for (better condition = higher value).

We also need to add an event handler to the button's click event. This event will kick off a request to the third-party service, but for now I'll leave it empty, as the following listing shows.

Listing 4.20   An event to handle a button click

```
public partial class CarValue : System.Web.UI.Page {
    protected void Page_Load(object sender, EventArgs e) {
        getValueButton.Click += getValueButton_Click;

        if (!IsPostBack)
            PopulateDropDowns();
    }

    void getValueButton_Click(object sender, EventArgs e) {

    }
}
```

⟵ Adds a method to the button-click event handler

⟵ The code here will be run when the page is processing the button click.

Finally, we need to write code that will display the entire contents of the Cache object (see the next listing). This code is for illustration purposes so that you can see exactly what is put in the Cache. Because I want the Cache to be displayed at the last possible moment before the page is rendered so that any items added by the click event will still show up, I'll put that code in the OnPreRender method of the page.

Listing 4.21   Show the entire contents of Cache

```
public partial class CarValue : System.Web.UI.Page {
    protected override void OnPreRender(EventArgs e) {
        DisplayCache();
    }
    void DisplayCache() {
        cachedItemsList.Items.Clear();
        foreach (DictionaryEntry cachedItem in Cache)
        {
            var cacheRecord = cachedItem.Key + " - " + cachedItem.Value;
```

⟵ OnPreRender is the last place to make changes to the content of the page before it's finished rendering.

Start with an empty list each time ⟶

Combine the cache key and value into a single string ⟶

⟵ Loop through each item in the Cache

```
            cachedItemsList.Items.Add(new ListItem(cacheRecord));
        }
        if(cachedItemsList.Items.Count == 0)
            cachedItemsList.Items.Add(new ListItem("None"));
    }
}
```

◁ Add the combined string to the list using a ListItem

If there's nothing in the Cache, display only one item that says "None".

At this point, if you compile and load CarValue.aspx in a browser, you should see a page like figure 4.15 that's ready to use.

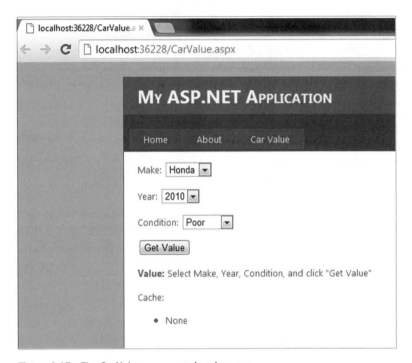

Figure 4.15   The CarValue.aspx page in a browser

If you click Get Value, the page will refresh in the browser, but it'll look the same because the click event isn't doing anything yet. I'm going to create a CarValue-Service class that can be called from the button click event handler. This class won't call a real web service but will simulate that a web service can be somewhat slow. I'm going to add a Thread.Sleep line to make the code pause:

```
public class CarValueService {
    readonly Random _rand;

    public CarValueService() {
        _rand = new Random();
    }
```

```
public decimal GetValue(int makeId, int conditionId, int year)
{
    Thread.Sleep(5000);
    return _rand.Next(10000, 20000);
}
}
```

This car service will pause for five seconds and return a value that's somewhere between $10,000 and $20,000. Now I just need the code (in the next listing) back in the button handler to use this service.

Listing 4.22 Clicking the Get Value button

```
void getValueButton_Click(object sender, EventArgs e) {

    var makeId = int.Parse(makeDropDown.SelectedValue);

    var year = int.Parse(yearDropDown.SelectedValue);

    var conditionId = int.Parse(conditionDropDown.SelectedValue);

    var carValueService = new CarValueService();

    var carValue = carValueService.GetValue(makeId, conditionId, year);

    valueLiteral.Text = carValue.ToString("c");

}
```

Get the ID of the selected make from the drop-down list

SelectedValues are always strings, so they must be parsed into integers.

I omitted validation from this web application; in a real web form, inputs should never be this trusted.

Create an instance of the CarValueService to call

Pass the user inputs to the service to retrieve the value

Display the value to the web page, with currency formatting via ToString

Now the application should display a (random) dollar amount on the page when you run it, as figure 4.16 shows.

Those extra five seconds of wait time (could be more or less, depending on the internet connection speed) may not seem like a lot, but if your company is doing thousands of these requests every hour, that time can add up—not to mention that our application is overly simplfied. In a more comprehensive piece of software

- Values would be much more integrated throughout the rest of the software.
- Reports and searches containing hundreds of cars could be generated.
- We might need to cache the results of many web services, not only one value service.

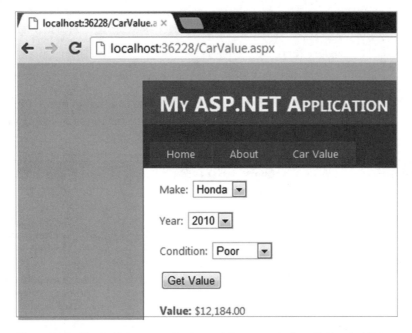

Figure 4.16 The CarValue.aspx showing a dollar amount after clicking Get Value

Because this third-party data is unlikely to change often, caching the data for a few hours (or even more) means that our cached data won't be out of date.

This seems like a great place not only to use caching, but also to use AOP to avoid all of the repetition and boilerplate that caching brings with it. Let's start by writing an aspect to cache the results of GetValue.

4.3.3 Caching a result

Getting the result of a method and putting it in the ASP.NET Cache is mostly straightforward. Create a class that uses PostSharp's OnMethodBoundaryAspect as a base class. Because we're interested in the results (the return value) of a method, OnSuccess seems to be the most logical place to put our code, as shown here.

Listing 4.23 Storing the results of the method in a cache

```
[Serializable]
public class CacheAspect : OnMethodBoundaryAspect {
    public override void OnSuccess(MethodExecutionArgs args) {
        var key = GetCacheKey(args);
        HttpContext.Current.Cache[key] = args.ReturnValue;
    }
}

public class CarValueService {
    readonly Random _rand;

    public CarValueService() {
```

The first step is to generate a unique key.

Use PostSharp's API to put the ReturnValue into the Cache

```
        _rand = new Random();
    }

    [CacheAspect]
    public decimal GetValue(int makeId, int conditionId, int year) {
        Thread.Sleep(5000);
        return _rand.Next(10000, 20000);
    }
```

Apply the aspect to GetValue by using an attribute

One important thing is omitted from the previous example: the GetCacheKey method. This method is responsible for generating a unique key that will be used to retrieve the data that's stored in the cache. It must be a key that's based on the arguments that are passed in to the bounded method. Therefore, if the user selects a Ford (ID: 2), 2010, in Average (ID: 1) condition, the results will be stored in the cache separate from the results if the user selects a Honda (ID: 0), 2012, in Mint (ID: 2) condition.

A naïve approach (you'll learn why it's naïve later) would be to combine all of those arguments into one string. To do that, write a GetCacheKey method, as shown next.

Listing 4.24 Naïve GetCacheKey implementation

```
    [Serializable]
    public class CacheAspect : OnMethodBoundaryAspect {
        public override void OnSuccess(MethodExecutionArgs args) {
            var key = GetCacheKey(args);
            HttpContext.Current.Cache[key] = args.ReturnValue;
        }

        string GetCacheKey(MethodExecutionArgs args) {
            var concatArguments = string.Join("_", args.Arguments);
            concatArguments = args.Method.Name + "_" + concatArguments;
            return concatArguments;
        }
    }
```

ToString is implicitly used here to join all of the argument values into one string.

Also prepend the name of the method to the string, in case other methods have similar parameters

Compile and load the CarValue.aspx again. Make a few requests for different cars, and you should see some values start to appear in the cache (see figure 4.17). Although we aren't retrieving any values out of the cache yet, you can see the values starting to build up in the cache.

In figure 4.18, you can see how GetCacheKey constructs the strings.

If we can construct this key the same way every time the same arguments are sent to the GetValue method, then we'll be able to retrieve the value using the same constructed key.

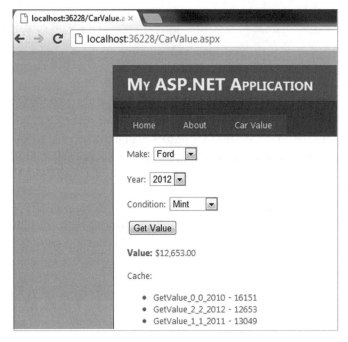

Figure 4.17   After three different requests, the cache contains three values

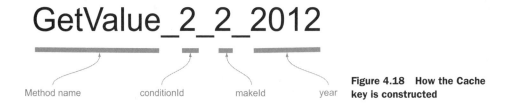

Figure 4.18   How the Cache key is constructed

4.3.4   *Retrieving from the cache*

Stored values in a cache aren't useful unless we retrieve the values when they're available. If GetValue is called with arguments for which we've already cached a value, then we can save a trip to the (slow) web service and retrieve the value out of cache instead of running the code inside of GetValue. If it turns out that the value hasn't been cached, only then do we need to run the (slow) GetValue method. To do this, let's add to CacheAspect by overriding the OnEntry method, as shown in the listing 4.25.

Think back to the metaphor of the boundary between two states. Instead of making the costly trip from Columbus, Ohio, to Philadelphia, Pennsylvania, to get a delicious cheesesteak, what this caching aspect is doing is putting the cheesesteak at the Ohio-Pennsylvania border.

Listing 4.25 Add an `OnEntry` override to the `CacheAspect` class

The code in
OnEntry will
run before
the method,
giving us a
chance to
check the
Cache.

```
[Serializable]
public class CacheAspect : OnMethodBoundaryAspect {
    public override void OnEntry(MethodExecutionArgs args) {

    }

    public override void OnSuccess(MethodExecutionArgs args) {
        var key = GetCacheKey(args);
        HttpContext.Current.Cache[key] = args.ReturnValue;
    }

    string GetCacheKey(MethodExecutionArgs args) {
        var concatArguments = string.Join("_", args.Arguments);
        concatArguments = args.Method.Name + "_" + concatArguments;
        return concatArguments;
    }
}
```

The same
CacheAspect
class as in
the last
section

In the `OnEntry` method, we check to see whether there's already a cached result (see listing 4.26). If there isn't, then there's nothing left to do: the slow method must be run. Someone has to go to get that cheesesteak.

If there's a value in the cache, then we need to set the return value of the bounded method and return immediately (without running the bounded method). Therefore, if there's a cheesesteak at the border, there's no reason to continue on to Philadelphia: the hard work has already been done.

Listing 4.26 Checking the cache in `OnEntry`

```
public override void OnEntry(MethodExecutionArgs args) {

    var key = GetCacheKey(args);

    if (HttpContext.Current.Cache[key] == null)

        return;

    args.ReturnValue = HttpContext.Current.Cache[key];

    args.FlowBehavior = FlowBehavior.Return;

}
```

Use the same
GetCacheKey
method to
generate
matching keys

If Cache returns
null, then there's no
cache of that object

Returning here means
that the (slow)
bounded method will
run as normal

Setting the
return value of
the bounded
method to be
the cached
value

Setting FlowBehavior.Return to make the
bounded method return immediately

There are two pieces of PostSharp API that warrant further explanation. The first is `args.ReturnValue`. This property gets and sets the return value of the method being bounded (`CarValueService`'s `GetValue` method). We want `GetValue` to return the value that's in the cache, and setting `args.ReturnValue` will accomplish that.

Second is `args.FlowBehavior`. If you set only `args.ReturnValue`, that isn't enough—because this is a boundary aspect, it's implicit that the bounded method will run. But because we have a cached value, we don't want it to run. Setting `args.Flow-Behavior` to `FlowBehavior.Return` will instruct PostSharp to make `GetValue` return immediately without running any of its code.

One more problem remains. In this simplified example, we can get only values of cars by model, year, and condition. In reality, the variables are much more comprehensive: color, number of doors, engine type, and so on can all be a factor in determining value. Adding more parameters to `GetValue` would quickly get out of control. It'd make sense to instead refactor `GetValue` to take a single parameter that encapsulates all the options, as shown next.

Listing 4.27   Refactored `CarValueService` to encapsulate options

```
public class CarValueService {
    readonly Random _rand;

    public CarValueService() {
        _rand = new Random();
    }

    [CacheAspect]
    public decimal GetValue(CarValueArgs args) {          The method body is
        Thread.Sleep(5000);                               the same as before;
        return _rand.Next(10000, 20000);                  only the parameter
    }                                                     has changed.
}

public class CarValueArgs {
    public int MakeId { get; set; }           You can now add
    public int Year { get; set; }             additional options
    public int ConditionId { get; set; }      without changing the
                                              parameters of GetValue.
}
```

If you make this change, though, you'll run into a problem with caching that goes back to the naïve `GetCacheKey` that I wrote:

```
string GetCacheKey(MethodExecutionArgs args) {                        Remember
    var concatArguments = string.Join("_", args.Arguments);          the implicit
    concatArguments = args.Method.Name + "_" + concatArguments;      ToString
    return concatArguments;                                          being called
}                                                                    here?
```

The cache key is being constructed by using `ToString` on each of the arguments. This approach works fine if all the arguments are types like `int`, `string`, `long`, and so on. But what happens if you call `ToString` on an argument of type `CarValueArgs`? You get a string `"CachingPostSharp.CarValueArgs"` (that is, the name of the type and its namespace). This string won't work well with caching, because `GetCacheKey` will always return the same string, regardless of the values of the `CarValueArgs` properties. We have to write a better `GetCacheKey`.

4.3.5 *A more robust cache key*

We want a cache key that will be unique for the values of the CarValueArgs parameter. This task may sound daunting, because it needs to be generic enough to use in an aspect.

One way is to perform shallow serialization on the argument(s) and use that serialization to generate the cache key. Shallow serialization means that only the values available through public properties will be serialized. All objects in .NET are available for shallow serialization without doing anything extra to them. For my CarValueArgs parameter, this is fine, because it's only public properties.

Next, we must determine how the serialization will be performed. XML is an option. We could use binary serialization and calculate a hash value. But let's keep it simple and straightforward and use JSON (JavaScript Object Notation) serialization.

Why JSON?

The caching aspect, ASP.NET Cache, and the CarValueService have nothing to do with JavaScript, so why are we using JSON?

- It's easy to read. When we see the contents of the cache on the screen, it'll be clear what's happening and what's being cached.

- It's compact. No offense to XML fans, but we don't need all the extra XML headers and namespace information to generate a caching key.

- It's easy to generate. We'll use the JavaScriptSerializer, which is in System.Web.Extensions.

It's okay to use some other kind of serialization, or to write your own, as long as it achieves the goal of generating a unique key that you can use to identify cached data.

Let's write a better GetCacheKey such as the one in the following listing. This one will serialize the arguments to a JSON string (and prepend the method name to provide additional uniqueness).

Listing 4.28 A more robust GetCacheKey using serialization

```
string GetCacheKey(MethodExecutionArgs args) {
    var serializedArguments = Serialize(args.Arguments);
    var concatArguments = string.Join("_", serializedArguments);
    concatArguments = args.Method.Name + "_" + concatArguments;
    return concatArguments;
}

string[] Serialize(Arguments arguments) {
    var json = new JavaScriptSerializer();
    return arguments.Select(json.Serialize).ToArray();
}
```

Instead of using ToString implicitly, serialize all of the arguments.

Make sure to add System.Web .Extensions to your project.

This code will call serialize on every argument and create an array.

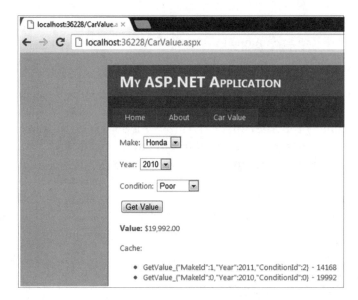

Figure 4.19   Serialized object used for cache keys

Now recompile and try getting some car values. You should see different-looking cache keys, as in figure 4.19.

Not only are we able to use a more flexible `CarValueArgs` parameter and have it still work with caching now, but we get a nice side effect whereby we have a more readable cache key on the demonstration page. I selected Honda (MakeId of 0), 2010 model year, and Poor condition (ConditionId of 0). The cached value is 19992 ($19,992).

4.4   Summary

In this chapter, I covered a common type of aspect: boundary aspects. Boundaries are like the borders between states. A boundary aspect gives you the opportunity to put behavior at the boundaries in your code. Two common examples of boundary aspects are before and after web pages and before and after method calls. Like method interception, boundary aspects give you another way to encapsulate cross-cutting concerns into their own classes.

PostSharp gives you the ability to write method interception aspects, and ASP.NET gives you the ability to write web page boundary aspects (via `HttpModules`). Both of their APIs give you contextual information (for example, information about the HTTP request or information about the method), as well as the ability to control the flow of the program (for example, redirects to another page or immediate returns from the method).

As I said, I believe it is beneficial to work through the two real-world aspects presented in this chapter. I recommend that you experiment with the `HttpModule`, the PostSharp `OnMethodBoundaryAspect`, and both of their APIs.

In the next chapter, we'll revisit both PostSharp and interception. But instead of methods, we'll look at intercepting properties and fields, known collectively as locations.

Get this instead: interceptiing locations

This chapter covers

- What is a location?
- Using PostSharp to intercept locations
- Writing lazy-loading aspects
- How noisy `INotifyPropertyChanged` makes your code
- Using AOP to make `INotifyPropertyChanged` clean and easy

In chapter 3, I wrote about method interception. In this chapter, we'll look at a different kind of interception: the interception of locations. I'll start by reviewing what a location is (field or property), then I'll show you a couple of examples of real-world aspects that you can use on locations. So far, the focus has been mainly on methods. But locations are an important part of your code and can be susceptible to the same types of repetitive boilerplate as methods.

Location interception is a less common feature of AOP frameworks, so most of the examples in this chapter use PostSharp, a framework that supports locations. Additionally, you'll look at a specialized AOP tool in this chapter (as opposed to a general AOP framework such as PostSharp) called NotifyPropertyWeaver that provides location-interception capabilities, but only for one narrow feature.

5.1   Location interception

You might not have heard the term location in reference to C#. A field is a location and a property is a location. The following code snippet contains two locations, one field and one property:

```
public class MyClass {
    public string MyField;
    public string MyProperty {get; set;}
}
```

A string field of MyClass called MyField

A string property of MyClass called MyProperty

Fields and properties are common in OOP. They give data and structure to a class, as well as the ability to share information among the methods of a class.

The next section is a quick refresher on how fields and properties in C# work. If you feel comfortable in your knowledge of fields and properties, you can skim the next section. Remember that properties are just syntactic sugar for getter/setter methods.

5.1.1   Fields and properties in .NET

Fields are members of a class. They can be declared public, private, protected, internal, and so on to restrict the access level (private by default).

Generally, public fields are frowned upon if encapsulation is important, so fields are most often set to private and used only outside the class via accessor methods (such as in the following listing). If I have a private _balance field, then—as the listing shows—only by calling Deposit or Withdrawal can the value of the field be changed by other objects.

Listing 5.1   Encapsulation of a private field with methods

```
public class BankAccount {
    decimal _balance;

    public void SetBalance(decimal amount) {
        _balance = amount;
    }

    public decimal GetBalance(decimal amount) {
        return _balance;
    }
}
```

In C#, you can use the properties syntax (get and set), which reduces the amount of code necessary to implement this common pattern. The following C# getter and setter code shows a private field (_balance) and a property that encapsulates access via Balance:

```
public class BankAccount {
    decimal _balance;
    public decimal Balance {
```

```
        get { return _balance; }
        set { _balance = value; }
    }
}
```

Using both `get` and `set` is optional: if a setter isn't necessary, you can leave it out (and vice versa). But behind the scenes, the .NET compiler still creates methods. If you use a decompiler tool such as ILSpy to examine `MyClass`'s CIL, as in the next listing, you'll see that it creates a `decimal get_Balance()` method and a `void set_Balance(decimal)`.

Listing 5.2   The compiled program viewed through the ILSpy tool

```
.class public auto ansi beforefieldinit MyBankingProject.BankAccount
    extends [mscorlib]System.Object
{
    .field private valuetype [mscorlib]System.Decimal _balance

    .method public hidebysig specialname
        instance valuetype [mscorlib]System.Decimal get_Balance ()
            cil managed {                                          The get_Balance()
IL instructions removed ──▷                                       getter is created.
        }

    .method public hidebysig specialname
        instance void set_Balance (                               The
            valuetype [mscorlib]System.Decimal 'value'           set_Balance(decimal)
        ) cil managed {                                           setter is created.
IL instructions removed ──▷
        }
}
```

Properties are called syntactic sugar because they make your life easier as a developer, even though they're implemented with methods and fields. In a way, this is similar to what AOP tools do for you: they make it easy to read/write code because they fill in all of the messy details later.

Autoproperties were introduced in C# 2. This new tool gives you the ability to create a property without having to create the backing field explicitly. You can now rewrite the previous code in a much more concise way:

```
public class MyClass {
    public string MyProperty {get; set;}
}
```

When using autoproperties, you must use both `get` and `set`, but you can put different access levels on them. For example, `get` could be public and `set` could be private.

This isn't brand-new or surprising information to a .NET developer, as properties and fields are part of your day-to-day work. But the most used features are often the ones you take for granted, so it's good to review some of those details before diving into new AOP code that involves interception of locations.

5.1.2 *PostSharp location interception*

In chapter 3, we talked about using AOP tools such as PostSharp to intercept methods, which might lead you to hypothesize that (because properties are methods underneath) you could use method interception aspects on properties. And you'd be correct. You can use PostSharp or Castle DynamicProxy to create method interception aspects on properties. The next listing shows an example that uses PostSharp to do so in a Console project.

Listing 5.3 Using a method interception aspect on a property

```
public class MyClass {
    public string MyProperty {
        get;
        [MyMethodAspect]            Apply aspect with
        set;                        attribute to
    }                               property's setter
}

[Serializable]                                                  Inheriting
public class MyMethodAspect : MethodInterceptionAspect {        MethodInterception-
    public override void OnInvoke(MethodInterceptionArgs args)  Aspect
    {
        Console.WriteLine("Hello from the aspect");
        args.Proceed();
    }
}

static void Main(string[] args) {                Here's where a set occurs.
    var myObj = new MyClass();                   Run the program; the
    myObj.MyProperty = "some string";            output should look like
}                                                that in figure 5.1.
```

But we should discuss a couple of issues with this approach. First, it's awkward. With this approach, you'd possibly have to write two aspects: one for getting and one for setting. Second, you can use this approach only with properties. Fields don't generate methods; they're like normal variables, except that they're scoped to the entire class instead of to only one method.

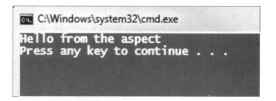

Figure 5.1 The Console output of method interception on a property

Fortunately, PostSharp gives us a more convenient way to write a single class that can handle both getting and setting, as well enable us to write aspects for both fields and properties: the `LocationInterceptionAspect`. The following listing shows similar example code as the last couple of examples, except this time it's written with a `LocationInterceptionAspect`.

Listing 5.4   Using a PostSharp location interception aspect

```
public class MyClass {
    [MyLocationAspect]
    public string MyProperty { get; set; }
}

[Serializable]
public class MyLocationAspect : LocationInterceptionAspect {
    public override void OnSetValue(LocationInterceptionArgs args) {
        Console.WriteLine("Hello from the aspect");
        args.ProceedGetValue();
    }
}

static void Main(string[] args) {
    var myObj = new MyClass();
    myObj.MyProperty = "some string";
}
```

⊲ **The attribute goes on the whole property now, not only the setter**

⊲ **Inheriting from LocationInterceptionAspect base class**

⊲ **The same set operation is taking place.**

In similar fashion to other PostSharp aspects, two overrides are available: `OnGetValue` and `OnSetValue`. Those methods run in place of the `get` or `set` operation, respectively. Therefore, as with method interception, you need to proceed if you want the operations to be called. Use `args.ProceedGetValue()` or `args.ProceedSetValue()`, respectively.

In addition to these simple proceed commands, the PostSharp API gives you ability to examine and change the underlying value of the field/property. If you want to modify or examine the value, you can do so with PostSharp. I'll demonstrate this usage with a real-world example of a lazy-loading aspect.

5.2   Real-world example: lazy loading

The purpose of lazy loading is to defer execution of a costly operation for as long as possible. For instance, if you have a service that takes a long time to initialize, you might want to wait to initialize until the service is used, particularly if there's a possibility that the service won't be used.

The opposite of lazy loading is eager loading, in which an operation or series of operations is performed every time before the results are needed, in case they might be needed.

NHibernate is one example of a database tool used in a persistence layer. When you retrieve an entity from the database with lazy loading, NHibernate would pull that entity but not the related entities. With eager loading, NHibernate could pull that entity, related entities, entities related to the related entities, and so on. In that case, it's a trade-off between performance and convenience.

I mention NHibernate only because it's a popular, mature tool with built-in configuration options to control lazy/eager loading with which you might be familiar. If you're working with resources or services for which lazy loading isn't already available, the next section will be helpful, as we'll look at a variety of approaches in .NET to implement it.

5.2.1 Lazy loading approaches in .NET

One approach to lazy loading involves using a property with a backing field. When you first use get, it creates a new instance. Subsequent uses of get will return the backing property as normal.

Suppose I have a class named SlowConstructor, which I've so named because instantiating an object of that type takes a long period of time (making it beneficial to be lazy when loading, and preventing the constructor penalty payment until it's absolutely necessary). This listing shows how lazy loading might look.

Listing 5.5 Lazy loading with a property and a backing field

```
SlowConstructor _myProperty;
public SlowConstructor MyProperty {
    get {
        if(_myProperty == null)
            _myProperty = new SlowConstructor();
        return _myProperty;
    }
}
```

A backing field is necessary to store the object after instantiation.

The constructor is called only when the getter is first used.

Not bad. You may have noticed that it's not thread-safe, so if that's a concern, put in a lock statement. This is an appropriate place to use double-checked locking, as shown in the next listing, because it's possible for a race condition to occur between the first check and the lock.

Listing 5.6 Thread-safe lazy loading with double-checked locking

```
readonly object _syncRoot = new object();
SlowConstructor _myProperty;
public SlowConstructor MyProperty {
    get {
        if(_myProperty == null)
            lock (_syncRoot)
                if (_myProperty == null)
                    _myProperty = new SlowConstructor();
        return _myProperty;
    }
}
```

It's possible for the value to be set between the first check and the lock in another thread, so double-check.

With that code in place, being lazy pays off. You can access the property in a normal way, and if it's never used, then that slow constructor never runs. Instead of using new, you could also use a factory or an IoC tool to instantiate an object. The surrounding code (the locks, the checking, and the backing field) would all remain the same.

Starting with .NET 4.0, the .NET framework provides System.Lazy<T>, which is a convenience class to accomplish the same thing as the previous listing with less code. The following listing is an example of that same lazy-loaded property with a Lazy field instead.

Listing 5.7   Using `System.Lazy<T>`

```
Lazy<SlowConstructor> MyProperty = new Lazy<SlowConstructor>(
    () => new SlowConstructor()
);
```

The factory code is passed in as a lambda (anonymous function) that tells `Lazy` to use this code to instantiate the object the first time that `Lazy` is accessed. `System.Lazy<T>` is also thread-safe (by default), so it's encapsulating all the locking.

However, unlike the previous example, this field is of the type `Lazy<Slow-Constructor>`, instead of being a property of the type `SlowConstructor`. To use the `SlowConstructor` object you need one additional step:

```
SlowConstructor c = MyProperty.Value;
```

Now you have two options when you want lazy loading. In the first example, you have a bunch of boilerplate code and backing fields. In the second example, with `System.Lazy<T>`, all of the boilerplate goes away, but now you have to go through a `Value` property to get at the lazy-loaded object. Let's use AOP to create an aspect that combines the best of both approaches.

5.2.2 *Implementing lazy loading with AOP*

In this example, we'll work toward a property that can be accessed directly (that is, without a `Value` property) and that has none of the boilerplate from the first example in the previous section. The following code represents what we want:

The body of the get will be the factory.

```
[LazyLoadGetter]
static SlowConstructor MyProperty {
    get { return new SlowConstructor();}
}
```

Use an attribute to tell PostSharp to make this property a lazy-loading property

The body of the `get` contains the factory for lazy loading. It won't be called until a `get` is performed, and the results of that operation will be used on subsequent `gets`.

Start by creating a Console project (I'm calling mine LazyLoading) and installing PostSharp via NuGet. I'll create a class called `SlowConstructor` that simulates a class or a service that's expensive to instantiate. Then, I'll make a property of that type in the `Main` class and use that property's `get` a couple of times to access the object and call its method. (I'll call it twice, just to demonstrate the lazy loading, as shown in this listing.)

Listing 5.8   Basic Console application with no lazy loading

```
public class SlowConstructor {
    public SlowConstructor() {
        Console.WriteLine("Doing something slow");
        Thread.Sleep(5000);
    }

    public void DoSomething() {
```

```
        Console.WriteLine("Hello, it's {0}", DateTime.Now);
    }
}

class Program {
    static SlowConstructor MyProperty {
        get { return new SlowConstructor();}
    }

    static void Main(string[] args) {
        MyProperty.DoSomething();
        MyProperty.DoSomething();
    }
}
```

The `SlowConstructor` object simulates a costly constructor operation. `MyProperty` contains only the code to instantiate the object. This would be a poor way to write a program, because the property gets reinstantiated every time it's used. But we're planning to make that `get` into a blueprint of how to lazily load the property. When you

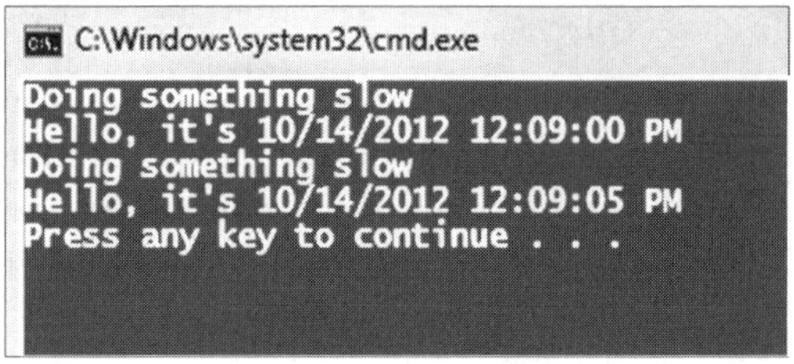

Figure 5.2   Output with no lazy-loading

run the program, you'd see output shown in figure 5.2.

Instead of adding all of the backing fields, double-checked locking, or switching to use `System.Lazy<T>`, I'm going to put an attribute on it that inherits from PostSharp's `LocationInterceptionAspect`:

```
class Program {
    [LazyLoadGetter]
    static SlowConstructor MyProperty {
        get { return new SlowConstructor();}
    }

    static void Main(string[] args) {
        MyProperty.DoSomething();
        MyProperty.DoSomething();
    }
}

[Serializable]
public class LazyLoadGetter : LocationInterceptionAspect
{

}
```

Nothing much changed in the previous code from the prior listing, except the addition of an (empty) aspect class, and the use of the attribute on `MyProperty` to indicate that you want that property to be lazy loading.

Next, in `LazyLoadGetter`, you want to intercept any `gets` to the property, so override `OnGetValue`:

```
[Serializable]
public class LazyLoadGetter : LocationInterceptionAspect {
    public override void OnGetValue(LocationInterceptionArgs args)
    {

    }
}
```

The backing field and double-check locking live in this aspect. Move the code from listing 5.6 (the code that uses double-checked locking to make the lazy-loading thread safe) into the aspect's `OnGetValue` method.

Listing 5.9 A lazy-loading aspect

```
[Serializable]
public class LazyLoadGetter : LocationInterceptionAspect {
    object _backingField;
    object _syncRoot = new object();

    public override void OnGetValue(LocationInterceptionArgs args) {
        if(_backingField == null)
            lock(_syncRoot)
                if(_backingField == null) {
                    args.ProceedGetValue();
                    _backingField = args.Value;
                }
        args.Value = _backingField;
    }
}
```

> **ProceedGetValue will continue to execute the get as normal.**

> **args.Value contains the value of the property, which should now be populated.**

> **Because the backing field has already been populated, set the value.**

This code looks similar to the original double-check locking code from the previous section. But the PostSharp API is being used in a few different places (specifically, the `ProceedGetValue` method and the `args.Value` property).

The first time that `get` is called, `OnGetValue` executes. The backing field will be null at first, so lock and double-check, as before. Now tell PostSharp to proceed to run the code inside of the `get`, which means that `SlowConstructor` will be executed. Once that's done, PostSharp's `args.Value` will be populated with the result of the `get`. Put that value into the backing field for use next time.

After all that, and on every subsequent call, all that PostSharp is doing is setting `args.Value` to be the value of the backing field. `args.ProceedGetValue()` is only called the first time. Run the code again and, as figure 5.3 shows, you'll see that lazy loading has kicked in.

With this aspect, you now have syntax that's similar to `System.Lazy<T>` (the body of the `get` acts as the factory instead of having to pass in a `Func` to Lazy's constructor) and still have the ability to access the property directly.

```
C:\Windows\system32\cmd.exe
Doing something slow
Hello, it's 10/14/2012 12:27:53 PM
Hello, it's 10/14/2012 12:27:53 PM
Press any key to continue . . .
```

Figure 5.3 Output with lazy-loading

As you know, for fields, you don't have a get, so using lazy loading will take on a bit of a different form.

5.2.3   *What about lazy-loading fields?*

A field is a class-level variable, which means you won't find a way to explicitly specify how a field should get lazy loaded. Let's make some assumptions to implicitly specify how the field should be loaded. First, let's write code similar to the last section, but use a field instead of a property:

```
class Program {
    static SlowConstructor MyField;

    static void Main(string[] args) {
        MyField.DoSomething();
        MyField.DoSomething();
    }
}
```

The simplest thing you can do is use Reflection's Activator to create an instance of the field's type. Let's create an aspect that does that. Start by creating a class that inherits LocationInterceptionAspect, and use it as an attribute on the field:

```
class Program {
    [LazyLoadActivator]
    static SlowConstructor MyField;

    static void Main(string[] args) {
        MyField.DoSomething();
        MyField.DoSomething();
    }
}

[Serializable]
public class LazyLoadActivator : LocationInterceptionAspect
{

}
```

Reflection's Activator

Reflection is a group of tools in the System.Reflection namespace that allows you to write code that reads and generates code as the program is running. The Activator class is able to create new instances of an object on the fly, which is useful when you want to instantiate a new object, but you won't know what type of object to instantiate until runtime. Using it in this aspect lets you reuse the aspect on a field of any type. With this flexibility comes a performance cost, so make sure that you use Reflection only when necessary.

The code in LazyLoadActivator will look similar to LazyLoadGetter, except that instead of args.ProceedGetValue(), you'll use Activator to invoke the parameterless constructor of SlowConstructor as shown in the next example.

Listing 5.10   Lazy loading using Activator

```
[Serializable]
public class LazyLoadActivator : LocationInterceptionAspect {
    object _backingField;
    object _syncRoot = new object();

    public override void OnGetValue(LocationInterceptionArgs args) {
        if (_backingField == null)
            lock (_syncRoot)
                if (_backingField == null)
                    _backingField = Activator
                        .CreateInstance(args.Location.LocationType);
        args.Value = _backingField;
    }
}
```

> **Activator is used with the location type to create a new object.**

PostSharp's `args.Location. LocationType` is able to tell us the `Type` of the location that's being intercepted (for both properties and fields). Once you have that information, use `System.Activator` to create a new instance of that type. Store the result in the backing field, as before.

This approach may be appropriate for some narrow situations, but a more realistic way would be to use a factory, service locator, or IoC container in place of `Activator`. For instance, if you use StructureMap (a popular .NET IoC tool), then you could replace `Activator` with `ObjectFactory.GetInstance`. This approach allows you to use lazy loading with more complex dependencies (that is, classes that don't have a parameterless constructor).

Suppose that `SlowConstructor` has only one constructor and that constructor has an `IMyService` parameter. Now you have a set of classes that looks something like the following code.

Listing 5.11   `SlowConstructor` with a dependency on `IMyService`

```
public class SlowConstructor {
    IMyService _myService;

    public SlowConstructor(IMyService myService) {
        _myService = myService;
        Console.WriteLine("Doing something slow");
        Thread.Sleep(5000);
    }

    public void DoSomething() {
        _myService.DoSomething();
    }
}
public interface IMyService {
    void DoSomething();
}
public class MyService : IMyService {
    public void DoSomething() {
```

> **There's only one constructor, and it needs a parameter.**

> **SlowConstructor expects an object that implements this interface**

> **Move the "Hello" message into the service implementation**

```
        Console.WriteLine("Hello, it's {0}", DateTime.Now);
    }
}
```

You could still use `Activator` to create an object, but then you'd have to use `Activator` to create the dependent object as well. In a real-world application, this chain of dependencies could be much longer and more complex, so typically you'd leave this task to a tool such as StructureMap. The following listing shows how I'd initialize StructureMap in the Console's `Main` method. Other IoC tools will be similar.

Listing 5.12   Initializing

```
static void Main(string[] args) {                      ObjectFactory.Initialize
                                                       tells StructureMap which
    ObjectFactory.Initialize(x =>              ◁──┘    implementations to use.

When a constructor       {
calls for IMyService,                                                  This line is
use MyService as the ┌▷     x.For<IMyService>().Use<MyService>();      optional;
implementation.                                                        StructureMap
                            x.For<SlowConstructor>().Use<SlowConstructor>(); ◁─┐ will self-bind
                                                                            automatically.
        });
}
```

Now that the dependencies are configured, add a field to the `Program` class, apply a new aspect to it, and use the `MyField`, as in the previous `Activator` example (listing 5.10). This listing shows the code to do that.

Listing 5.13   Lazy loading with StructureMap

```
class Program {
    [LazyLoadStructureMap]                              ◁──┐ Using a new aspect as
      static SlowConstructor MyField;                       an attribute on a field

StructureMap    static void Main(string[] args) {
configuration └─▷   ObjectFactory.Initialize(x => {
                        x.For<IMyService>().Use<MyService>();
                        x.For<SlowConstructor>().Use<SlowConstructor>();
                    });

        MyField.DoSomething();                          ◁──┐ Invokes the equivalent
        MyField.DoSomething();                               of a get on the field
    }
}

[Serializable]
public class LazyLoadStructureMap : LocationInterceptionAspect {
    public override void OnGetValue(LocationInterceptionArgs args) {
                                      ◁──┐ The lazy-loading code that
        }                                  uses ObjectFactory goes here.
    }
}
```

I'm using StructureMap's `ObjectFactory.Initialize` method to specify the dependencies. If StructureMap is asked for an implementation of `IMyService`, it will return a new `MyService` object. If it's asked for an implementation of `SlowConstructor`, it will use `SlowConstructor`. More important, when creating an instance of `Slow-Constructor`, it'll recognize that `SlowConstructor`'s constructor has a single parameter (`IMyService`) and will automatically use the configured dependency and pass a new instance of `MyService` to it.

Once again, the lazy-loading code will look similar to previous iterations, but this time it'll use `ObjectFactory.GetInstance` (that is, it'll ask StructureMap to provide the object) instead of using `Activator` as shown here.

Listing 5.14 Using StructureMap in place of Activator

```
[Serializable]
public class LazyLoadStructureMap : LocationInterceptionAspect {
    object _backingField;
    object _syncRoot = new object();

    public override void OnGetValue(LocationInterceptionArgs args) {
        if (_backingField == null)
            lock (_syncRoot)
                if (_backingField == null) {
                    var locationType = args.Location
                        .PropertyInfo.PropertyType;
                    _backingField = ObjectFactory
                        .GetInstance(locationType);     ◁──┐ GetInstance returns
                }                                            a new instance of
            args.Value = _backingField;                      MyService
    }
}
```

Run the Console application, and you'll see that figure 5.4 outputs similar results as before (figure 5.3).

The main difference is that it's a much more real scenario: classes have dependencies on interfaces, the configuration of which is defined through a DI tool.

Judicious use of lazy loading can improve the performance of your code by performing expensive operations only when they're necessary. AOP makes it painless to use lazy loading by intercepting the accessing of fields and properties and moving boilerplate code out of the property and into its own aspect class. Another place where fields and properties can get bogged down with boilerplate is in a responsive GUI.

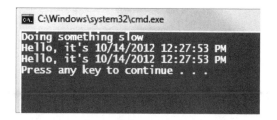

Figure 5.4 Lazy loading with dependencies via StructureMap

5.3   *Real-world example: INotifyPropertyChanged*

If you're a web developer, as I am, then you don't write many desktop or rich client applications. But if you aren't a web developer, you might be writing rich UI applications with UI frameworks such as WPF, Silverlight, Windows 8, or even standard Windows Forms (WinForms).

If you've spent your days working with such frameworks, then you've probably used the `INotifyPropertyChanged` interface a few times. Implementations of this interface raise an event that signals to the UI that one of the properties has been changed and to update the UI accordingly. This interface is helpful and can save a lot of code; it also requires a lot of repetitive boilerplate code to get it working, so it is a great place to use AOP.

Let's first review how `INotifyPropertyChanged` works (in a desktop WPF app) without the help of any AOP.

5.3.1   *Using INotifyPropertyChanged in a desktop application*

In this section, I'll walk you through a refresher on how `INotifyPropertyChanged` works in WPF.

Create a WPF project in Visual Studio. I'm going make MainWindow a window with two text boxes: one for first name and one for last name. There will be a label on the window that shows the combination of first name with last name. Use a simple set of StackPanels to lay this out, something like figure 5.5.

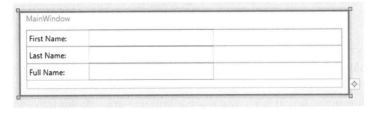

**Figure 5.5
MainWindow layout
with text boxes and
labels**

You can drag and drop your way to that, or if you're more comfortable with XAML, you might put together something like this listing.

Listing 5.15   XAML to create textbox, button, and textblocks

```
<Window x:Class="NotifyPropertyChanged.MainWindow"
    xmlns="http://schemas.microsoft.com/winfx/2006/xaml/presentation"
    xmlns:x="http://schemas.microsoft.com/winfx/2006/xaml"
    Title="MainWindow" Height="130" Width="525">
  <StackPanel Orientation="Vertical">
    <StackPanel Orientation="Horizontal">
      <Label Content="First Name:" Width="100" />       ◁──┐ A textbox for the
      <TextBox Width="200" />                                first name
    </StackPanel>
    <StackPanel Orientation="Horizontal">
```

```
            <Label Content="Last Name:" Width="100" />
            <TextBox Width="200" />                          A textbox for the
        </StackPanel>                                        last name
        <StackPanel Orientation="Horizontal">
            <Label Content="Full Name:" Width="100" />
            <Label Width="200" />                            The label that will
        </StackPanel>                                        show the combination
    </StackPanel>                                            of first and last name
</Window>
```

You want the "Full Name" field to be populated with the combination of first and last name as the user is typing. A common approach to doing this in WPF is to create a view model to encapsulate the data (first name and last name) and derived data (full name).

Create a `NameViewModel` class with three properties, as in the following listing. `FirstName` and `LastName` will be standard autoproperties. Create another property called `FullName`, which will be a derived property that appends `LastName` to `FirstName` with a space between them.

Listing 5.16   A view model class representing the data

```
public class NameViewModel {
    public string FirstName { get; set; }
    public string LastName { get; set; }
    public string FullName {
        get {
            return string.Format("{0} {1}", FirstName, LastName);
        }
    }
}
```

There are just a couple more steps to get this to work. First, bind the `DataContext` of the WPF window to a new instance of this type. Do this in the MainWindow.xaml.cs code-behind class by assigning an instance of the object to the WPF Window's `DataContext` property.

Listing 5.17   Binding a `NameViewModel` object to MainWindow's DataContext

```
public partial class MainWindow : Window {           Bind a new
    public MainWindow() {                             NameViewModel
        InitializeComponent();                        object to the
                                                      DataContext
        DataContext = new NameViewModel();
    }
}
```

Next, you need to bind the individual text boxes and label to the properties of the `ViewModel` by specifying the binding in the `Text` and `Content` properties of the TextBoxes and `Label`s, respectively, as in the next listing.

Listing 5.18 Binding controls to `ViewModel` properties

```
<StackPanel Orientation="Horizontal">
    <Label Content="First Name:" Width="100" />
    <TextBox Width="200" Text="{Binding Path=FirstName}"/>
</StackPanel>
<StackPanel Orientation="Horizontal">
    <Label Content="Last Name:" Width="100" />
    <TextBox Width="200" Text="{Binding Path=LastName}"/>
</StackPanel>
<StackPanel Orientation="Horizontal">
    <Label Content="Full Name:" Width="100" />
    <Label Width="200" Content="{Binding Path=FullName}" />
</StackPanel>
```

Bind the first TextBox's Text attribute to the FirstName property

Bind the final label's Content attribut to the FullName property

Bind the second TextBox's Text attribute to the LastName property

We're getting closer. Next, tell the two `TextBox` bindings that they should trigger an update whenever they change (that is, when the user types something in). Modify the FirstName and LastName text boxes, specify `UpdateSourceTrigger` in the bindings, and set it to `PropertyChanged`:

```
<TextBox Width="200"
    Text="{Binding Path=FirstName,
        UpdateSourceTrigger=PropertyChanged}"/>
```

and

```
<TextBox Width="200"
    Text="{Binding Path=LastName,
        UpdateSourceTrigger=PropertyChanged}"/>
```

`TextBoxes`, by default, will update the source data when losing focus. What we're doing here is telling them to update the source data as the user is typing. To make that work, you need to do one last thing: make the `NameViewModel` class implement `INotifyPropertyChanged`. The only thing that you need to implement this interface is an event of type `PropertyChangedEventHandler`. With the binding that you've added to the TextBoxes, WPF will look for this event to be fired, which means that you have to code the setters of each property to trigger that event with the name of the property that has been changed. This listing shows how to do it.

Listing 5.19 Implementing `INotifyPropertyChanged` on `NameViewModel`

```
public class NameViewModel : INotifyPropertyChanged {
    public event PropertyChangedEventHandler PropertyChanged;

    void OnPropertyChanged(string propertyName) {
        if (PropertyChanged != null)
            PropertyChanged(this,
                new PropertyChangedEventArgs(propertyName));
    }

    string _firstName;
    public string FirstName {
        get { return _firstName; }
```

This event is required to implement INotifyProperty-Changed.

A convenience method to raise the event, given a property name

```
        set {
            if(value != _firstName) {
                _firstName = value;
                OnPropertyChanged("FirstName");
                OnPropertyChanged("FullName");
            }
        }
    }

    string _lastName;
    public string LastName {
        get { return _lastName; }
        set {
            if (value != _lastName) {
                _lastName = value;
                OnPropertyChanged("LastName");
                OnPropertyChanged("FullName");
            }
        }
    }

    public string FullName {
        get {
            return string.Format("{0} {1}", _firstName, _lastName);
        }
    }
}
```

When FirstName is changed, raise the event for FirstName

Also raise the event for FullName (which is derived from FirstName)

Nothing terribly new going on here, if you're used to WPF: whenever a `set` is used on these properties, the `PropertyChanged` event is triggered. Because this object is bound to the WPF window, WPF is listening for that `PropertyChanged` event. For instance, if you type a single letter in the `FirstName` text box, that causes the `FirstName` property to be set. During the `set`, the `PropertyChanged` event is fired twice: first to announce that the `FirstName` property has changed and then to announce that the `FullName` property has changed.

Compile and run this application, then type in a first name such as Alan and a last name such as Turing. As you type, you'll see the full name appear (shown in figure 5.6).

Although this demonstration isn't terribly complex, in a real-world WPF window, there could be many more fields and complex relationships between those fields. If you're familiar with the MVVM (Model-View-ViewModel) pattern (as many WPF developers are), you know that this type of binding is important in making that pattern easy to implement.

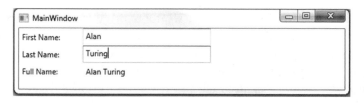

Figure 5.6 Type in first and last name, and watch the full name populate

Also notice that even with a trivial demonstration application, the `NameViewModel` went from a small class with autoproperties to a class that's more than five times the size, with backing fields and logic in every `set`. You get a nice clean separation between the View and the ViewModel, but now you face pitfalls and issues with using `INotifyPropertyChanged`.

5.3.2 *Problems and constraints with INotifyPropertyChanged*

Even though using `INotifyPropertyChanged` brings some benefits, it has drawbacks that leave you with potentially a lot of boilerplate, brittle code, and code that may be difficult to refactor.

You've certainly noticed the boilerplate already: the basic `NameViewModel` class went from having two small autoproperties to having explicit backing fields and `set`s with logic in them. As you can see, there is a lot of repetition, which you can reduce through the use of AOP.

Second, notice that to trigger the `PropertyChanged` event, you need a `Property-ChangedEventArgs` object, which needs a string to identify the property that has changed. So each time you call `OnPropertyChanged`, you need to pass in a string corresponding to the name of the property. If you make a typo or any other kind of mistake, it will fail to trigger the event correctly.

Finally, using `INotifyPropertyChanged` can be difficult to refactor. Because it uses strings, if you change the name of the property, you need to remember to change the strings as well. (Refactoring tools such as ReSharper can do this for you if you use them to rename the property.) Also note that because you have a derived property (`FullName`), you need to remember to include that property when you're sending notification about what properties have been changed.

> ### Refactoring with ReSharper
> Even though a property name such as `FirstName` and a string such as `"FirstName"` look the same to a human reading the code, to a compiler they're different symbols. If you change one symbol, the compiler won't be smart enough to realize that the other symbol is related, and you'll end up with errors when you run the code.
>
> Refactoring tools such as JetBrains ReSharper, Telerik JustCode, and many others will attempt to find related symbols using intelligent analysis and deduction. When you use ReSharper to rename the `FirstName` field, for example, it might also ask if you want to change the value of the `"FirstName"` string.

You can mitigate these issues in a number of ways, without using AOP. You can write unit tests or defensive programming that will verify that all the correct notifications are being sent. That could potentially be a lot of code, though some use of Reflection could make things easier. (For example, you could use Reflection to loop over the properties, get the property names, and make sure they match when the event is triggered.)

If you're using .NET 4.5, check out a new tool to help you deal with INotify-PropertyChanged called CallerMemberName. CallerMemberName is an attribute that you can use to set a parameter to be the name of the property that called it. I could use CallerMemberName to reduce my dependency on strings in the NameViewModel class. This listing shows how it would look.

Listing 5.20 Using CallerMemberName attribute

```
public class NameViewModel : INotifyPropertyChanged {
    public event PropertyChangedEventHandler PropertyChanged;

    void OnPropertyChanged([CallerMemberName] string propertyName = "")
     {
        if (PropertyChanged != null)
            PropertyChanged(this,
                new PropertyChangedEventArgs(propertyName));
    }

    string _firstName;
    public string FirstName {
        get { return _firstName; }
        set {
            if(value != _firstName) {
                _firstName = value;
                OnPropertyChanged();
                OnPropertyChanged("FullName");
            }
        }
    }

    string _lastName;
    public string LastName {
        get { return _lastName; }
        set {
            if (value != _lastName) {
                _lastName = value;
                OnPropertyChanged();
                OnPropertyChanged("FullName");
            }
        }
    }

    public string FullName {
        get {
            return string.Format("{0} {1}", _firstName, _lastName);
        }
    }
}
```

I've added the CallerMemberName attribute and set propertyName to have a default value.

I was able to remove "FirstName" here.

I can also remove "LastName" here.

This is an improvement: renaming FirstName and LastName properties becomes less of an issue, because you're allowing the .NET framework to fill in the blanks. Typos and misspellings are also not an issue, because CallerMemberName will use only the names of the properties. But you still have to notify that FullName is changed, because it's a derived property. You still have a lot of boilerplate, including explicit backing fields and a lot of code in all the sets.

You can tackle both of these issues with AOP. In the next section, I'll introduce a new AOP tool that was created specifically to help with INotifyPropertyChanged.

5.3.3 *Reducing boilerplate with AOP*

I've shown a lot of code examples using general-purpose AOP frameworks such as PostSharp and Castle DynamicProxy. But I want to introduce a more specific, single-minded AOP tool that was created just for working with INotifyPropertyChanged: NotifyPropertyWeaver. After walking through NotifyPropertyWeaver, we'll also look at how we might write something similar with PostSharp.

To install NotifyPropertyWeaver, in Visual Studio go to Tools -> Extension Manager (see figure 5.7). Click Online Gallery and search for NotifyPropertyWeaver. Click Download to install it. You may need to restart Visual Studio after that.

Once you've installed it, you can configure/disable it in Visual Studio by clicking Project -> NotifyPropertyWeaver. But the default behavior is good enough for this demonstration. Now you can remove all the boilerplate, strings, and backing fields from NameViewModel. All you need are the bare essentials of the properties, the derived property, and the one PropertyChanged event, as in listing 5.21. NotifyPropertyWeaver will fill in the rest in a postcompile step, like PostSharp.

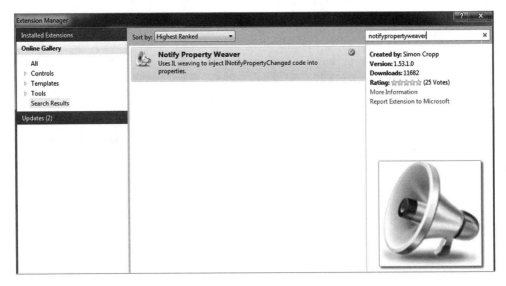

Figure 5.7   Installing NotifyPropertyWeaver

Listing 5.21   Boilerplate-free use of `INotifyPropertyChanged`

```
public class NameViewModel : INotifyPropertyChanged {
    public event PropertyChangedEventHandler PropertyChanged;
    public string FirstName { get; set; }
    public string LastName { get; set; }
    public string FullName {
        get {
            return string.Format("{0} {1}", FirstName, LastName);
        }
    }
}
```

And so can LastName

The derived property remains the same

You still need to implement INotifyPropertyChanged, which is only one event.

FirstName can be an autoproperty

NotifyPropertyWeaver fills in all the gaps, and it's even smart enough to detect the derived property and fill in the notification gaps for it.

NotifyPropertyWeaver isn't the only AOP tool that provides this level of narrow bolt on/plug-and-play functionality. PostSharp also offers similar functionality in the form of PostSharp Ultimate.

PostSharp Ultimate

PostSharp Ultimate is a growing open source collection of ready-to-use aspects. At the time of writing, it includes ready-made aspects for:

- Threading
- Diagnostics (logging)
- The definitive `INotifyPropertyChanged` aspect

These toolkits are free, but they require the full commercial edition of PostSharp.

The advantage to these toolkits (and any of the other similar ready-made AOP tools such as NotifyPropertyWeaver or Fody) is that you get all the benefits of AOP to solve a specific problem without having to write a production-ready aspect from scratch.

I definitely recommend that you use a tool like NotifyPropertyWeaver or PostSharp Ultimate, because they offer a set of well-tested functionality, intelligent static analysis, and configurability. But writing a basic `INotifyPropertyChanged` aspect is a good way to explore location interception in PostSharp as we wrap up this chapter.

In this example, you aren't going to build in any intelligence or analysis for derived properties, but you still need to allow for that possibility. Therefore, let's make it an option on the aspect to specify which derived properties use a particular location. As with NotifyPropertyWeaver, you want to remove all the boilerplate and end up with a minimal view model. Shoot for something like the following listing.

Listing 5.22   NameViewModel with a custom PostSharp aspect

```
public class NameViewModel : INotifyPropertyChanged {
    public event PropertyChangedEventHandler PropertyChanged;

    [NotifyPropertyChangedAspect("FullName")]
    public string FirstName { get; set; }

    [NotifyPropertyChangedAspect("FullName")]
    public string LastName { get; set; }

    public string FullName {
        get {
            return string.Format("{0} {1}", FirstName, LastName);
        }
    }
}
```

⟵ **Changes to this property will notify that FirstName and FullName have been changed.**

⟵ **Changes to this property will notify that LastName and FullName have been changed.**

Add PostSharp to the project via NuGet, as before. Create a new class called Notify-PropertyChangedAspect that inherits from LocationInterceptionAspect. It should have a constructor that can accept any number of strings as parameters, as in this listing.

Listing 5.23   Constructor that accepts derived property names

```
[Serializable]
public class NotifyPropertyChangedAspect : LocationInterceptionAspect {
    readonly string[] _derivedProperties;

    public NotifyPropertyChangedAspect(params string[] derived) {
        _derivedProperties = derived;
    }
}
```

If you think back to implementing INotifyPropertyChanged, all the hard work was done in the setters, so override the OnSetValue method. The code in OnSetValue will be run when the property's setter is used, and it will be run instead of the setter:

```
[Serializable]
public class NotifyPropertyChangedAspect : LocationInterceptionAspect
{
    readonly string[] _derivedProperties;

    public NotifyPropertyChangedAspect(params string[] derived) {
        _derivedProperties = derived;
    }
```

Override OnSetValue ⌎⟶
```
    public override void OnSetValue(LocationInterceptionArgs args)
    {

    }
}
```

Think back to the WPF example with FirstName and LastName. When you type a letter into the FirstName textbox (like "A"), the WPF binding means that the FirstName property is set to "A." Before that value gets assigned, the old value of FirstName is still null. If you type another letter (like "l"), FirstName gets set to "Al," and the old value is "A."

Inside OnSetValue, you need to do three things: compare the old value and the new value (using an if statement). If they're different, then you need to allow the set action to go through (using the args.ProceedSetValue method of the PostSharp API). And finally, you need to notify that the property has been changed (including any of the derived properties that were specified by the constructor). Create a RaisePropertyChanged method that you can reuse to perform the last step, and loop through any derived properties that were specified and call RaisePropertyChanged for those, too. (In the following listing notice that RaisePropertyChanged is called, but you haven't written the details of it yet.)

Listing 5.24   Perform all the steps of property notification in OnSetValue

```
public override void OnSetValue(LocationInterceptionArgs args) {
    var oldValue = args.GetCurrentValue();
    var newValue = args.Value;
    if (oldValue != newValue) {
        args.ProceedSetValue();
        RaisePropertyChanged(args.Instance, args.LocationName);   ⟵   Always raise
        if(_derivedProperties != null)                                  the property
            foreach (var derivedProperty in _derivedProperties)         changed
                RaisePropertyChanged(args.Instance, derivedProperty);   ⟵  event for the
    }                                                                   property
}
```

Raise the property changed event for any specified derived properties

Let's go over all of the PostSharp API usage here, because I haven't shown some pieces yet. args.GetCurrentValue() gets the current value of the location, but it doesn't put that value into args.Value. I store this value in the appropriately named oldValue variable. args.Value returns the incoming location value. args.ProceedSetValue() then instructs PostSharp to allow the set operation to happen.

If the values don't match (that is, the property has changed), then you want to raise the property changed event. Look at the arguments being passed in. args.Instance returns the object that the property is in (for example, an instance of the NameViewModel class), which should be a class that implements INotify-PropertyChanged. args.LocationName returns the name of the property (or field) being intercepted. For instance, it could be FirstName or LastName.

After that property changed notification is sent out, you then loop through any derived properties that were specified (like FullName) and call the same Raise-PropertyChanged method for those.

Let's finish this aspect and write the RaisePropertyChanged method now. In this method, you would expect to find the PropertyChanged event on the instance object that was passed in and raise that event using the location name that was passed in.

However, only a plain `object` is being passed in, so you have to resort to Reflection to do that.

Listing 5.25   `RaisePropertyChanged` method

```
private void RaisePropertyChanged(object instance, string propertyName)
{
    var type = instance.GetType();
    var propertyChanged = type.GetField("PropertyChanged",
        BindingFlags.Instance | BindingFlags.NonPublic);
    var handler = propertyChanged.GetValue(instance)
        as PropertyChangedEventHandler;
    handler(instance, new PropertyChangedEventArgs(propertyName));
}
```

None of the PostSharp API is used in this method—only the System.Reflection API. Reflection retrieves the `Type` of the instance. From that `Type`, Reflection can find the `PropertyChanged` event field. Use that field to invoke the event.

I'm using Reflection because that's the only way to raise the event from outside the class. It's not a good idea to do this because Reflection is a slow process and writing the aspect this way means that Reflection will be performed every time a property changes. Additionally, if this aspect is somehow used on a class that doesn't have a `PropertyChanged` event, then it will fail (You'll see ways to avoid that problem in chapter 8; specifically, the `CompileTimeValidate` feature of PostSharp).

5.4   *Summary*

This chapter covered a new type of interception: interception of properties and fields (locations). As with methods, location interception aspects act as middlemen between the getters/setters and the code doing the getting/setting.

Because properties offer a succinct way of writing getter/setter methods in C#, tools that can intercept methods can intercept properties (Castle DynamicProxy, for instance). But PostSharp has special aspects created for locations, with an API that's geared toward properties and fields. As with method interception, you get the ability to proceed to the get/set operation, as well as the ability to get information about the location (for example, field name or property name), its instance object, and so on.

I also introduced a new tool in this chapter, albeit a tool with a narrow focus. NotifyPropertyWeaver is an AOP tool that does only one thing, unlike PostSharp or Castle DynamicProxy, which are general-purpose frameworks. The advantage to such a tool is that you don't have to write an aspect from scratch; the disadvantage is that such tools are good for only a single purpose.

Showing tools like NotifyPropertyWeaver to developers who've been implementing `INotifyPropertyChanged` the hard way is often an exciting moment: for developers because the tool lifts a weight from their shoulders, and for me because it demonstrates the power of AOP to save time and simplify code in an immediate way.

In these last three chapters, we've been going full steam ahead and writing many different types of aspects. You now know how to write aspects for method boundaries, for intercepting methods, and for intercepting locations. But learning AOP isn't only about quantity—it's about quality, too. In the next chapter, you'll look at how unit testing and aspects fit together.

Unit testing aspects

All of the code you write should be tested. If you believe that, then writing automated unit tests should be important to you, because it makes your code much faster and easier to test. In earlier chapters, I mentioned that one of the benefits of using AOP is that it makes testing easier. For code that's heavily tangled, this should be obvious: small classes that do only one thing are easier to test than big classes that do multiple things.

But for code that's less tangled, and still uses a lot of dependency inversion (for example, more than one or two dependencies), AOP can make that code easier to test by completely moving cross-cutting concern dependencies into aspects. Now you don't have to worry about mocking/stubbing those dependencies and can focus on the code under test. Is it that straightforward? Yes and no. And what about testing the aspects themselves?

When I think of unit testing, I think of code that tests a small piece of functionality in an automated way. Other types of testing that are important but not discussed in this chapter include integration tests (which test multiple pieces of code working together) and functional tests (which are tests that run against the software specifications).

The reasons why you should write unit tests are many. If you practice test-driven development (TDD), then writing tests helps drive the design and architecture of your code. But at the most basic level, writing unit tests helps you prove that the code you wrote does what you want it to do. Unit tests can also provide the benefit of catching bugs and edge cases early on, when they're much cheaper and easier to fix. Tests give you a safety net when refactoring, so you know that your code still works when you change something.

6.1 Writing tests with NUnit

If you're already writing unit tests, you should be comfortable with this chapter. I'm going to review unit testing using a common unit test tool for .NET called NUnit. If you prefer other testing tools or frameworks, that's perfectly okay; it shouldn't be difficult to follow along with the examples in this chapter.

Why NUnit?

I use NUnit and the NUnit Runners for this book because they're free, popular, and well documented. I usually favor a test runner that's more closely integrated with Visual Studio, for the sake of convenience and to reduce context switching. And even though NUnit is a popular unit testing framework, other frameworks such as MSTest, MSpec, xUnit.net, and so on are all good unit-testing frameworks. You can do everything that I'm doing in this chapter as well using those other tools, so feel free to use the tool you're most comfortable with to follow along.

If you aren't already in the habit of writing unit tests, or if you've never written a unit test, I suggest that you start as soon as possible. Unit testing is a rich topic whose surface I'll barely scratch in this chapter, so after you finish this book, I suggest that you pick up another book on unit testing (perhaps *The Art of Unit Testing* by Roy Osherove [Manning, 2009] or *Test-Driven Development* by Kent Beck [Addison-Wesley Professional, 2002]) and come back to this chapter to review.

In either case, so that we're all on the same page, I'll quickly review unit testing and get you up and running with a new project that has a basic NUnit setup.

6.1.1 Writing and running NUnit tests

Create a new project in Visual Studio. A Class Library project should be sufficient. I'm calling my project UnitTestingReview. Next, create a class in this project called `MyStringClass`. In this class, create a method called `Reverse` and have it accept a single string parameter and return a string. This method is going to reverse the string that's passed in, but for now have it return the same string that was passed in, as this code shows:

```
public class MyStringClass {
    public string Reverse(string str) {
        return str;
    }
}
```

Now we want to start writing tests, so use NuGet to install NUnit. You can do so via the NuGet UI, or you can use the Package Manager Console, as follows:

```
PM> Install-Package NUnit
Successfully installed 'NUnit 2.6.2'.
Successfully added 'NUnit 2.6.2' to UnitTestingReview.
```

The first step in writing tests is to write a *test fixture*. A test fixture is a class that contains tests (and possibly setup/teardown code). To write a fixture with NUnit, use the Test-Fixture attribute on a class:

```
[TestFixture]
public class MyStringClassTests {

}
```

Inside that fixture, write a simple test to see if the `Reverse` method works as you expect it to. Tests generally follow an arrange, act, assert pattern. First, create a new instance of the class that we're testing (the arrange step). Then, pass in a short string to `Reverse` (for example, "hello") and get the result (the act step). Then examine the result to see if it's reversed (the assert step). Write a `TestReverse` method, as shown in this listing.

Listing 6.1 Writing a test of the `Reverse` method

```
[TestFixture]
public class MyStringClassTests {
    [Test]
    public void TestReverse() {
        var myStringObject = new MyStringClass();
        var reversedString = myStringObject.Reverse("hello");
        Assert.That(reversedString, Is.EqualTo("olleh"));     ⟵
    }
}
```

> The assert syntax can vary widely based on the tool being used and the preference of the developer.

We already know that this test should fail (because we didn't reverse the string in the `Reverse` method). But let's run it to see what happens. If you have a tool such as ReSharper or TestDriven.net already installed, you can use those to run the test. If you don't have them installed, you can use the free NUnit.Runners tools. Install NUnit.Runners via NuGet:

```
PM> Install-Package NUnit.Runners
Successfully installed 'NUnit.Runners 2.6.2'.
Successfully added 'NUnit.Runners 2.6.2' to UnitTestingReview.
```

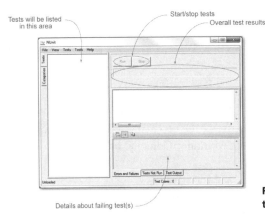

Figure 6.1   The NUnit
test runner UI

The NUnit.Runners package comes with a variety of tools to run NUnit tests. Let's find and use the UI test runner. Look in the packages folder of your project (for instance, if your project folder is Z:\projects\UnitTestingReview, the folder you want is Z:\projects\UnitTestingReview\packages\NUnit.Runner.2.6.2\tools). If you look at the files, you'll see some Console-based test runners, but let's use the UI tool, nunit.exe (or nunit-x86.exe). Run it, and you should see the NUnit UI, as shown in figure 6.1.

Now go to File->Open and find the .dll file of the project you want to test. If your project is Z:\projects\UnitTestingReview, then the .dll file is probably Z:\projects \UnitTestingReview\UnitTestingReview\bin\Debug\UnitTestingReview.dll). Once you open that file, click the Run button. You should see something like figure 6.2: one failed test, a red (in the ebook) bar, and a message that indicates why the test failed.

Now go back to the `MyStringClass` code and make the test pass. You can do this in a couple of different ways, but here's an example that uses Linq:

```
public string Reverse(string str) {
    return new string(str.Reverse().ToArray());
}
```

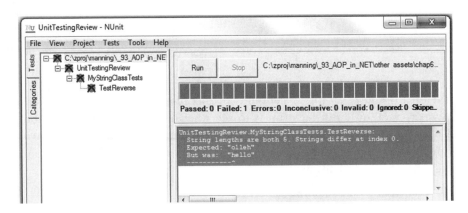

Figure 6.2   One failing test

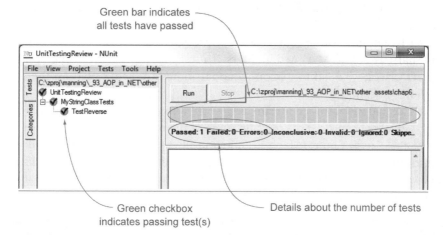

Green bar indicates all tests have passed

Green checkbox indicates passing test(s)

Details about the number of tests

Figu **ʼɪʼɴɢ test**

No   pile, the NUnit UI will automati-
cal   d will reload the .dll for you. Click
ru   figure 6.3.

w   ing more test cases. For instance,
w   want it to return only null, but
b   argument of null would cause a
N   for it, and I'll leave it to you to fix
F   eceives null:

```
se(null);
```

on, so if you aren't comfortable with
vn this book and pick up another one
ie next chapter if you promise to look

. Now let's look into unit testing when

6.1.2

test one of two main things: whether
s (testing the pointcut), and whether
e doing (testing the advice). In this sec-
tion, I'...   iefly. This is probably the easiest thing
about aspects to test.   r, we'll look at testing the advice code in

both DynamicProxy and PostSharp, as well as testing the code to which advices are applied.

.NET AOP tools often make use of attributes to apply aspects. We've seen this in PostSharp as well as MVC ActionFilters. To test that aspects are being applied to the correct places, we need to test only that attributes are being used on the classes and methods we expect.

Recall that when you create an ASP.NET MVC project in Visual Studio, you automatically get an `AccountController`, and some of the methods in `AccountController` use the `Authorize` attribute (which is an action filter). Suppose that you want to write a test to prove that those attributes are in the correct place. The following listing shows how you'd test that the `ChangePassword` methods have the `Authorize` attribute on them, using `System.Reflection` in an NUnit test.

> **Listing 6.2   Testing for the presence of attributes**

```
[TestFixture]
public class AccountControllerTests {
    [Test]
    public void ChangePassword_should_be_restricted_by_Authorize() {
        var classUnderTest = typeof (AccountController);
        var allMethods = classUnderTest.GetMethods();
        var changePwdMethods = allMethods
            .Where(m => m.Name == "ChangePassword");
        foreach (var changePwdMethod in changePwdMethods) {
            var attr = Attribute.GetCustomAttribute(
                changePwdMethod, typeof (AuthorizeAttribute));
            Assert.That(attr, Is.Not.Null);
        }
    }
}
```

Start with the AccountController Type ⊳ (points to `var classUnderTest = typeof (AccountController);`)

Get all its methods ◁ (points to `var allMethods = classUnderTest.GetMethods();`)

Limit the methods to the ones called ChangePassword ⊳ (points to `.Where(m => m.Name == "ChangePassword");`)

Look for an Authorize-Attribute on the method ◁ (points to `changePwdMethod, typeof (AuthorizeAttribute));`)

If it's there, the test passes; otherwise it fails ◁ (points to `Assert.That(attr, Is.Not.Null);`)

This code uses `System.Reflection` to examine the class, find the `ChangePassword` method(s), find an attribute of type `AuthorizeAttribute` (if it exists) on those methods, and then assert that it exists (that is, `GetCustomAttribute` doesn't return null). Note that this test isn't testing what the `AuthorizeAttribute` does, only that it's present in the correct places.

Some might consider this overkill, redundant, or verging on testing the framework. I believe those to be defensible points of view. But with a large team and/or a large code base, it's sometimes hard to keep track of what aspects should be used, and it's easy to be forgetful, so these types of tests can be useful.

For tools such as DynamicProxy that use IoC containers instead of attributes, testing for the presence of aspects takes a different approach but presents a similar situation. If you already write tests to verify that your IoC tool of choice is initialized correctly, then you should also test the dynamic proxies while you're at it. But again, this starts bordering on testing the framework, so use your best judgment.

The way you write tests against aspects can differ from tool to tool, developer to developer, and framework to framework, so your mileage will vary. I will cover the two main tools that I've been using in this book (Castle DynamicProxy and PostSharp) and some approaches you might take to writing unit tests.

6.2 Castle DynamicProxy testing

Aspects written with Castle DynamicProxy implement only the `IInterceptor` interface. In every other way, they're like any other class: they are compiled and are instantiated and executed only at runtime (this is much different than PostSharp aspects, which are instantiated at compile time and can be partially executed at compile time). Because of this, testing aspects is as easy as testing any Plain Old CLR Object (POCO).

First, we'll look at testing an extremely simple aspect that's self-contained and has no dependencies. Then, we'll look at an aspect that uses DI to resolve its dependencies. If you're already familiar with the role that DI can play with unit testing, testing DynamicProxy classes should be familiar to you.

6.2.1 Testing an interceptor

It's not a realistic scenario, but let's start with a simple interceptor that uses a static `Log` class to log before and after messages. First, we need a static `Log` class that can store strings, as shown here.

Listing 6.3 A static `Log` class

```
public static class Log {
    public static List<string> _messages = new List<string>();
    public static List<string> Messages {
        get { return _messages; }
    }

    public static void Write(string message) {
        _messages.Add(message);
    }
}
```

Next, we need to write an interceptor that makes use of this class. It should write a before message, proceed, and write an after message. These messages will use the `invocation` argument passed in to record the method name:

```
public class MyInterceptor : IInterceptor {
    public void Intercept(IInvocation invocation) {
        Log.Write("Before " + invocation.Method.Name);
        invocation.Proceed();
        Log.Write("After " + invocation.Method.Name);
    }
}
```

This works like many examples you've already seen. But how to test it? Well, because it's a regular class, why not instantiate a `MyInterceptor` object, call the `Intercept` method, and check that the correct messages made it into the `Log` (which is what `TestIntercept` attempts to do in this listing).

Listing 6.4   NUnit fixture to test `MyInterceptor`

```
[TestFixture]
public class MyInterceptorTest {
    [Test]
    public void TestIntercept() {                              There's something
        var myInterceptor = new MyInterceptor();               missing: invocation
        IInvocation invocation;                                is null
        myInterceptor.Intercept(invocation);

        Assert.IsTrue(Log.Messages                             The two assertions
            .Contains("Before " + invocation.Method.Name));    mirror the code
        Assert.IsTrue(Log.Messages                             inside of Intercept
            .Contains("After " + invocation.Method.Name));
    }
}
```

Hold the phone: in that code, the invocation object wasn't set to anything. If you try to compile that code, you'll get an error: "Use of unassigned local variable invocation." If you have experience with unit testing, you already know the next tool/concept that needs to be used to make this test work: mocking.

When the interceptor class runs in a program, DynamicProxy creates that invocation object. But we haven't even put this interceptor to work—it's floating out there in isolation for the test. We've got to come up with an object that mimics the real invocation object, only for the purposes of testing. To do this, I'll use a mocking tool. Although many are available, I'll use Moq by installing it with NuGet:

```
PM> Install-Package Moq
Successfully installed 'Moq 4.0.10827'.
Successfully added 'Moq 4.0.10827' to UnitTestingCastleDynamicProxy.
```

Now I can create a mock object that implements the `IInvocation` interface and pass that in to the `Intercept` method. Because the `Intercept` code cares only about `invocation.Method.Name`, that's the only property of the mock object that I define (see the following listing). Everything else will be set to a default value by Moq.

Listing 6.5   Using Moq

```
[Test]
public void TestIntercept() {
    var myInterceptor = new MyInterceptor();
    var invocationMock = new Mock<IInvocation>();
    invocationMock.Setup(i => i.Method.Name).Returns("MyMethod");
```

Create a mock object that implements the IInvocation interface

Arrange for the Name property of the Method property to be "MyMethod"

```
var invocation = invocationMock.Object;
myInterceptor.Intercept(invocation);
Assert.IsTrue(Log.Messages
    .Contains("Before " + invocation.Method.Name));
Assert.IsTrue(Log.Messages
    .Contains("After " + invocation.Method.Name));
}
```

Use the Object
property to get
the object to pass

invocation is of type
IInvocation, so it
can be passed in

Now the test code should compile, and when you run the test with NUnit, it should pass. We've created an interceptor and tested it completely in isolation (well, almost completely; we had to use that ugly static Log class).

Let's consider the bit of irony taking place here, because if you take a closer look at Moq, you'll realize that Moq itself uses DynamicProxy. Therefore, in a way, we're using DynamicProxy aspects to test other DynamicProxy aspects. This is perfectly okay—we're not testing the framework itself but the code built with the framework.

Let's look at a more realistic situation. I hope you aren't using a lot of static classes like Log in the previous example and are instead using DI.

6.2.2 *Injecting dependencies*

In a real code base, using a class like Log results in tight coupling between Log and whatever code uses it. Instead, a logging interface should be used and the implementation details should be hidden from the rest of the code.

It's the same with writing aspects: you want dependencies to be passed in to the MyInterceptor class. Aspects, like any other module, should follow the Dependency Inversion principle and should depend on abstractions, not on implementations.

PUTTING INVERSION OF CONTROL TO WORK

A complex domain is where an IoC tool becomes helpful, so let's create a more complex example domain to illustrate.

There's a Program that needs to use a service (MyService, which implements IMyService). That service needs to use another service (MyOtherService, which implements IMyOtherService). You also want some logging on MyService, so you write an aspect called MyLoggingAspect. The MyLoggingAspect itself uses a service (LoggingService, which implements ILoggingService). It's starting to get complicated; see figure 6.4.

With the diagram in mind, let's start writing the code.

IMPLEMENT THE SERVICES

Create a Console project in Visual Studio. Add NUnit, Castle.Core, StructureMap, and NUnit.Runners. Let's start at the bottom of the diagram and create the IMyOtherService interface and its implementation MyOtherService. I'll create one method, DoOtherThing, but for this demonstration, it's not important that this method (listing 6.6) has any code in it at all: I'm trying to show a realistic scenario in which complex dependencies are present.

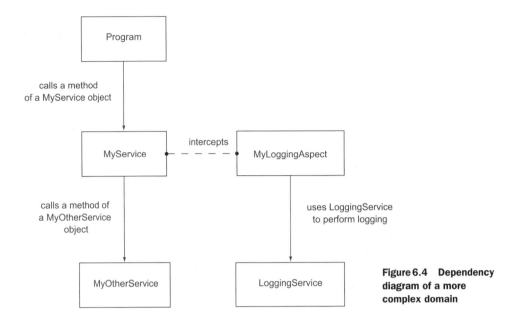

Figure 6.4 Dependency diagram of a more complex domain

Naming convention

I'm using the naming convention of ServiceName and IServiceName because that's the default convention that StructureMap uses. When I configure these dependencies, I won't have to explicitly list every single interface-implementation pair as long as I follow that convention.

Listing 6.6 `MyOtherService` service implementation and interface

```
public interface IMyOtherService {
    void DoOtherThing();
}

public class MyOtherService : IMyOtherService {        This class doesn't
    public void DoOtherThing() {                        need any
        // nothing                                      implementation
    }
}
```

Next, create the LoggingService implementation and interface. In reality, this service would use NLog, log4net, and so on in its implementation, but to keep things simple, it's going to log to the Console (as shown in the next listing). This code is a logging service that could be used from anywhere in the application but will be used only by the logging aspect in this project.

Listing 6.7 `LoggingService` implementation and interface

```
public interface ILoggingService {
    void Write(string message);
}

public class LoggingService : ILoggingService {
    public void Write(string message) {
        Console.WriteLine("Logging: " + message);
    }
}
```

The logging aspect (`MyLoggingAspect`) is shown on the diagram to be dependent on `LoggingService`, so that's the next thing to write.

WRITE THE LOGGING ASPECT

In the next listing, the aspect will use constructor injection to get the `ILogging-Service` dependency. In its `Intercept` method, it will log the start and the end of the method being logged.

Listing 6.8 `MyLoggingAspect` implementation

```
public class MyLoggingAspect : IInterceptor {
    private readonly ILoggingService _loggingService;

    public MyLoggingAspect(ILoggingService loggingService) {
        _loggingService = loggingService;
    }

    public void Intercept(IInvocation invocation) {
        _loggingService.Write("Log start");
        invocation.Proceed();
        _loggingService.Write("Log end");
    }
}
```

Writing a test for this aspect will be slightly more involved than in the last section, because now we have a dependency.

UNIT TESTING THE ASPECT

We want to test only `MyLoggingAspect`, and not the dependency, so we need to use a mocking tool (shown in the following listing) to create a substitute object to pass in to `MyLoggingAspect`'s constructor so that you're testing `MyLoggingAspect` in total isolation.

Listing 6.9 Testing `MyLoggingAspect`

```
[TestFixture]

public class MyLoggingAspectTest {

    [Test]

    public void TestIntercept() {                                Create a mock
                                                                 object for
        var mockLoggingService = new Mock<ILoggingService>();;)  ILoggingService
```

Create a
mock object
for
IInvocation
like before

Use the mock
object to
verify that
the Write
method was
called as
expected

Instantiate
MyLogging-
Aspect using
the mock
object

Execute the
Intercept
method

```
var loggingAspect

   = new MyLoggingAspect(mockLoggingService.Object);

var mockInvocation = new Mock<IInvocation>();

loggingAspect.Intercept(mockInvocation.Object);

mockLoggingService.Verify(x => x.Write("Log start"));

mockLoggingService.Verify(x => x.Write("Log end"));

  }

}
```

Testing is still easy with DynamicProxy. But we don't quite have the whole picture yet, so let's keep going and complete the code that goes along with the dependency diagram. The aspect we wrote needs to intercept any calls to MyService objects.

CREATE THE MYSERVICE CLASS

Create the MyService implementation and interface. This service won't do much; it only writes to Console. The diagram indicates that it's dependent on MyOther-Service's interface, so I'll be sure to pass that in to the constructor. I won't use the dependency, because it's only in this listing for illustrative purposes.

Listing 6.10 `MyService` implementation and interface

```
public interface IMyService {
    void DoSomething();
}

public class MyService : IMyService {
    public MyService(IMyOtherService other)
    {
    }

    public void DoSomething() {
        Console.WriteLine("Something was done");
    }
}
```

Even though the code doesn't
use the IMyOtherService
dependency, this object can't
be instantiated without it.

With a more complex domain, the use of StructureMap is going to be different than it was in earlier examples that had no dependencies. To start, let's look at how the Program class would use MyService. To instantiate a MyService object in Main, we need to first instantiate a MyOtherService object, as seen here.

Listing 6.11 Using `MyService` object in `Main`

```
static void Main(string[] args) {
    var myOtherObj = new MyOtherService();
    var myObj = new MyService(myOtherObj);
    myObj.DoSomething();
}
```

Compile and run, and you should see "Something was done" displayed on the Console.

USING AN IOC TOOL TO MANAGE THE DEPENDENCIES

This code looks okay, but we're violating the Dependency Inversion principle by making the `Main` method in the `Program` class depend on specific implementations. That is, `new MyOtherService()` and `new MyService()` tightly couple `Program` to those implementations. Not only is this a bad idea architecturally, but imagine having an even more complex dependency graph: you could spend five-plus lines of code instantiating all the objects you need every time you need to call one method on one service.

What we should do instead is use StructureMap in `Main` and throughout the entire program manage the dependencies and instantiate the correct services. Then, instead of newing specific implementations, you can ask StructureMap for an implementation of an interface. The following listing shows a basic StructureMap setup that uses default conventions.

Listing 6.12   Initializing and using StructureMap

```
static void Main(string[] args) {
    ObjectFactory.Initialize(x => {
        x.Scan(scan => {
            scan.TheCallingAssembly();
            scan.WithDefaultConventions();
        });
    });

    var myObj = ObjectFactory.GetInstance<IMyService>();
    myObj.DoSomething();
}
```

I mentioned StructureMap's default conventions earlier.

If you prefer other IoC tools, the initialization code will look different.

Main is now dependent only on IMyService, not MyService and MyOtherService.

Compile and run that code, and you should see the same thing as before: "Something was done." StructureMap is doing all the work of wiring up the dependencies in the diagram.

Except that we forgot one thing: the logging aspect. It should intercept any calls to `MyService`.

USING DYNAMICPROXY WITH STRUCTUREMAP

As you might remember from earlier chapters, you needed to use a `ProxyGenerator` to apply a DynamicProxy aspect to the class. As in earlier chapters, this can be done within the StructureMap configuration, but because `MyService` has a dependency (that is, no parameterless constructor), it's not as straightforward as before.

StructureMap interception

If you're already familiar with StructureMap, then you might know that it has its own interception abilities, such as its `InstanceInterceptor` interface. For certain types of decorators, this is an adequate tool, but I find DynamicProxy to be a more feature-rich interception tool, so I use it instead of StructureMap's `InstanceInterceptor`.

One approach (used in the next listing) is to instantiate the aspect (along with its dependencies), instantiate the service class (along with its dependencies), and finally apply the aspect to the service.

Listing 6.13 One approach to using aspects with a complex domain

```
ObjectFactory.Initialize(x => {

        x.Scan(scan => {

            scan.TheCallingAssembly();

            scan.WithDefaultConventions();

        });

        var proxyGenerator = new ProxyGenerator();

        var aspect = new MyLoggingAspect(new LoggingService());

        var service = new MyService(new MyOtherService());

        var result = proxyGenerator

            .CreateInterfaceProxyWithTargetInterface(

            typeof(IMyService), service, aspect);

        x.For<IMyService>().Use((IMyService) result);

    });
```

Instantiate an aspect and its dependency → `var aspect = new MyLoggingAspect(new LoggingService());`

Instantiate the target service and its dependency → `var service = new MyService(new MyOtherService());`

Create a ProxyGenerator as before ← `var proxyGenerator = new ProxyGenerator();`

Apply the aspect ←

Tell StructureMap to use the resulting dynamic proxy ← `x.For<IMyService>().Use((IMyService) result);`

There are several problems with this approach. The first and most obvious is the aesthetic: it's a lot of code to apply one aspect to one service class. Second, there should be a way to leverage StructureMap to take care of the dependencies for us instead of a bunch of news. Third, which is probably less obvious right now, what if we want to use this aspect (or other aspects) multiple times? This StructureMap initialization could turn into a huge mess if we continue with this approach.

REFACTOR USING ENRICHWITH

Fortunately, we can clean up this situation using a combination of a helper class and a StructureMap feature called EnrichWith.

StructureMap has an EnrichWith method you can use to register a method that then will be used to substitute an object in the place of the normal service—sounds like a perfect place to inject an interceptor. Let's start by moving most of the messy code into an EnrichWith statement. I'll use a lambda, as shown here.

Listing 6.14 Using EnrichWith feature of StructureMap

```
ObjectFactory.Initialize(x => {
        x.Scan(scan => {
            scan.TheCallingAssembly();
            scan.WithDefaultConventions();
        });
        var proxyGenerator = new ProxyGenerator();
        x.For<IMyService>().Use<MyService>().EnrichWith(svc => {
```

EnrichWith expects a Func (lambda) argument → `x.For<IMyService>().Use<MyService>().EnrichWith(svc => {`

Still have to instantiate the aspect and its dependency

```
var aspect = new MyLoggingAspect(new LoggingService());
var result = proxyGenerator
    .CreateInterfaceProxyWithTargetInterface(
        typeof(IMyService), svc, aspect);
return result;
});
});
```

Use the svc parameter that the lambda defines as the second parameter to the proxy generator

This code is starting to look better, but it's still a lot to type in every time you want to use an aspect.

Let's move that `Func` that gets passed into `EnrichWith` into its own reusable class to encapsulate the proxy creation as much as possible. It would be better if we could see something like this listing.

Listing 6.15 More concise use of `EnrichWith`

```
ObjectFactory.Initialize(x => {
    x.Scan(scan =>
    {
        scan.TheCallingAssembly();
        scan.WithDefaultConventions();
    });
    var proxyHelper = new ProxyHelper();
    x.For<IMyService>().Use<MyService>()
        .EnrichWith(proxyHelper
        .Proxify<IMyService, MyLoggingAspect>);
});
```

Note the syntax carefully: the Proxify method itself is being passed as the argument

With this code, all we need to do to use an aspect is to use `EnrichWith`, the proxy-Helper's `Proxify` method, and the aspect's type (`MyLoggingAspect`).

A PROXYHELPER

That's what we'd like to see. To accomplish this, let's move the proxy generator code into a `ProxyHelper` class (in the next listing). We'll also use StructureMap within this helper to resolve the interceptor object, by using `ObjectFactory`.

Listing 6.16 `ProxyHelper`

```
public class ProxyHelper {

    readonly ProxyGenerator _proxyGenerator;

    public ProxyHelper() {

        _proxyGenerator = new ProxyGenerator();

    }

    public object Proxify<T, K>(object obj) where K: IInterceptor {

        var interceptor = (IInterceptor) ObjectFactory.GetInstance<K>();
```

The ProxyGenerator is moved to this helper class.

Constrain K to only allow IInterceptor type arguments

Leverage StructureMap to handle the aspect's dependencies

```
    var result = _proxyGenerator

        .CreateInterfaceProxyWithTargetInterface(

        typeof (T), obj, interceptor);

    return result;

  }

}
```

> ◁ **This is the same proxyGenerator usage as before**

A couple of things to point out in this helper: the `where K: IInterceptor` syntax may not be something you see or use often, but it's telling the compiler that only classes that implement `IInterceptor` (that is, DynamicProxy aspects) *can* be used in place of `K`. This approach makes it safe to cast any objects of type `K` to `IInterceptor`.

Another difference is that instead of instantiating `MyLoggingAspect` with `new`, `Proxify` is leveraging StructureMap to instantiate the aspect and handle the dependencies (make sure that you use `ProxyHelper` after scanning the assembly).

What if I don't use StructureMap?

I favor StructureMap because it has many nice features, it's the tool I've been using the longest, and it has the helpful `EnrichWith` method. But IoC offers a wide world of tools available for .NET. As long as those tools have functionality similar to StructureMap's `EnrichWith`, you can write a similar helper for the IoC container of your choice.

In fact, a helper may already be written for you. SNAP (Simple .NET Aspect-oriented Programming) provides this helper functionality for a number of IoC tools, including Ninject, Autofac, Castle Windsor, and others. Look for it on NuGet.

In this section, we explored unit testing aspects written with DynamicProxy and found that testing isn't terribly difficult (or at least not different than testing any other type of class). We also wrote `ProxyHelper`, which will definitely see more use in the rest of the book. In the next section, we'll look at writing similar tests against PostSharp aspects, where unit testing gets more difficult.

6.3   *PostSharp testing*

Aspects written with PostSharp inherit from abstract base classes like `OnMethod-BoundaryAspect`. They're also attributes, which are metadata. Thus, without the Post-Sharp postcompiler tool, they don't do anything and don't execute. The postcompiler tool instantiates the aspects at compile time, serializes them, and then deserializes them. Therefore, it's more difficult to test these aspect classes directly, and in some cases, it's not feasible at all due to the nature of postcompilation weaving and the way that the PostSharp framework is written.

But we're going to look at writing similar tests to the ones in the previous section. We'll look at a simple self-contained aspect first and then the use of an aspect in a more complex domain. DI will still be used, but it plays less of a role because aspects are assigned with attributes instead of using a proxy generator.

6.3.1 Unit testing a PostSharp aspect

As before, we'll be writing an (unrealistic) aspect that uses a static `Log` class. The `Log` class is the same. The aspect class is different: it will inherit from PostSharp's `OnMethodBoundaryAspect` base class. I'll override `OnEntry` and `OnSuccess` and write to the log within those methods:

```
[Serializable]
public class MyBoundaryAspect : OnMethodBoundaryAspect {
    public override void OnEntry(MethodExecutionArgs args) {
        Log.Write("Before: " + args.Method.Name);
    }
    public override void OnSuccess(MethodExecutionArgs args) {
        Log.Write("After: " + args.Method.Name);
    }
}
```

The unit test will be similar to the test used in the previous section. As shown in listing 6.17, we don't need to use Moq yet; we can instantiate a `MethodExecutionArgs` object directly. The constructor expects an instance object and a list of arguments, but because `MyBoundaryAspect` doesn't use these, we can use `null` and `Arguments.Empty`, respectively. `MyBoundaryAspect` does use the `Method` property, so we'll need to set that to some object that implements `MethodBase`. `System.Reflection` gives us a convenient way to do this by using a `DynamicMethod` object. For testing, only the method name is important, so the return type and parameter types (the remaining two parameters in the `DynamicMethod` constructor) can be set to `null`.

Now we've gotten the arrange portion of the unit test written, so let's write the act. I'll instantiate a `MyBoundaryAspect` object and call the `OnEntry` and `OnSuccess` methods, simulating what would happen at runtime when the aspect is used.

Finally, I'll assert that the two log messages I expect to be written to `Log` were written.

Listing 6.17 A test of a PostSharp aspect

```
[TestFixture]
public class TestMyLoggerCrossCuttingConcern {

    [Test]
    public void TestMyBoundaryAspect() {

        var args = new MethodExecutionArgs(null, Arguments.Empty);

        args.Method = new DynamicMethod("FooBar",null,null);

        var aspect = new MyBoundaryAspect();

        aspect.OnEntry(args);
```

Instantiate a MethodExecutionArgs object directly

Pass the args object into OnEntry and OnSuccess

Set the method property, because the aspect uses it

```
        aspect.OnSuccess(args);

        Assert.IsTrue(Log.Messages
            .Contains("Before: " + args.Method.Name));    ◁─┐  Assert that log
                                                             │  entries were
        Assert.IsTrue(Log.Messages                          │  written correctly
            .Contains("After: " + args.Method.Name));

    }

}
```

You could use a mocking tool to create a substitute `MethodExecutionArgs` object, but because it's not an interface or abstract class, you'll have to use a more sophisticated mocking tool like TypeMock, because Moq isn't capable of doing that.

Let's revisit the complex domain example from DynamicProxy and see what happens when we use PostSharp instead.

6.3.2 *Injecting dependencies*

When we used StructureMap with DynamicProxy in the previous section, the dependencies were injected using constructor injection. With PostSharp, the aspect constructors are called at compile time, before StructureMap has a chance to initialize. Therefore, constructor injection won't work, which means that testing becomes much more difficult. In order to work around this issue, I'm going to use the service locator pattern.

Service locator is a form of dependency inversion that makes it the job of the class to ask for a service, as opposed to the service being passed in via a constructor. Sometimes the service locator pattern is considered a bad idea (or an antipattern), but it's certainly better than no dependency inversion at all.

We're going to revisit the same complex dependencies as outlined in the dependency diagram from the previous section. Create a new Console project (I call mine UnitTestingPostSharpAspect). Again, add PostSharp, NUnit, NUnit.Runners, and StructureMap via NuGet.

Because we're using PostSharp, StructureMap won't play a role in applying aspects. Thus, the `Main` method will be much smaller and will be scanning only for the default conventions (as in this listing).

Listing 6.18   Program's `Main` method

```
static void Main(string[] args) {
    ObjectFactory.Initialize(x => {
        x.Scan(scan => {
            scan.TheCallingAssembly();
            scan.WithDefaultConventions();
        });
    });

    var myObj = ObjectFactory.GetInstance<IMyService>();
    myObj.DoSomething();
}
```

The service classes and interfaces remain the same: IMyService, MyService, IMyOtherService, MyOtherService, ILoggingService, and LoggingService are identical to the code in the previous section.

MyLoggingAspect has OnMethodBoundaryAspect as a base class now, instead of implementing Castle's IInterceptor interface. It must still use an ILoggingService implementation, so that should be a private field, as in this listing.

Listing 6.19   MyLoggingAspect with PostSharp

```
[Serializable]
public class MyLoggingAspect : OnMethodBoundaryAspect {
    ILoggingService _loggingService;

    public override void OnEntry(MethodExecutionArgs args) {
        _loggingService.Write("Log start");
    }

    public override void OnSuccess(MethodExecutionArgs args) {
        _loggingService.Write("Log end");
    }
}
```

PostSharp constructors can be used only in attributes. C# attribute constructors can accept only static values, so you can't inject the logging service dependency that way. Instead, you'll use a part of the PostSharp API that hasn't been mentioned yet: an override of the RuntimeInitialize method (see listing 6.20). This method is executed by PostSharp at runtime before runtime methods such as OnEntry or OnSuccess. (It's available for LocationInterceptionAspect and MethodInterceptionAspect, too.) Now override that method and use StructureMap as a service locator to initialize _loggingService. You also need to mark _loggingService as NonSerialized with an attribute, because it won't be initialized until after the aspect is deserialized anyway (more on this process in chapter 7).

Listing 6.20   Dependency inversion via RuntimeInitialize

```
[Serializable]
public class MyLoggingAspect : OnMethodBoundaryAspect {
    [NonSerialized] ILoggingService _loggingService;

    public override void RuntimeInitialize(MethodBase method) {
        _loggingService = ObjectFactory.GetInstance<ILoggingService>();
    }

    public override void OnEntry(MethodExecutionArgs args) {
        _loggingService.Write("Log start");
    }

    public override void OnSuccess(MethodExecutionArgs args) {
        _loggingService.Write("Log end");
    }
}
```

Now this aspect is ready to use, so apply it to the `DoSomething` method of `MyService` using an attribute:

```
public class MyService : IMyService {
    public MyService(IMyOtherService other) { ... }

    [MyLoggingAspect]
    public void DoSomething() {
        Console.WriteLine("Something was done");
    }
}
```

Execute the program, and you should see the appropriate text written to the Console, as shown in figure 6.5.

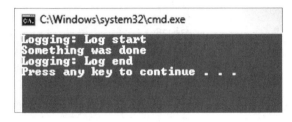

Now you've achieved some measure of dependency inversion: not as good as DynamicProxy, but it's a start.

Figure 6.5   Correct Console output

It also makes it possible to write a decent unit test of the aspect. It will take a little more work, but it can be done. Create a test fixture (class) and a test (method). In the test, as before, you need to start by creating a `Mock` object of `ILoggingService`. (Add Moq to your project with NuGet if you haven't already done so):

```
[TestFixture]
public class MyLoggingAspectTest {
    [Test]
    public void TestIntercept() {
        var mockLoggingService = new Mock<ILoggingService>();
    }
}
```

Create another `MethodExecutionArgs` object to pass in: it doesn't need to have the `Method` property defined because we aren't using it this time.

```
[TestFixture]
public class MyLoggingAspectTest {
    [Test]
    public void TestIntercept() {
        var mockLoggingService = new Mock<ILoggingService>();
        var args = new MethodExecutionArgs(null, Arguments.Empty);
    }
}
```

With Castle, the next step would be to instantiate the aspect object and pass in the `mockLoggingService` object to the constructor. With PostSharp, we can't pass that to a constructor. Instead, we have to pass the `mockLoggingService` object to Structure-Map, instantiate the aspect object, and execute the `RuntimeInitialize` method (which will then ask StructureMap for an `ILoggingService` object). This roundabout path is coded here.

Listing 6.21   Creating an aspect object for the test

```
[TestFixture]
public class MyLoggingAspectTest {
    [Test]
    public void TestIntercept() {
        var mockLoggingService = new Mock<ILoggingService>();
        var args = new MethodExecutionArgs(null, Arguments.Empty);
        ObjectFactory.Initialize(x =>
            x.For<ILoggingService>()
              .Use(mockLoggingService.Object));
        var loggingAspect = new MyLoggingAspect();
        loggingAspect.RuntimeInitialize(null);
    }
}
```

Instantiate the aspect we want to test — `var loggingAspect = new MyLoggingAspect();`

Tell StructureMap that if it gets asked for an ILoggingService object, to return the mock object — `.Use(mockLoggingService.Object));`

Call RuntimeInitialize so that the logging dependency is loaded — `loggingAspect.RuntimeInitialize(null);`

Yes, `RuntimeInitialize` must be explicitly called, because we're executing the aspect outside of the PostSharp framework, so it won't perform that for us automatically. That concludes the arrange portion of the test. Now we must act to run the code that we're testing. Execute the `OnEntry` and `OnSuccess` methods of the aspect.

Listing 6.22   Call `OnEntry` and `OnSuccess` to execute the aspect

```
[TestFixture]
public class MyLoggingAspectTest {
    [Test]
    public void TestIntercept() {
        var mockLoggingService = new Mock<ILoggingService>();
        var args = new MethodExecutionArgs(null, Arguments.Empty);

        ObjectFactory.Initialize(x =>
            x.For<ILoggingService>()
              .Use(mockLoggingService.Object));
        var loggingAspect = new MyLoggingAspect();
        loggingAspect.RuntimeInitialize(null);

        loggingAspect.OnEntry(args);
        loggingAspect.OnSuccess(args);
    }
}
```

When `OnEntry` executes, we expect that the logging service's `Write` method will be called with the message Log start. Similarly, when `OnSuccess` executes, we expect the logging service's `Write` method to be called again with the message Log end. In the next listing, the `Mock` object is used to verify that these two operations did take place.

Listing 6.23   Verify that the logging operations happened

```
[TestFixture]
public class MyLoggingAspectTest {
    [Test]
    public void TestIntercept() {
        var mockLoggingService = new Mock<ILoggingService>();
        var args = new MethodExecutionArgs(null, Arguments.Empty);

        ObjectFactory.Initialize(x =>
            x.For<ILoggingService>()
              .Use(mockLoggingService.Object));
        var loggingAspect = new MyLoggingAspect();
        loggingAspect.RuntimeInitialize(null);

        loggingAspect.OnEntry(args);
        loggingAspect.OnSuccess(args);

        mockLoggingService.Verify(x => x.Write("Log start"));
        mockLoggingService.Verify(x => x.Write("Log end"));
    }
}
```

Execute that test with an NUnit test runner, and it will pass. It took a little more work, but you achieved a similar level of testing to what could be accomplished with DynamicProxy.

Unfortunately, the full story is a little more complicated when it comes to unit testing and PostSharp.

6.3.3   *Problems with PostSharp and testing*

When trying to write unit tests for PostSharp aspects, you're going to run into obstacles that don't have elegant solutions, particularly when trying to test code that has aspects applied to it.

The first problem is that PostSharp does its weaving at compile time. Writing tests against code that later becomes modified becomes complicated.

COMPILE-TIME WEAVING

Consider a small, easy-to-test piece of code: a class with one method that reverses a string.

Listing 6.24   A class/method that reverses a string, and its unit test

```
public class MyClass {
    public void string Reverse(string str) {
        return new string(str.Reverse().ToArray());
    }
}

[TestFixture]
public class MyStringClassTests {
    [Test]
    public void TestReverse() {
        var myStringObject = new MyStringClass();
```

```
        var reversedString = myStringObject.Reverse("hello");
        Assert.That(reversedString, Is.EqualTo("olleh"));
    }
}
```

This is the method we wrote a test for at the beginning of the chapter. Pass in a string such as "hello," get the result, and confirm that the result is "olleh." Now consider the same method with the `MyLoggingAspect` PostSharp aspect applied to it as shown here.

Listing 6.25   Reverse method with aspect applied

```
public class MyClass {
    [MyLoggingAspect]
    public void string Reverse(string str) {
        return new string(str.Reverse().ToArray());
    }
}
```

The `Reverse` method that is executed at runtime will now be executing the code in the `MyLoggingAspect` class. Therefore, the `RuntimeInitialize` method will be executed and the aspect will use StructureMap to get the `ILoggingService` dependency. Now the `TestReverse` test gets a little more complex. You need to mock `ILogging-Service` again and initialize StructureMap to use the substitute object (shown in the following listing). This is done because it's a unit test; we're not interested in testing the logging—only the `Reverse` method.

Listing 6.26   Mocking `ILoggingService` to satisfy the aspect

```
[Test]
public void TestReverse() {
    var mockLoggingService = new Mock<ILoggingService>();
    ObjectFactory.Initialize(x =>
        x.For<ILoggingService>()
         .Use(mockLoggingService.Object));

    var myStringObject = new MyStringClass();
    var reversedString = myStringObject.Reverse("hello");
    Assert.That(reversedString, Is.EqualTo("olleh"));
}
```

You've used aspects to have a nice separation of concerns: one class for reversing a string and one class for logging, but when it comes time to run the unit test, they're still coupled together, so you still have to put in extra work to isolate the code under test using mock objects. Additionally, when writing unit tests, it's not obvious what services need to be mocked, because you aren't the one instantiating the aspect. If you forget one, then the test will fail because StructureMap will throw an exception.

Finally, we have the issue of service locator. In this demonstration, it's not a problem to put `ObjectFactory.Initialize` directly in the unit test, because it only has one unit test. But because this is a `static` method, you now have to worry about shared state when writing multiple unit tests. For instance, when I initialized the mock of `ILoggingService` in `ObjectFactory`, that mock object will stay registered for every other unit test. The solution is a layer of indirection between your code (`Runtime-Initialize`, unit tests) and StructureMap. It will thus take even more work to write unit tests.

Overall, when writing unit tests when PostSharp is involved, it's difficult. You gain the benefits of splitting out cross-cutting concerns into their own classes, but the unit tests have to deal with the code after it's been combined by PostSharp. It's a pay-me-now-or-pay-me-later situation that isn't a problem when using DynamicProxy.

WORKAROUND BY TURNING OFF POSTSHARP

PostSharp can be turned off by changing a setting in the project properties in Visual Studio. You could turn off PostSharp temporarily, run a unit test, and turn PostSharp back on after the test passes. This solution is hardly ideal—it's cumbersome and discourages you from running unit tests.

Another workaround is to use compiler symbols. For instance, if you define a custom symbol such as `UNITTESTING`, you can wrap the aspect code in an `#if` statement (as shown in the next listing). An empty aspect will be compiled if `UNITTESTING` is defined, which means that you can run the unit test without the extra mocking.

Listing 6.27   Workaround with custom symbols

```
#define UNITTESTING                                           Define a custom symbol
                                                              with whatever name you
[Serializable]                                                wish
public class MyLoggingAspect : OnMethodBoundaryAspect
{
#if !UNITTESTING                                              If that symbol is
    [NonSerialized] ILoggingService _loggingService;         defined, this code
                                                              won't be compiled
    public override void RuntimeInitialize(MethodBase method) {
        _loggingService = ObjectFactory.GetInstance<ILoggingService>();
    }

    // ... etc ...
#endif
}

[TestFixture]
public class MyStringClassTests {                             The unit test can run
    [Test]                                                    without worrying about
    public void TestReverse() {                               the aspect
        var myStringObject = new MyStringClass();
        var reversedString = myStringObject.Reverse("hello");
        Assert.That(reversedString, Is.EqualTo("olleh"));
    }
}
```

This situation is hardly ideal, either. You still have to turn PostSharp on and off by defining (or not defining) the `UNITTESTING` symbol (or at least finding a way to automate this). On top of that, you have to wrap #if/#end around all the code inside your aspect classes.

A similar option that doesn't involve compiler symbols is defining a global variable that indicates whether aspect code should be run. This value will be true by default, but in your unit tests (as shown next), you could set it to false.

Listing 6.28 A global variable setting for unit testing

```
public static class AspectSettings {
    public static bool On = true;                    ⊲─┐  Aspects are
}                                                         │  on by default

[Serializable]
public class MyLoggingAspect : OnMethodBoundaryAspect {      If aspect settings are
    [NonSerialized]                                          off, return without
    ILoggingService _loggingService;                         doing anything

    public override void RuntimeInitialize(MethodBase method) {
        if (!AspectSettings.On) return;
        _loggingService = ObjectFactory.GetInstance<ILoggingService>();  ⊲──┈┈
    }

    public override void OnEntry(MethodExecutionArgs args) {
        if (!AspectSettings.On) return;              ⊲─┐
        _loggingService.Write("Log start");          │  If aspect settings are off,
    }                                                 │  return without doing anything

    public override void OnSuccess(MethodExecutionArgs args) {
        if (!AspectSettings.On) return;              ⊲─┐
        _loggingService.Write("Log end");            │  If aspect settings are off,
    }                                                 │  return without doing anything
}

[Test]
public void TestReverse() {
    AspectSettings.On = false;                       ⊲─┐  When testing, turn
                                                          │  aspects off
    var myCode = new MyNormalCode();
    var result = myCode.Reverse("hello");

    Assert.That(result, Is.EqualTo("olleh"));
}
```

This last workaround is probably the easiest of all because you don't have to worry about mocking, shared state, service locator problems, or other such issues. Aspects are turned off when testing. It's still inconvenient, because you have to modify the aspects to check for this setting and make sure that your unit tests always turn off aspects. With one of these workarounds, it becomes possible to test code to which aspects are applied.

INACCESSIBLE CONSTRUCTORS

If all that weren't enough to make you say yuck, you have yet one more problem with writing unit tests of the PostSharp aspects themselves.

In this chapter's examples, I've been using `OnMethodBoundaryAspect`. The argument class I've been using is `MethodExecutionArgs`, which (fortunately) has a public constructor. The other two PostSharp aspect base classes that we've seen before (location interception and method interception) use `LocationInterceptionArgs` and `MethodInterceptionArgs`, which don't have public constructors. This makes it difficult to create mock or substitute objects for use in testing and could require you to use a more advanced (and not free) mocking tool such as TypeMock.

TESTING POSTSHARP INDIRECTLY

When all is said and done, it might not be worth the effort to test PostSharp aspect classes directly. What you should do instead is keep the code in the aspects to a minimum (thin). An aspect might contain only code to instantiate and execute another class that does the work. That is, you could create a layer of indirection between the PostSharp aspects and the code that performs the cross-cutting concern. In figure 6.6 I show an example for PostSharp, but the same principle can be applied to Dynamic-Proxy or any aspect framework.

This approach is similar to the MVP pattern in some ways. The view is the Post-Sharp aspect itself: the `OnEntry` method, the `OnSuccess` method, and so on. The presenter is a separate class that does the work (logging before, logging after, and so on). The code inside of the aspect would be extremely minimal: you delegate its work to a cross-cutting concern object (the `concern`), as shown in the following listing. The

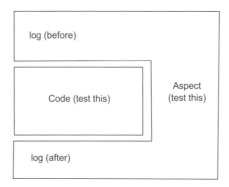

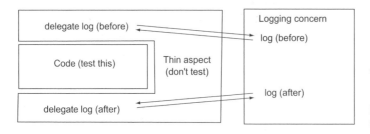

Figure 6.6   **A fat aspect and a thin aspect**

cross-cutting concern object, being a POCO—for example, an object that doesn't inherit from a PostSharp base class—would be much easier to test on its own.

Listing 6.29 A thin aspect and the interface to which it's delegating

```
public class MyNormalCode {                        A PostSharp aspect is
    [MyThinAspect]                                  applied to Reverse
    public string Reverse(string str) {
        return new string(str.Reverse().ToArray());
    }                                                       This aspect has one
}                                                              dependency on
                                                        IMyCrossCuttingConcern,
[Serializable]                                                      supplied by
public class MyThinAspect : OnMethodBoundaryAspect {           StructureMap
    IMyCrossCuttingConcern _concern;

    public override void RuntimeInitialize(MethodBase method)  {
        if (!AspectSettings.On) return;
        _concern = ObjectFactory.GetInstance<IMyCrossCuttingConcern>();
    }

    public override void OnEntry(MethodExecutionArgs args) {
        if (!AspectSettings.On) return;
        _concern.BeforeMethod("before");       ⊲─── Delegate to BeforeMethod
    }

    public override void OnSuccess(MethodExecutionArgs args) {
        if (!AspectSettings.On) return;
        _concern.AfterMethod("after");
    }
}

public interface IMyCrossCuttingConcern {    ⊲─── Delegate to AfterMethod
    void BeforeMethod(string logMessage);
    void AfterMethod(string logMessage);
}
```

The advice code can be put entirely within an implementation of IMyCrossCutting-Concern, like MyCrossCuttingConcern in the following code:

```
public class MyCrossCuttingConcern : IMyCrossCuttingConcern {
    ILoggingService _logService;

    public MyCrossCuttingConcern(ILoggingService logService) {
        _logService = logService;
    }

    public void BeforeMethod(string logMessage) {
        _logService.Write(logMessage);
    }

    public void AfterMethod(string logMessage) {
        _logService.Write(logMessage);
    }
}
```

MyCrossCuttingConcern is easy to test because it isn't coupled to PostSharp (or any AOP framework), and constructor injection again becomes possible. It's more work to get to this point, but even if you use DynamicProxy, having this extra layer of indirection between advice code and the AOP tool that performs it has architectural benefits (as you'll see in chapter 9). The aspect class (MyThinAspect) itself would go untested (at least by unit testing), but this could be an acceptable trade-off as long as the code in the aspect is kept very thin, as in this example.

In this example, I'm passing a string to BeforeMethod and AfterMethod, but in a more realistic example, you might need to construct data transfer objects (DTOs) or use the adapter pattern to pass information from MethodExecutionArgs as you need it (there is an example of this in chapter 9).

6.4 *Summary*

When it comes to unit testing, Castle DynamicProxy has the clear advantage. Unit testing with PostSharp is at least mildly difficult and certainly requires more work.

Good software architecture, then, largely consists of knowing the correct trade-offs to make; these vary widely based on the type of software you're writing and your development goals.

If you find unit testing to be important (as I do), don't count PostSharp completely out yet. In later chapters, we're going to look at some ways in which PostSharp can provide forms of testing that a runtime weaving tool can't. PostSharp provides compile-time validation and architectural validation, which are both forms of testing that take place at compile time. You could use PostSharp to prevent you (and your team) from using aspects in the wrong way (for example, using a NotifyProperty-Changed aspect on a class that doesn't implement INotifyPropertyChanged). You can use PostSharp to validate code at the architectural level (for example, to make sure that all your NHibernate entities' properties are properly defined as virtual).

One thing that this chapter starts to expose is the large difference between a runtime weaving tool such as DynamicProxy and a post-compile weaving tool such as PostSharp. Until the beginning of this chapter, PostSharp had been the clear favorite: it's more powerful and more flexible, but with unit testing now involved, you're learning the price that we pay for such power. In the next chapter, we'll start to look under the hood of these two classes of tools (runtime and compile time).

Part 3

Advanced AOP concepts

In parts 1 and 2, you gained a basic understanding of PostSharp, Castle DynamicProxy, and AOP. In chapter 7, we'll learn about the details of compile-time and runtime weaving (with PostSharp and Castle DynamicProxy respectively).

Failing is a fact of life in programming but failing early is much better than failing later. In chapter 8, the focus is on PostSharp through the eyes of an architect and how it can help you identify failures at compile time, so you can address them more efficiently.

The goal of chapter 9 is to create projects that demonstrate the composition of multiple, complex aspects that keep individual components loosely coupled and testable. This chapter introduces new concepts, but also ties together many of the those introduced throughout the book to show a complete, cohesive view of using AOP.

AOP implementation types

7

This chapter covers

- How runtime weaving works
- The difference between proxy and dynamic proxy
- Defining a postcompiler
- What postcompiled code looks like
- The trade-offs between runtime and compile-time weaving

After reading this chapter, you might still not be able to implement your own AOP tool, but you should have a basic understanding of how the two main types of AOP tools work. These two main tools, which I've been using in this book, are PostSharp and Castle DynamicProxy.

PostSharp is a postcompiler that performs weaving at compile time; Castle DynamicProxy generates proxy classes at runtime. I've glossed over some of the details of how these tools work in favor of how to use them. But the more you use AOP tools in your code, the more important it is to know exactly how they work.

For the purposes of this chapter, PostSharp will be representing compile-time weaving and DynamicProxy will be representing runtime weaving. These tools are first-class representatives, and their implementations will teach you a lot about how AOP works.

7.1   How does AOP work?

Recall the figure from chapter 1 (repeated here in figure 7.1).

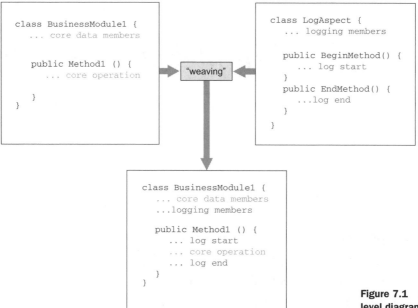

Figure 7.1   A high-level diagram of AOP

In chapter 1 the goal of including this figure was to show that AOP was able to split a cross-cutting concern into its own class, separated and encapsulated from the business logic class(es). The end result was that as a developer, you wouldn't have to deal with the tangled and scattered code—you could leave the work of combining the aspect to the AOP tool. You, the developer, read, write, and maintain the separate classes, whereas the rest of code uses the code that's been woven together.

Until this chapter, I've been entirely focused on the top half of the previous figure. Weaving is the process that an AOP framework uses to combine the separate classes. In this chapter, we'll focus on the weaving and the lower half of the figure.

Weaving must take place at some point before the class is used. With .NET, that means that you can do the weaving right after compiling the code (compile-time weaving), or you can do it at some point during execution (runtime weaving). Let's start by looking at runtime weaving, because it's the easiest to explore.

7.2   Runtime weaving

Runtime weaving means that weaving takes place after the program starts running. The aspects are instantiated at the same time as the code to which it's applied. This is what made Castle DynamicProxy so test friendly in the previous chapter: nothing happens until runtime.

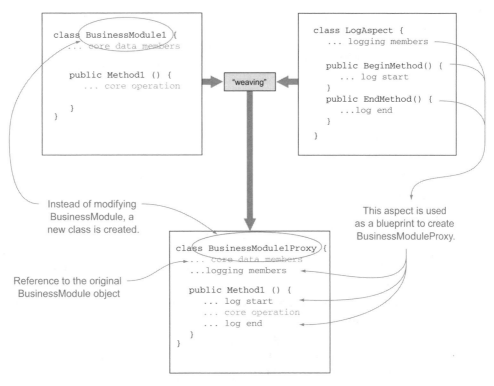

Figure 7.2   A proxy class constructed at runtime

The way runtime weaving works is similar to the decorator/proxy pattern that I covered in chapter 1 (and which I'll review in the next section). But instead of creating decorator classes by hand, a runtime weaver creates these classes at runtime.

Look at the weaving chart again, this time with runtime weaving specifically in mind. You'll still create separate classes, a `BusinessModule1` and a `LogAspect`, but at runtime, another class (let's call it `BusinessModuleProxy`) will be created and used to decorate `BusinessModule1`, as figure 7.2 shows.

If you've used the proxy/decorator pattern, this figure should look familiar. The key difference is that instead of writing the `BusinessModuleProxy` class yourself, it's generated for you. If you aren't familiar with this pattern, don't worry; the next section gives a crash course on this useful software design pattern.

7.2.1   *Proxy pattern revisited*

Let's review how the proxy pattern works before talking about dynamic proxies. The proxy pattern and its close relative the decorator pattern are patterns that have slightly different purposes and implementations, but from the perspective of AOP they're practically the same. They both allow you to add functionality to a class without changing the class itself. Typically, a proxy is used as a stand-in for another object: it's often responsible for instantiating the real object, it has the same interface as the real object,

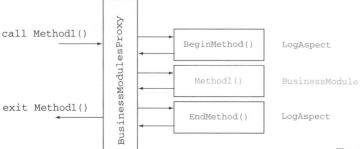

Figure 7.3   The proxy pattern

and it may control access to or provide additional functionality and control around that real object.

All the program knows is that it's calling Method1 on an object with a certain interface. That object is a proxy (see figure 7.3) that has a chance to run code of its own. Then it will call the real Method1. Once Method1 is finished, it has another opportunity to run some code of its own before returning execution to the original program.

The proxy pattern is often used to represent objects or services external to the program (for example, a web service). You may be given a generated WCF proxy class that represents an object in some other program. You could use and manipulate that object as if it were running in your program, but behind that interface, the proxy could be making HTTP calls to carry out your commands.

A decorator object is similar to a proxy object in that it has the same interface as the real object but usually isn't responsible for instantiating the object, and therefore multiple decorators can be layered on top of the real object. Instead of only LogAspect, you could also have LogAspect and CacheAspect, for instance, each of which has the same interface as BusinessModule and each of which has its own BeginMethod and EndMethod code.

For the purposes of this section, the decorator and proxy patterns have nearly the same pattern in terms of their AOP-like features.

Let's look at some C# that shows how the proxy pattern works in a new Console project. Let's start with a real class, BusinessModule, that implements an interface (IBusinessModule). The interface (and its implementation) have only one method, Method1:

```
public interface IBusinessModule {
    void Method1();
}

public class BusinessModule : IBusinessModule {
    public void Method1() {
        Console.WriteLine("Method1");
    }
}
```

Instantiate `BusinessModule` in `Main`, and call `Method1`, and it will output `Method1` to the Console, as you'd expect. In this `Main` code, notice that the module is of type `IBusinessModule`, the interface:

```
static void Main(string[] args) {
    IBusinessModule module = new BusinessModule();
    module.Method1();
}
```

Now let's create a class that acts as a proxy to `BusinessModule`. The proxy class (`BusinessModuleProxy`) will implement the same interface (`IBusinessModule`), which means that you can slot it into `Main` just by changing the `new` statement (or the IoC configuration in a real-world scenario):

```
static void Main(string[] args) {
    IBusinessModule module = new BusinessModuleProxy();
    module.Method1();
}
```

As far as `Main` is concerned, it doesn't care what object it gets for the module, as long as it implements the `IBusinessModule` interface.

Now let's create the `BusinessModuleProxy` class. Remember that its job is to be a stand-in for `BusinessModule`, so it will instantiate `BusinessModule` and forward any `Method1` calls to `BusinessModule`'s `Method1`:

```
public class BusinessModuleProxy : IBusinessModule {
    BusinessModule _realObject;

    public BusinessModuleProxy() {
        _realObject = new BusinessModule();
    }

    public void Method1() {
        _realObject.Method1();
    }
}
```

This class is nearly useless. It serves no purpose other than being a middleman between `Main` and `BusinessModule`. But note that you can put some code before and after calling the real `Method1` if you want, as in the following example:

```
public void Method1() {
    Console.WriteLine("BusinessModuleProxy before");
    _realObject.Method1();
    Console.WriteLine("BusinessModuleProxy after");
}
```

Look familiar? This proxy object is acting as an interceptor aspect. We could use it for caching, logging, threading, or anything else that we've done with an interception aspect. As long as `Main` gets an `IBusinessModule` object (through an IoC container, most likely), it will work regardless of whether we use a proxy, and we can add cross-cutting concerns to the real `BusinessModule` without changing any code in `BusinessModule`.

But hold on: if a proxy class can do the work of an AOP tool, then what's the point of all this AOP? Well, in a narrow, limited situation, use of the proxy pattern alone can be effective. But if you need to write an aspect to work with multiple classes that have different interfaces, then you need to write a proxy class for each interface.

If you have only a small number of classes that each have a small amount of methods, then you can probably use a proxy. For a cross-cutting concern such as logging or caching, coding a lot of similar functioning proxy classes becomes repetitive. For example, it wouldn't be that difficult to write proxy classes for two interfaces that have two methods each, but consider having to write proxy classes for a dozen interfaces that each have a dozen methods (144 nearly identical proxy methods). Also consider a situation in which you need cross-cutting concerns for an indeterminate number of classes—a logging project that could itself be reused for multiple solutions. By using a dynamic proxy, you no longer have to write out all of those proxies yourself; let a dynamic proxy generator do the work for you instead.

7.2.2   *Dynamic proxies*

Although the proxy pattern is a great way to implement cross-cutting concerns without involving a dependency on a third-party tool, at some point you might make a determination that the proxy pattern itself is becoming too repetitive and too boilerplate. If you find yourself writing nearly the same proxy classes with slightly different names and interfaces many times, then it's time to let a tool do that work for you.

Castle DynamicProxy (and other AOP tools that use runtime weaving) generates these classes for you by using Reflection, specifically Reflection.Emit. Instead of defining a class in a code file, a proxy generator uses the Reflection.Emit API to create a class.

Let's look at a scenario similar to the proxy pattern from the last section. I'll define a simple ITwitterService interface for Twitter, with one method to send a tweet. I'll create an implementation of it called MyTwitterService. (It'll write to console, but only for demonstration purposes.)

```
public interface ITwitterService {
    void Tweet(string message);
}

public class MyTwitterService : ITwitterService {
    public void Tweet(string message) {
        Console.WriteLine("Tweeting: {0}", message);
    }
}
```

To use the decorator or proxy pattern, we'd have to create a class that implements ITwitterService; maybe something like MyTwitterServiceProxy, which will only write a before and after message to the Console (but could do logging, caching, and so on in a real-world program):

```
public class MyTwitterServiceProxy {
    MyTwitterService _realObject;
```

```
    public MyTwitterServiceProxy(MyTwitterService svc) {
        _realObject = svc;
    }

    public void Tweet(string message) {
        Console.WriteLine("Hello before!");
        _realObject.Tweet(message);
        Console.WriteLine("Hello after!");
    }
}
```

That works, but suppose that instead of only sending a message on Twitter, you need a dozen other methods with additional functionality. And suppose that you need similar classes for Facebook, LinkedIn, Pinterest, and whatever other social networking services come into fashion. Every time you create a class or add a new method, you have to add/modify the proxy classes, too. Instead, generate those classes on the fly.

> ### Your own personal proxy generator
>
> What we're creating in this section is a primitive way to generate a proxy class using Reflection.Emit. It's not dynamic, as it'll only create a proxy for MyTwitterService. If Castle DynamicProxy is an express train, our tool is a stone wheel.
>
> The idea with this example isn't to teach you to write your own dynamic proxy generator from scratch but to provide insights into how a sophisticated tool like DynamicProxy works.

Because Reflection.Emit will generate MyTwitterServiceProxy, we won't have MyTwitterServiceProxy in the source code. Instead, we'll create a method that returns a Type named "MyTwitterServiceProxy", with which we can create a new instance using Activator.CreateInstance.

Let's start with Main so that when we're done coding our proxy generator, we'll be able to see how the end result looks, as this listing shows.

Listing 7.1   A Console program that uses a proxy generator

```
class Program {
    static void Main(string[] args) {
        var type = CreateDynamicProxyType();        This method generates
                                                    and returns a Type object.
        var dynamicProxy = (ITwitterService)Activator.CreateInstance(
            type, new object[] { new MyTwitterService() });      Use Activator
                                                                 with a Type to
        dynamicProxy.Tweet("My tweet message!");                 instantiate the
    }                                                            proxy object

    static Type CreateDynamicProxyType() {
                                                 Where all the
                                                 Reflection.Emit
    }                                            code will go
}
```

Call the Tweet method

Building a new type at runtime is similar to building a new type at compile time: you need to create an assembly. In the assembly, you create a module. With the Reflection.Emit API, start by creating an `AssemblyName`, use that to define an `AssemblyBuilder` in the current domain, and use the `Assembly-Builder` to create a `ModuleBuilder`, as the next listing shows.

> **Dynamic?**
> Don't get `DefineDynamicModule` confused with the C# 4.0 `dynamic` keyword. They aren't related. `DefineDynamic-Module` has been available in the `System.Reflection.Emit` namespace since the early days of .NET.

Listing 7.2   Creating an `AssemblyBuilder` and a `ModuleBuilder`

```
static Type CreateDynamicProxyType() {
    var assemblyName = new AssemblyName("MyProxies");   ◁── Define the AssemblyName
    var assemblyBuilder = AppDomain.CurrentDomain
        .DefineDynamicAssembly(              ◁──  DefineDynamicAssembly returns
            assemblyName,                          an AssemblyBuilder for the
            AssemblyBuilderAccess.Run);            assembly that you named
    var modBuilder = assemblyBuilder.DefineDynamicModule("MyProxies");
    // ...
}
```

Use the AssemblyBuilder to create a ModuleBuilder

The module name and assembly name don't have to be the same; I've used the same name to keep it simple.

> **Assemblies and modules**
> If you're getting a little lost in all these .NET structures, here's a simplified reminder of the various levels of .NET packaging:
>
> - Assemblies are compiled code libraries, which can be EXE or DLL files.
> - Assemblies contain some metadata and can contain one or more modules, but in practice they rarely contain more than one.
> - Modules contain classes.
> - Classes contain members (methods (functions) and/or fields).

Once you have a `ModuleBuilder`, you can use it to start building a proxy class. To build a `Type`, you need a type name, its attributes (`public` and `class`), its base class (all classes have a base class, even if it's `object`), and any interfaces the type will implement (you want to implement `ITwitterService`). Use this information with the

ModuleBuilder's `DefineType` method, and it will return a `TypeBuilder` object, as this listing shows.

Listing 7.3 Define a `Type` and get a `TypeBuilder`

```
static Type CreateDynamicProxyType() {
    // ...                                                    ◁─ This code follows the code to
                                                                 create a Module Builder.

    var typeBuilder = modBuilder.DefineType(
        "MyTwitterServiceProxy",
        TypeAttributes.Public | TypeAttributes.Class,   ◁── The Type's attribute(s)
        typeof (object),                                ◁── A base class
        new[] {typeof (ITwitterService)});              ◁─ Interface(s) to
    // ...                                                  implement (optional)
}
```

The name of the Type being created. → `"MyTwitterServiceProxy"`

You've now defined a class, but it's empty. We still need to create a field, a constructor, and a method. Let's start with the field. This field will be where the real object is stored so that it can be called when the proxy wants to call it.

To create a field, you need a field name, its type (`MyTwitterService`), and its attributes (we need only `private`). Give this information to the `TypeBuilder`'s `Define-Field` method, and it will return a `FieldBuilder` object, as shown here.

Listing 7.4 Define a field and get a `FieldBuilder`

```
static Type CreateDynamicProxyType() {
    // ...                                                    ◁─ This code follows the code
    var fieldBuilder = typeBuilder.DefineField(                  to create a TypeBuilder.
        "_realObject",
        typeof (MyTwitterService),                      ◁── The type of the field
        FieldAttributes.Private);                       ◁── The field's attribute(s)

    // ...
}
```

The name of the field being created. → `"_realObject"`

This method at this point generates code that corresponds to about three lines of C#, but it's much more verbose because we're doing similar work that the compiler would normally do for us.

Next, we need a constructor. This constructor will have one parameter, and the body of that constructor will set the field to the argument passed in to the constructor.

We can again use the `TypeBuilder` to define a constructor. To define it, we need its attributes (`public` only), its calling convention (whether it's an instance constructor or a static constructor), and the `Type` of each parameter (we'll have only one parameter of the type `MyTwitterService`). Call the TypeBuilder's `DefineConstructor` method with this information. Once the constructor is defined, we need a way to put code in that method, so we'll get an `ILGenerator` object for the constructor by calling `GetILGenerator`, as this listing shows.

Listing 7.5 Define a constructor and get an `ILGenerator`

```
static Type CreateDynamicProxyType() {                    This code follows the code
                                                          to create a TypeBuilder.
    // ...

    var constructorBuilder = typeBuilder.DefineConstructor(    The constructor
                                                               is public.
        MethodAttributes.Public,

        CallingConventions.HasThis,                       The constructor's only
                                                          parameter is of the
        new[] {typeof (MyTwitterService)}});              type MyTwitterService.

    var contructorIl = constructorBuilder.GetILGenerator();
    // ...                                                Get an ILGenerator to add
                                                          code to the constructor.
}
```

The constructor is an instance constructor, so it has access to this.

Inside the constructor, we need only one statement to assign the argument to the field (two statements if you count `return`, which is implicit in C#). We created a parameter by specifying an array of types when calling `DefineConstructor`, but note that the argument doesn't have a name. As far as .NET is concerned, it's only argument 1. (Why argument 1 instead of argument 0? Because argument 0 is `this`—the current instance).

To put code inside the constructor, we need to use `constuctorBuilder` to emit Common Intermediate Language (CIL) OpCodes. If you thought everything up to this point was complicated, here's where it really gets difficult. I'm far from an expert on Reflection.Emit, but because this is such a simple operation, I was able to piece together the correct OpCodes for an assignment operation. It will contain three parts: argument 0 (`this`), argument 1 (the incoming value of the parameter), and the field to which it'll be assigned. They're emitted to an evaluation stack (in the following listing), so the ordering may seem awkward.

Listing 7.6 Emitting CIL code for the constructor

```
contructorIl.Emit(OpCodes.Ldarg_0);           Load argument 0 (this)
                                               onto the evaluation stack

contructorIl.Emit(OpCodes.Ldarg_1);           Load argument I (the
                                               constructor's argument)

contructorIl.Emit(OpCodes.Stfld, fieldBuilder);   Store the evaulation result on
                                                   the specified field

contructorIl.Emit(OpCodes.Ret);               Return from the constructor
                                               (end its execution)
```

Now we've generated a type that has a name, a named private field, and a constructor that sets the private field. To make sure this type implements the ITwitterService interface, we need to define a void method called Tweet that has a string parameter, as shown in the following listing. Use this information with the TypeBuilder's DefineMethod and DefineMethodOverride. We also need another ILGenerator to emit code into this method's body.

Listing 7.7 Tweet method for the interface with an ILGenerator

```
static Type CreateDynamicProxyType() {

    // ...                                              This code follows the code
                                                        to create a TypeBuilder.

    var methodBuilder = typeBuilder.DefineMethod("Tweet",

        MethodAttributes.Public | MethodAttributes.Virtual,

        typeof (void),

        new[] {typeof (string)});

    typeBuilder.DefineMethodOverride(methodBuilder,

        typeof (ITwitterService).GetMethod("Tweet"));

    var tweetIl = methodBuilder.GetILGenerator();

    // ...

}
```

The Tweet method is public and we call it virtual so that it can implement the interface.

It's a void method.

It has a single string parameter.

Specify that the method being built implements the Tweet method of the interface.

Get an ILGenerator to add code to the Tweet method.

Now that we have a Tweet method, we need to fill it with code. In MyTwitterService-Proxy, the Tweet method wrote "Hello before!" to Console, called the real Tweet method, and wrote "Hello after!" to the Console. We need to do all of that by emitting OpCodes, as shown in this listing.

Listing 7.8 Writing to Console and calling the real Tweet method with OpCodes

```
tweetIl.Emit(OpCodes.Ldstr, "Hello before!");              Load the literal string
                                                           onto the evaluation stack.

tweetIl.Emit(OpCodes.Call, typeof (Console)

    .GetMethod("WriteLine", new[] {typeof (string)}));

tweetIl.Emit(OpCodes.Ldarg_0);

tweetIl.Emit(OpCodes.Ldfld, fieldBuilder);

tweetIl.Emit(OpCodes.Ldarg_1);
```

Call the static WriteLine method of the Console class.

Load argument 0 (this) onto the stack.

Load the field (_realObject) onto the stack next.

Load argument I (Tweet's string argument) onto the stack.

```
tweetIl.Emit(OpCodes.Call,

    fieldBuilder.FieldType.GetMethod("Tweet"));
```

⊲ **Call the Tweet method on the field. . .**

```
tweetIl.Emit(OpCodes.Ldstr, "Hello after!");
```

⊲ **. . . you did the first use of Console's WriteLine with a different string.**

```
tweetIl.Emit(OpCodes.Call, typeof (Console)

    .GetMethod("WriteLine", new[] {typeof (string)}));

tweetIl.Emit(OpCodes.Ret);
```

That's it. The `TypeBuilder` object has all of the information it needs to build the proxy class we want. The final step is to use the builder to create the `Type` (and return it):

```
return typeBuilder.CreateType();
```

Compile and run the program. After all that work, you'll see (in figure 7.4) simultaneously satisfying and disappointing output.

As I said earlier, we're far from building a full dynamic proxy generator in this chapter. To make this little demonstration into a somewhat respectable dynamic

```
C:\Windows\system32\cmd.exe
Hello before!
Tweeting: My tweet message!
Hello after!
Press any key to continue . . .
```

Figure 7.4   The output after creating a proxy class at runtime

proxy generator would take a lot of work, including (but not limited to):

- Making it able to proxy any type instead of only `MyTwitterService` objects
- Making it able to handle any method(s) in those objects, not only the `Tweet` method
- Making it able to execute arbitrary aspect code instead of only writing before and after to the Console
- Wrapping it all up in a nice, encapsulated, easy-to-use API

Fortunately, tools such as DynamicProxy have blazed this trail for us, so we don't have to do all this tedious plumbing ourselves. By showing you this oversimplified version of a dynamic proxy, I hoped to accomplish two things: to have you appreciate the expertise and intricate work that has gone into the making of these tools, and to give you the chance to take a look under the hood of dynamic proxy generation. When you implement an `IInterceptor` and give it to a DynamicProxy `ProxyGenerator`, you're kicking off a series of complex assembly, module, type, field, and method building with Reflection.Emit to create a new `Type` at runtime that otherwise doesn't exist in your source code.

The work that a compile-time weaving tool does is similar to the runtime weaving we've been discussing in this chapter, except that it doesn't create a new `Type` at runtime—it modifies the `Type` in the assemblies that are created by the normal .NET compiler before the code is executed.

7.3 Compile-time weaving

When you create a .NET project in C#, it's compiled into CIL (also referred to as MSIL, IL, and bytecode) as an assembly (a DLL or an EXE file). Figure 7.5 illustrates the flow of this process. The Common Language Runtime (CLR) is then able to convert the CIL into real machine instructions (via a process known as just-in-time compilation, or JIT). As a .NET developer, this process should be familiar to you.

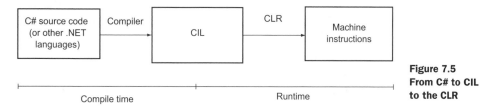

Figure 7.5 From C# to CIL to the CLR

An AOP tool that uses compile-time weaving introduces another step to this process known as postcompiling (hence the name *Post*Sharp). Right after you complete compilation, PostSharp (or other compile-time AOP tools) then examine the assembly for aspects you've created and where you've indicated that the aspects should be used. It then directly modifies the CIL in the assembly to perform the weaving, as figure 7.6 illustrates.

A nice side effect of this approach is that any errors PostSharp can detect can also be displayed in Visual Studio as if they were errors from the compiler (more on this in the next chapter).

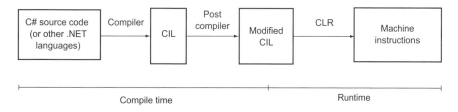

Figure 7.6 The same process from figure 7.5 with PostSharp added

Immediately after the compiler finishes creating the CIL code, the postcompiler process runs and modifies the CIL code, based on the aspects you wrote and where you applied those aspects. This process of modifying the CIL is the general basis of any compile-time AOP tool, but in the rest of this section you'll see some of the details of how PostSharp in particular works and what the resultant modified CIL looks like.

7.3.1 Postcompiling

To help you understand PostSharp, let's start by looking at the work that PostSharp does, step by step. The first step comes before compile time, of course—you'll use the PostSharp.dll library to write aspects and indicate where those aspects should be used (specifying pointcuts with attributes, for instance). All PostSharp aspects are attributes, which don't usually execute on their own (they are just metadata). The next step comes immediately after you compile your project.

The compiler will look at your source code and turn it into an assembly that contains CIL. Immediately thereafter, the PostSharp postcompiler program takes over. It'll examine the aspects you wrote, where you specified the aspects should be applied, and the CIL of the assembly. PostSharp will then do several things: instantiate the aspects, serialize the aspects, and modify the CIL to place the appropriate calls to the aspect.

When PostSharp has finished its work, the serialized aspects will be stored as a binary stream in the assembly (as a resource). This stream will be loaded at runtime for execution (and will also execute its `RuntimeInitialize` method).

To help visualize this process, figure 7.7 is a diagram that uses pseudocode to represent the three major states of your project: the source code that you write, the assembly that's created by the compiler in cooperation with PostSharp, and the program execution, carried out by the CLR.

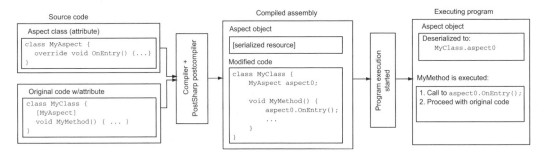

Figure 7.7 From source to assembly to execution

That all may sound and look a bit complex, so to further demonstrate, let's review the code both before and after PostSharp does its work. We'll compare the source code that you write to the compiled assembly by using a decompiler.

7.3.2 Before and after

A decompiler is a tool that can analyze a .NET assembly (such as a DLL or an EXE file) and convert it from CIL back into C# code. It's compiling in reverse (CIL to C# instead of C# to CIL). You can use a variety of decompiling tools to do this, and they all tend to have a common set of features, but the tool I use in this book is called ILSpy; it's a free, open source tool available at http://ilspy.net.

To demonstrate, I'm going to write a simple program, compile it, and use ILSpy on it. At first, I won't use any AOP, which means I expect to see that my C# and my decompiled C# are identical. Here's a simple class with one method in Visual Studio:

```
public class MyClass {
    public void MyMethod() {
        Console.WriteLine("Hello, world!");
    }
}
```

I then compile it (into a DLL or an EXE file in the bin folder of my project). If I open it with ILSpy and navigate to `MyClass`, then ILSpy will show me figure 7.8.

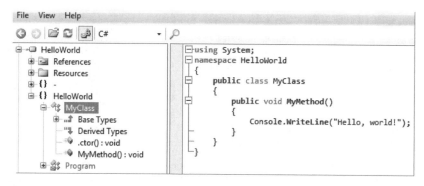

Figure 7.8 Decompiling an assembly with ILSpy

If you use a different tool, you might not see exactly the same thing. A default parameterless constructor might appear. Every class needs a constructor, and because I didn't define one explicitly, the compiler assumes a public, empty, parameterless constructor. ILSpy happens to make the same assumption when decompiling. Other than that, the decompiled C# should look similar to the original C#, regardless of which tool you use.

Now let's use PostSharp to add an aspect to the code in this project. PostSharp will modify the CIL, which means that I wouldn't expect the decompiled C# to look the same as the C# that I see in Visual Studio. The following listing shows `MyClass` again, this time with a simple PostSharp aspect applied to `MyMethod`.

Listing 7.9 Introducing a PostSharp aspect

```
public class MyClass {
    [MyAspect]
    public void MyMethod() {
        Console.WriteLine("Hello, world!");
    }
}

[Serializable]
```

```
public class MyAspect : OnMethodBoundaryAspect {
    public override void OnEntry(MethodExecutionArgs args) {
        Console.WriteLine("Before the method");
    }

    public override void OnExit(MethodExecutionArgs args) {
        Console.WriteLine("After the method");
    }
}
```

After compiling, I open the assembly with ILSpy again and look at the decompiled code for MyMethod. If you're using the free PostSharp Express, you'll see a long method (compared to the full commercial edition).

PostSharp feature: Aspect optimizer

PostSharp Express doesn't include the aspect optimizer. The aspect optimizer examines the aspect you've written and modifies the IL only enough to accomplish what you want to do. For instance, if you don't use the args object at all, then the aspect optimizer will discover this, and when OnEntry and OnExit are called, a null will be passed to the args parameter. Another example: because we didn't override OnSuccess or OnException, the aspect optimizer would see this and wouldn't bother creating code to call those empty base methods.

PostSharp Express does no such interrogation—it assumes that you'll need everything, which is why the decompiled version of MyMethod is so long.

Don't be frightened by what ILSpy shows you: it's not as bad as it looks. Most of the code you see is to build the object for the args parameter that OnEntry, OnExit, OnSuccess, and OnException use, and the code to respond to any changes you make to that object. PostSharp also adds a try/catch/finally structure, which is how it calls OnEntry, OnSuccess, and so on in the correct places (see lines 9, 15, 20, 40 in figure 7.9). If you look closely at line 14, you'll see that the Console.WriteLine("Hello, world!") is still in there, surrounded by all of the code that PostSharp has woven with it.

Some of the naming may also look strange. These are weird names, but they're just names, like any other class or method name. OnEntry is a method on an object named a0, which is of the type MyAspect. The object a0 is an internal static member of an internal subclass called <>z__Aspects.

You've now seen the new, modified MyMethod. To get the full picture, let's also examine the rest of the decompiled MyClass in listing 7.10, which contains the weirdly named subclass and its static members.

```
 1   // HelloWorld.MyClass
 2   public void MyMethod()
 3   {
 4       Arguments empty = Arguments.Empty;
 5       MethodExecutionArgs methodExecutionArgs = new MethodExecutionArgs(this, empty);
 6       MethodExecutionArgs arg_17_0 = methodExecutionArgs;
 7       MethodBase m = MyClass.<>z__Aspects.m1;
 8       arg_17_0.Method = m;
 9       MyClass.<>z__Aspects.a0.OnEntry(methodExecutionArgs);
10       if (methodExecutionArgs.FlowBehavior != FlowBehavior.Return)
11       {
12           try
13           {
14               Console.WriteLine("Hello, world!");
15               MyClass.<>z__Aspects.a0.OnSuccess(methodExecutionArgs);
16           }
17           catch (Exception exception)
18           {
19               methodExecutionArgs.Exception = exception;
20               MyClass.<>z__Aspects.a0.OnException(methodExecutionArgs);
21               switch (methodExecutionArgs.FlowBehavior)
22               {
23               case FlowBehavior.Default:
24               case FlowBehavior.RethrowException:
25                   IL_81:
26                   throw;
27               case FlowBehavior.Continue:
28                   methodExecutionArgs.Exception = null;
29                   return;
30               case FlowBehavior.Return:
31                   methodExecutionArgs.Exception = null;
32                   return;
33               case FlowBehavior.ThrowException:
34                   throw methodExecutionArgs.Exception;
35               }
36               goto IL_81;
37           }
38           finally
39           {
40               MyClass.<>z__Aspects.a0.OnExit(methodExecutionArgs);
41           }
42       }
43   }
```

— OnEntry (pointing to line 9)

— Original code (pointing to line 14)

— OnExit (pointing to line 40)

Figure 7.9 Decompiling an assembly that's been modified with PostSharp

Listing 7.10 ILSpy decompile of `MyClass`

```
namespace HelloWorld {
    public class MyClass {
        [DebuggerNonUserCode, CompilerGenerated]
        internal sealed class <>z__Aspects {
            internal static MethodBase m1;
            internal static readonly MyAspect a0;
            public static void Initialize() { }
            [CompilerGenerated]
            static <>z__Aspects() {
                MyClass.<>z__Aspects.m1 = MethodBase.
                    GetMethodFromHandle(methodof(MyClass.MyMethod())
                        .MethodHandle);
                MyClass.<>z__Aspects.a0 = (MyAspect)
                    <>z__AspectsImplementationDetails2971080271
                        .aspects1[0];
                MyClass.<>z__Aspects.a0.RuntimeInitialize(
                    MyClass.<>z__Aspects.m1);
            }
        }
```

This subclass of **MyClass** was created by PostSharp. (pointing to internal sealed class)

The aspect object is a static member of the subclass. (pointing to internal static readonly MyAspect a0)

The a0 member gets an instance of MyAspect (post-deserialization). (pointing to MyClass.<>z__Aspects.a0 = (MyAspect)...)

The RuntimeInitialize member also gets executed at this time. (pointing to MyClass.<>z__Aspects.a0.RuntimeInitialize(...))

```
    }

    [CompilerGenerated]
    static MyClass() {
        MyClass.<>z__Aspects.Initialize();
    }

    public void MyMethod() { // ... }
}
}
```

PostSharp created almost everything in this code at compile time by adding and manipulating CIL, as it interrogated the aspects you wrote. Some of the generated CIL doesn't correspond directly to C#. The name `<>z__Aspects` isn't valid in C#, and `methodof` isn't part of the C# language. ILSpy is doing its best to interpret.

This section and the previous one may seem to be a deep dive into the depths of .NET, but in reality we've barely scratched the surface of Reflection.Emit and CIL manipulation. Fortunately, you and I—as users of AOP tools—don't need to be terribly concerned with such complexities most of the time. But it's important to have some level of understanding of the inner workings of each of these AOP implementation approaches, as we're responsible for making a good decision about which type of AOP implementation to use. Should we use runtime weaving or should we use compile-time weaving?

7.4   *Runtime versus compile-time weaving*

One factor that developers always seem to get hung up on is performance, so let's start by comparing the performace of the two approaches. In my experience, the reality is that the performance bottleneck in a program is rarely caused by the use of AOP tools, and any performance hit caused by AOP is insignificant when compared to the gains in developer productivity and maintainable code.

As you've seen, runtime AOP tools such as DynamicProxy use Reflection.Emit, which can be a somewhat slow operation that a user could notice, but once a `Type` is created, it doesn't need to be created again, so this performance hit is relatively negligible. A compile-time tool doesn't use the slow Reflection.Emit operations because it does its work at compile time. This increased build time can be noticeable to the developers when they have a large number of projects in a solution that all use Post-Sharp, and this is the most common complaint about postcompiling tools. But Post-Sharp's performance continues to improve with newer versions, and you can configure a large multiproject solution so that PostSharp isn't executed on a project that doesn't use aspects. If performance is your primary concern, both types of tools will slow down performance in one way or another, though it may not be slow enough to notice in practice.

Therefore, how do you decide which AOP implementation is better: runtime weaving or compile-time weaving, based on performance alone? Which one should you use? I hate to give the classic weaselly answer, but it's as true as it is annoying: it depends.

If you aren't using a lot of aspects or you aren't using them on many classes, you can probably get away with writing proxy or decorator classes and not use any third-party AOP tool at all.

But if your project uses a lot of cross-cutting concerns and/or uses them on a lot of different classes, AOP will definitely be of benefit to you. Perhaps dynamically generated types at runtime, perhaps CIL modifications at compile time. Perhaps both. Let's examine the benefits of each approach.

7.4.1 Pros of runtime weaving

One of the key benefits to using a tool like DynamicProxy that you've already seen is that it's easy to test (see chapter on unit testing). A DynamicProxy interceptor can be easily injected with dependencies at runtime, making it easy to write tests that keep the aspect in isolation.

Second, compared to a tool like PostSharp, a runtime tool like DynamicProxy doesn't require a postcompile process. You don't need a separate EXE to make it compile correctly on every team member's machine and on the build server. Thus it may be easier to introduce AOP to a project team and/or to the project's build server.

Third, because aspects aren't instantiated until runtime, you also retain the ability to configure aspects after the build is complete. You retain a measure of flexibility at runtime—you could change the aspect configuration with an XML file, for instance.

Finally, even though licensing and costs are complex issues, DynamicProxy, a world-class AOP framework, is a free and open source tool, so I'd definitely count that as a pro in the runtime weaving camp. These are the key areas in which runtime has the advantage over compile time.

7.4.2 Pros of compile-time weaving

Compile-time weaving has a different set of benefits. Because of the nature of how tools like PostSharp work (by directly manipulating CIL in assembly files), they can be much more powerful.

First, with runtime weaving, the interceptor typically gets applied to every method on a class—even if you're interested in only one. With a tool such as PostSharp, you can use more fine-grained control over where to apply aspects.

Second, with runtime weaving, you typically need to use an IoC container to use the interceptor aspects. But it's not always the case that every object in your program is instantiated via an IoC tool. UI objects and domain objects, for instance, may not be suitable or possible for a container to instantiate. Therefore, a tool such as PostSharp has additional reach that a runtime AOP tool doesn't have.

If the project you're working on doesn't use an IoC tool, then in order to use runtime AOP you'll need to rearchitect the code to use an IoC tool before you can start using AOP. With a compile-time AOP tool, you start reaping the benefits of AOP immediately. I'm not saying you shouldn't use an IoC or other dependency injection tool: far from it. Dependency injection is an incredibly useful tool that allows you to create loosely coupled, easily testable code, regardless of whether you use AOP. But not every code base you work on will have the good fortune of being built with DI in mind, and that refactoring process may be slow and costly.

One final way that a compile-time tool is more powerful is that it gives you the ability to use AOP with any code: including `static` methods, `private` methods, and fields (which you saw in chapter 5 on location interception).

7.5   *Summary*

Ultimately, I can't unilaterally prescribe one approach over the other: only you can make this decision. Besides the technical pros and cons that I've mentioned, you have to consider a whole world of nontechnical factors, including licensing, pricing, and support. I've used a broad brush to describe the two main approaches: runtime weaving and compile-time weaving. In practice, the individual tools you evaluate can vary a lot as well. How mature is the tool? Is its API likely to change? Does its API make sense to you? What is the rest of your team most comfortable with? Are you working on a legacy code base or starting a new project from scratch?

These are all critical attributes that must factor into your decisions. But these factors are all beyond the scope of this book, because every team, every company, every AOP tool, and every project is different. Now that you're familiar with using AOP and how the AOP tools work, you're in a much better position to make overall decisions about the architecture of your project or code base.

In addition to the aspects I've been describing for common cross-cutting concerns, AOP has features that an architect would be interested in. Because PostSharp examines your code right after it's compiled, it's in a unique position to provide additional capabilities that many other AOP tools can't provide. In the next chapter, we'll look at how to put PostSharp to work on your architecture.

Using AOP as an
architectural tool

8

This chapter covers

- Aspect initialization
- Aspect validation
- Improving a threading aspect using validation and initialization
- Dealing with architectural constraints
- Using architectural constraints to help with NHibernate
- Working with multicasting attributes

AOP's own architecture and its effect on the architecture of a large code base are important concepts to understand in order to use AOP effectively. When you're designing and implementing an architecture, failing earlier in the process may reduce costs from rework, and PostSharp can help you quickly and automatically identify failures at compile time.

Until this point, we've been looking at PostSharp and AOP in a narrow way: one aspect and one class at a time. Let's look at PostSharp through the eyes of an architect, viewing an entire system and how it fits together. PostSharp contains tools to make an architect's job easier, as well as tools to make sure that the aspects themselves are well-architected.

One thing about PostSharp that may have concerned you at some point is that all of my examples involve putting attributes on individual methods and properties, which may seem tedious and repetitive, and if you had to do that with a large code base, it would be. Fortunately, PostSharp doesn't require that you always do that. We'll look at ways in which we can multicast aspect attributes so that we can reuse aspects without a lot of attribute repetition.

Because PostSharp is implemented as a compile-time tool (as explored in the previous chapter), it opens the door for us to write code that can run immediately after the normal compile time. We can use this opportunity to write code that validates that aspects are being used in the right places and won't cause problems during runtime, as well as the structure and architecture of a project as a whole. This approach allows problems to be identified earlier (or, as I like to call it, to fail faster).

We'll also take this opportunity to perform aspect initialization. If you have an expensive operation (such as the use of Reflection), better to get that out of the way during the build than wait until runtime.

8.1   *Compile-time initialization and validation*

Let's review the PostSharp build process (illustrated in figure 8.1 [a repeat of figure 7.6]) from the previous chapter and look at how it fits into the normal .NET build process. Recall that you have the compile-time phase (in which code is compiled into CIL) and the runtime phase (in which CIL is compiled to machine instructions just in time to be executed). Compile-time AOP tools like PostSharp add one more step (the post compiler) and modify the CIL after it's compiled but before it's executed.

The post-compiler portion of the previous diagram is where PostSharp does its work. Let's zoom into the post-compiler step of the build process (shown in figure 8.2).

PostSharp performs several steps for each aspect that you write. Each aspect is instantiated using the aspect's constructor. PostSharp can then perform a validation step (calling a `CompileTimeValidate` method in your aspect) to check whether the aspect is being used properly. Then PostSharp can perform an initialization step (calling a `CompileTimeInitialize` method in your aspect) to perform any expensive computations now instead of waiting until runtime. Finally, PostSharp will take the aspect instance and serialize it (to a binary stream) so that it can be deserialized and executed later at runtime.

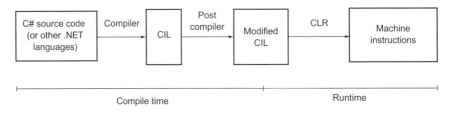

Figure 8.1   Build process with PostSharp

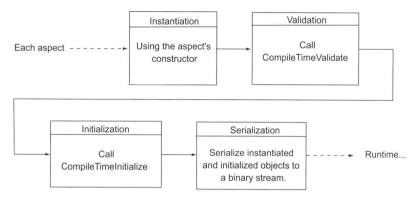

Figure 8.2 Zooming into the post-compiler steps of PostSharp aspects

This section focuses on the validation and initialization steps of the process. Until this chapter, I hadn't defined any `CompileTimeValidate` or `CompileTimeInitialize` code in the examples in order to keep them simple. All of these steps are still performed, but because we didn't define `CompileTimeValidate` or `CompileTimeInitialize`, those steps didn't do anything.

> **NOTE** Aspects are serialized by default, but unless you use `CompileTime-Initialize`, you can turn serialization off at the individual aspect level to get an improvement in runtime performance.

With `CompileTimeValidate`, PostSharp lets us fail faster. If we can validate something at compile time, we don't have to wait until runtime to find a bug or get an exception. `CompileTimeInitialize` lets us do costly work ahead of time. If we can do a (potentially costly) operation before running the program, let's get it out of the way.

8.1.1 Initializing at compile time

Often, an aspect needs to know some information about the code to which it's being applied, such as a method name, some parameter information, or other information. All of this information can be supplied by the PostSharp API, which uses Reflection to populate the information that is passed to your aspect (for example, the `args` parameters). Reflection information is the most common thing I've seen initialized, but any other costly information that can be obtained and instantiated before the entire program is executed is also fair game.

For a quick example, let's look at a basic logging aspect (of which you've seen multiple examples in the book so far). Instead of logging a `string`, let's log the name of the method. If I used a PostSharp `OnMethodBoundaryAspect`, and did this at runtime, the next listing shows how I could log that `MyMethod` was being executed.

Listing 8.1 Logging the method that was called

```
class Program {
    static void Main(string[] args) {
        var obj = new MyClass();
```

```
            obj.MyMethod();
        }
}

public class MyClass {
    [MyLoggingAspect]
    public void MyMethod() {
        Console.WriteLine("Code in MyMethod");
    }
}

[Serializable]
public class MyLoggingAspect : OnMethodBoundaryAspect {
    public override void OnEntry(MethodExecutionArgs args) {
        Console.WriteLine("Method was called: {0}", args.Method.Name);
    }
}
```

Aspect attribute is applied to MyMethod.

Using args.Method.Name to get the method name

If you examine `args.Method`, you'll notice that it's an object of the type `MethodBase`, which is in `System.Reflection`. Although it's not a big deal for our example, which has only one bounded method, using Reflection every time the aspect is used could add up in terms of performance in a large application.

But paying this performance price at runtime shouldn't be necessary. The method name won't change when the program is running, so why not interrogate the method names at compile time instead, within PostSharp's post compiler process? In the following listing, we override `CompileTimeInitialize` in this aspect and store the method name in a private `string` field. In `OnEntry`, use that `string` field instead of `args.Method.Name`.

Listing 8.2 Using `Initialize` to get the method name at compile time

```
[Serializable]
public class MyLoggingAspect : OnMethodBoundaryAspect {

    string _methodName;

    public override void CompileTimeInitialize(MethodBase method,

                                       AspectInfo aspectInfo) {

        _methodName = method.Name;

    }

    public override void OnEntry(MethodExecutionArgs args) {

        Console.WriteLine("Method was called: {0}", _methodName);

    }

}
```

A MethodBase object is made available to CompileTimeInitialize.

You can ignore AspectInfo for now; it's reserved for future use in PostSharp.

Store the method name in a private string field.

When the method is called, use _methodName instead of Reflection.

> ### PostSharp licensing
> One note about PostSharp licensing: this initialization won't have much effect on performance if you're using the Express (free) edition because it doesn't do any optimization and `args.Method` will still be populated for `OnEntry` using Reflection regardless of whether `OnEntry` uses it. But it's still a good idea to follow this practice of using `CompileTimeInitialize` in case you end up needing the aspect optimization, which the full version of PostSharp can give you.

Use of Reflection is only one type of operation that can be performed at compile time instead of runtime. If you want to perform other slow or costly operations, `Compile-TimeInitialize` is the place to do it.

Because PostSharp is already running this initialization code at compile time, why not also take the opportunity to run some validations on the aspect while you're at it?

8.1.2 Validating the correct use of an aspect

The use of `CompileTimeValidate` in PostSharp allows us to check the context of where and how an aspect is applied to make sure that it will work correctly at runtime. To use `CompileTimeValidate`, override it in an aspect—for instance, a `LocationInterceptionAspect`.

Let's start with a simplistic example, shown in the next listing, and then I'll show you a more realistic scenario in the next section. I have a `Program` class with one string property called `MyName`. I'll apply an aspect to it called `MyAspect`, which will log to Console whenever the property's getter is used.

Listing 8.3 A `LocationInterceptionAspect` to log usage of get

```
class Program {
    [MyAspect]
    public static string MyName { get; set; }          ◁─┐ The aspect attribute is
                                                           │ applied to a property.
    static void Main(string[] args) {
        MyName = "Matthew D. Groves";
    }
}

[Serializable]
public class MyAspect : LocationInterceptionAspect {
    public override void OnGetValue(LocationInterceptionArgs args) {
        Console.WriteLine("Property 'getter' was used");   ◁─┐ When a get is
        args.ProceedGetValue();                              │ used, a string
    }                                                        │ will be written
}                                                            │ to Console.
```

But as the author of this aspect, I have a (strange) rule that I only want the aspect to be used on properties that are named `Horse`. Otherwise, the aspect is being used improperly, and therefore the project shouldn't compile. I'll override the `Compile-TimeValidate` method (see the next listing) and check the location's name. If it's not `"Horse"`, then I'll use the PostSharp API's `Message` class to write an error message.

> **Listing 8.4 Using `CompileTimeValidate` to check the location name**

There are multiple levels of Severity; I've chosen Error.

An arbitrary error code

```
[Serializable]
public class MyAspect : LocationInterceptionAspect {
    public override bool CompileTimeValidate(
                         LocationInfo locationInfo) {
        if (locationInfo.Name != "Horse") {
            Message.Write(locationInfo,
                         SeverityType.Error,
                         "MYERRORCODE01",
                         "Location name must be 'horse'");
            return false;
        }
        return true;
    }

    public override void OnGetValue(LocationInterceptionArgs args) {
        Console.WriteLine("Property 'getter' was used");
    }
}
```

LocationInfo is Reflection information about the property.

An error message

When I create this aspect and try to compile my project, because my property name isn't `'Horse'`, I'll get an error message. And because I'm using Visual Studio, it'll appear to be a normal compiler error message (figure 8.3).

I'm not going to comprehensively document this PostSharp feature here, but I will point out a couple of interesting things. First, notice that `CompileTimeValidate` returns a `bool`. If `CompileTimeValidate` returns false, the aspect won't be applied to that particular location. If I put the aspect attribute on 100 properties, and only one of them is named `'horse'`, the aspect will only be applied once.

Second, notice that the `SeverityLevel` I chose was "Error." By doing this, I'm telling PostSharp to write a compiler error, and thus Visual Studio will treat it as such. If I instead used a `SeverityLevel` like "Warning," the message would be shown as a warning and wouldn't keep the project from being compiled. In my experience, warnings are often ignored, so generally I like to stick with "Error." One other thing to mention

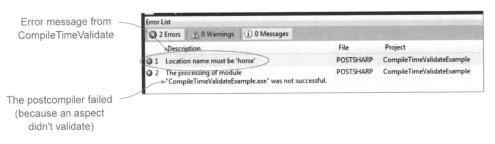

Error message from CompileTimeValidate

The postcompiler failed (because an aspect didn't validate)

Figure 8.3 `CompileTimeValidate`-generated error message

about errors: the post compiler will not stop at the first error it finds—it will continue to process all aspects and write out each `Message`.

Finally, the error code and the message are strings that can be whatever you want. It's a good idea to make these as descriptive and as useful as possible so that anyone encountering these `CompileTimeValidate` errors can find the offending code easily, as line number and filename are not included by PostSharp in the `Message`. Including the full class name, full property type, and property name in your error message and creating meaningful error codes are good ideas (and use similar information for method aspects, of course).

Now you've seen a few basic examples of `CompileTimeInitialize` and `Compile-TimeValidate`. Let's put `CompileTimeValidate` to work in a real aspect.

8.1.3 *Real-world example: Threading revisited*

Let's revisit the threading example from chapter 3. Recall that we created a `Work-erThread` aspect to spin up another thread, and a `UIThread` aspect to make sure that any UI code called from that thread will be run on the UI thread. Let's take another look at `UIThread` in particular, and look for anything that might be a problem with the way that aspect was written:

```
[Serializable]
public class UIThread : MethodInterceptionAspect {
    public override void OnInvoke(MethodInterceptionArgs args) {
        var form = (Form) args.Instance;
        if (form.InvokeRequired)
            form.Invoke(new Action(args.Proceed));
        else
            args.Proceed();
    }
}
```

This aspect depends on `args.Instance` being an object of type `Form`. What if it's not? Casting `args.Instance` to `Form` would then cause an `InvalidCastException` to be thrown. We could add runtime checks to avoid that. Instead of hard casting the object, we could use the C# as operator to soft cast the object and then check to make sure the cast is valid before trying to call `InvokeRequired` and `Invoke`. When using as, if the cast isn't able to be performed, then a `null` is returned and no exception is thrown, as shown here.

Listing 8.5 Runtime checks on casting

```
[Serializable]
public class UIThread : MethodInterceptionAspect {
    public override void OnInvoke(MethodInterceptionArgs args) {
        var form = args.Instance as Form;              ◁—— Soft cast
        if(form == null)
            args.Proceed();                            ◁——┐ If the cast fails, proceed
        if (form.InvokeRequired)                           │ without checking
            form.Invoke(new Action(args.Proceed));         ┘ InvokeRequired.
```

```
        else
            args.Proceed();
    }
}
```

Doing that would at least keep the aspect from throwing exceptions. But it still raises a question: why was `UIThread` being used on a class that didn't inherit from `Form` in the first place? Is there some code that was moved to another class? Is there a new team member who's unfamiliar with how threading works? Is someone trying to use this aspect with a UI framework other than Windows Forms? If we put in that runtime check, it solves the exception issue, but it kicks those other questions down the road.

Instead of enabling procrastination, let's make this aspect force us to deal with such an issue immediately. Instead of that soft cast, let's use `CompileTimeValidate` to ensure, at compile time, that the `UIThread` aspect is always being used on methods in a `Form` class (see the next listing). If it's not, we'll write an error message with information about where `UIThread` is being used incorrectly and prevent the build from succeeding.

Listing 8.6   Threading aspect of compile-time validation

```
public override bool CompileTimeValidate(MethodBase method) {
    if (!typeof (Form).IsAssignableFrom(method.DeclaringType)) {
        var errorMessage =
            string.Format("UIThread aspect must be used in a Form.
                [Assembly: {0}, Class: {1}, Method: {2}]",
            method.DeclaringType.Assembly.FullName,
            method.DeclaringType.FullName,
            method.Name);
        PostSharp.Extensibility
            .Message.Write(method,
            SeverityType.Error,
            "UIThreadFormError01",
            errorMessage);
        return false;
    }
    return true;
}
```

Use **IsAssignableFrom** to see if **DeclaringType** inherits Form.

Full type name of the class

Full assembly name of the class

Name of the method

Error will prevent build from finishing.

Succinct but helpful error code

All assembly, class, and method information

I wrote out a message explaining the error, as well as the assembly, class, and method name where the aspect is failing to validate (see figure 8.4 for an example error message). You could also write out parameters or any other information you think might be helpful to find the problem.

> **Message confusion?**
>
> If you're following along with a Windows Forms application, make sure that you don't confuse `System.Windows.Forms.Message` with `PostSharp.Extensibility` `.Message`. For clarity, I've written the full name in the previous example.

Now, instead of waiting for a crash or another consequence, you can use this `Compile-TimeValidate` code to fail faster. I'll put the aspect on a class that doesn't inherit from `Form` (I'll put a `UIThread` attribute on a method in class `NotAWindowsForm` called `MyMethod`) and see what happens when I try to build, as shown in figure 8.4.

The use of `CompileTimeValidate` doesn't eliminate the need for communication and teamwork around the use of AOP; it will cause that communication to happen sooner, when it's easier and cheaper to fix. The last thing you want to do is have the discussion the day before deploying to production (or even afterwards).

Compile-time validation is one of the more interesting and powerful features available in all versions of PostSharp. In fact, it led many developers to write aspects that contained only compile-time validation. These validation aspects could be used to examine the code of the project and treat any mistakes it finds as compiler errors. They have no pointcut and contain no code that will run after the program starts. This was such a common technique that the PostSharp developers decided to make it a first-class feature called architectural constraints (compile-time validation still remains its own feature, though).

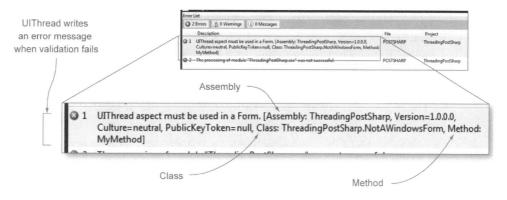

UIThread writes an error message when validation fails

Assembly

Class

Method

Figure 8.4 `UIThread` validation error message

8.2   *Architectural constraints*

In PostSharp, the architectural constraint feature helps you to write sanity checks for your project. Think of it as a unit test for your project's architecture.

> **PostSharp licensing**
>
> Before we get too far into this chapter, let's address some licensing and technical concerns. This feature (architectural constraints) isn't strictly related to AOP. It's also not available in the free Express edition of PostSharp. But it's still an interesting way to demonstrate the power of post-compiler IL manipulation, so that's why I've decided to leave it in the book. Compile-time validation from the previous section is available in all versions of PostSharp, including the free version.

In this section, I'll give you an overview of the types of constraints that PostSharp allows you to create, and I'll show you a real-world example of how architectural constraints might come in handy if you're using NHibernate.

8.2.1 *Enforcing architecture*

The main idea behind architectural constraints is that you can examine the code in your project in an automated way by writing other code. We all know that even though a project compiles, that doesn't mean it won't fail. If we can build in additional checks to run when compiling, then we'll know about problems sooner (continuing the theme of this chapter of failing faster).

PostSharp gives us the ability to write two different types of architectural constraints: scalar and referential. This separation is partially a semantic one and partially a technical one. Both types of constraints can enforce rules at compile time that the C# compiler itself doesn't give you, but referential constraints are checked on all assemblies processed by PostSharp that reference the code element.

SCALAR CONSTRAINTS

A *scalar constraint* is a simple constraint that's meant to affect a single piece of code written in isolation. This is most like using a `CompileTimeValidate` method in an aspect (except without the aspect part).

For instance, when you use NHibernate, all of the properties of entities must be marked as `virtual` (which was covered in an earlier chapter—NHibernate uses Castle DynamicProxy). I often forget to make properties virtual, and when I do, I don't find out until I run the program and use the entity, which might not happen right away.

I'd rather get an error message when compiling. We'll look at that in more detail in the next section, with a real-world example of an NHibernate `virtual` constraint.

Examples aren't limited to NHibernate. If you've used Windows Communication Foundation (WCF) before, then maybe you've created a `DataContract` class, added a new property, and forgotten to put the `DataMember` attribute on it. Or, have you created a `ServiceContract` interface and forgotten to put the `OperationContract` attribute on a new method that you've added to it? These are frustrating issues that the normal C# compiler won't detect but that a scalar constraint can detect early.

REFERENTIAL CONSTRAINTS

A *referential constraint* is a more wide-reaching form of architectural constraint. Referential constraints are meant to enforce architectural design across assemblies, references, and relationships. This form of constraint can be useful for architects, particularly if you're developing an API.

PostSharp comes with three out-of-the-box constraints that you can use for some specific scenarios: ComponentInternal, InternalImplements, and Internal. In table 8.1, I don't go into too much documentation-level detail, but in addition to being useful, they serve as good examples for when you can use referential constraints.

Table 8.1 PostSharp out-of-the-box architectural constraints

Constraint	What does it do?	Why would I use it?
ComponentInternal	Enforces that the code it's applied to can't be used outside of its own C# namespace	Allows you to simulate the behavior of C# internal at the namespace level for more organizational control
InternalImplements	Enforces that an interface can be implemented only by classes inside its own assembly	Allows you to expose an interface to API consumers, who might find it useful (in unit tests, for instance) without allowing them to write their own implementations
Internal	Enforces that a public item will remain public, but can't be used by another assembly	Allows you to keep an item of code as visible as a public item and still restrict its use as with C# internal

Of course, the door is wide open for you to write your own custom referential constraints. One annoyance I often come across is that sealed can be overused and that it limits extensibility. Sometimes there is a good reason to use sealed, but not often. It can make testing difficult, too. Therefore, in order to prevent sealed from sneaking into a project, I created a referential constraint called Unsealable.

To write this constraint, I created a class called Unsealable, which inherits from PostSharp's ReferentialConstraint base class (see the next listing). Inside this class, I override the ValidateCode method, which receives a target object as well as an Assembly. I scan the entire assembly to look for classes that are sealed and derived from the target class. I also need to use an attribute (MulticastAttributeUsage) to tell PostSharp to exactly which items this constraint should be applied.

Listing 8.7 Unsealable referential constraint

```
[Serializeable]
[MulticastAttributeUsage(MulticastTargets.Class)]
public class Unsealable : ReferentialConstraint {
```

```
public override void ValidateCode(object target,
                                  Assembly assembly) {
    var targetType = (Type)target;
    var sealedSubClasses = assembly.GetTypes()
            .Where(t => t.IsSealed)
            .Where(t => targetType.IsAssignableFrom(t))
            .ToList();
    sealedSubClasses.ForEach(c =>
        Message.Write(c, SeverityType.Error,
        "UNSEAL001",
        "Error on {0}: subclasses of {1} cannot be sealed.",
        c.FullName,
        targetType.FullName));
    }

}
```

The target type is the class(es) I mark as Unsealable. . .

Get all the types

. . . that are sealed

. . . and inherit from target type.

Go through the list

Write out an error for each

Output the offending class name and the unsealable class name

Any class that I mark Unsealable with that attribute means that any other class that inherits from it can't be sealed and will cause an error that prevents the build from completing.

A demonstration of this constraint is shown next. Write a class called MyUnsealableClass; put the Unsealable attribute on it; write another class that inherits from MyUnsealableClass called TryingToSeal; make TryingToSeal a sealed class; and try to compile.

Listing 8.8   Unsealable demonstration

```
[Unsealable]
public class MyUnsealableClass {
    protected string _value;

    public MyUnsealableClass() {
        _value = "I'm unsealable!";
    }

    public string GetValue() {
        return _value;
    }
}
public sealed class TryingToSeal : MyUnsealableClass {
    public TryingToSeal() {
        _value = "I'm sealed!";
    }
}
```

This is the class in which I don't want any derived classes to be sealed.

The C# compiler would normally have no problem with this

When I try to compile, because I was trying to make the class sealed, I'll get an error message in Visual Studio (as in figure 8.5).

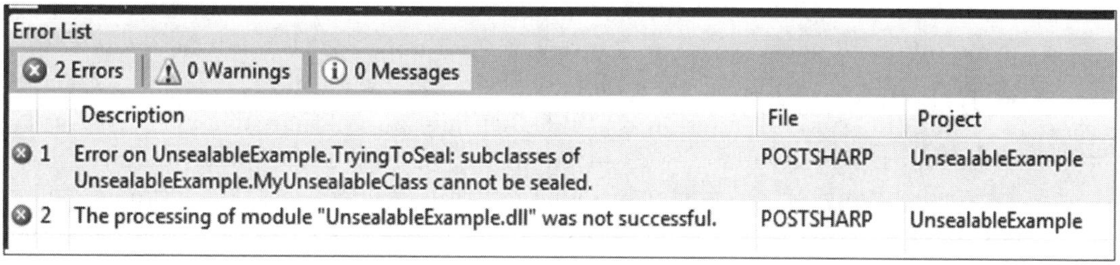

Figure 8.5   Error caused by trying to seal an `Unsealable` **class**

Again, these architectural constraints don't eliminate the need for communication on your team. As an architect, if you don't want developers sealing their classes, this makes the conversation about appropriate use of C#'s `sealed` keyword happen sooner. The faster the fail, the better.

And speaking of failing fast, let's look at creating a scalar constraint to deal with the `virtual` keyword in NHibernate entity classes.

8.2.2   *Real-world example: NHibernate and virtual*

Each property of an NHibernate entity must be `virtual`. But often when creating new properties and making changes to data access code, I forget to put `virtual` on properties.

Must be virtual?

You can have an NHibernate entity property that isn't virtual, if you disable lazy loading. But lazy loading is an important feature of NHibernate, so by default, NHibernate will assume that you want lazy loading unless you configure things otherwise in your .hbm mapping files.

The C# compiler doesn't care (nor should it) and lets me continue compiling and running the code. But over time it catches up to me, and when I try to build a session factory, I'll get the all-too-familiar `InvalidProxyTypeException` (as in figure 8.6).

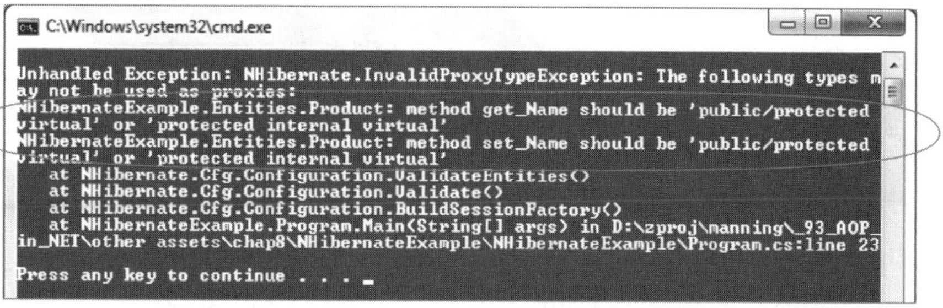

Figure 8.6   The `InvalidProxyTypeException` **of death**

Now I have to stop what I was doing—whatever feature I was trying out or website I was demo'ing—and add virtual to a property. And hope that I didn't forget any other properties. Because if I did, then I'll have to do it all over again.

I want to avoid this annoyance; I'd rather fail fast. Let's create a PostSharp scalar constraint so that I'm made aware of these mistakes right when I'm compiling.

Writing a ScalarConstraint is similar to writing a ReferentialConstraint. In figure 8.9, I create a class that inherits from the PostSharp ScalarConstraint base class. Override the ValidateCode method. In that method, get all of the properties from the targeted item(s) (in our case, the target(s) will be each of the entity class Types). For each property of the target type, check to make sure that it's virtual. If it's not, write a Message. Again, use a MulticastAttributeUsage attribute to indicate to which items this constraint can be applied.

Listing 8.9   NHibernate ScalarConstraint

```
[Serializable]
[MulticastAttributeUsage(MulticastTargets.Class)]            ⟵┐ This constraint can
                                                                be used on classes.
    public class NHEntityAttribute : ScalarConstraint
    {
        public override void ValidateCode(object target) {   ⟵┐ Note that we only
            var targetType = (Type)target;                      get a target—no
                                                                assembly this time.
            var properties = targetType
                .GetProperties(BindingFlags.Public | BindingFlags.Instance)
                .Where(p => !p.GetGetMethod().IsVirtual);  ⟵ ... that aren't virtual.
            foreach (var propertyInfo in properties) {
                Message.Write(propertyInfo,
                    SeverityType.Error,
                    "NHVIRTUAL001",
                    "Property {0} in Entity class {1} is not virtual",
                    propertyInfo.Name, targetType.FullName);
            }
        }
    }
```

Because the target is a class, the target will be a Type object. → (points to `var targetType = (Type)target;`)

Get all public instance properties . . . → (points to `.GetProperties(...)`)

Write the property name and class name in the error. → (points to the Message.Write block)

To use this constraint, you could put an [NHEntity] attribute on each entity class in your domain model. But what if you create a new entity and forget to put an attribute on it? Instead, I'm going to use another feature of PostSharp: attribute multicasting. This feature allows me to specify more than one class at a time.

We'll explore how multicasting works more in the next section, but here's a little preview. If I put all of my NHibernate model entities into the same namespace (for instance, NHibernateExample.Entities), I can multicast this NHEntity scalar constraint with one assembly directive:

```
[assembly: NHEntity(AttributeTargetTypes =
    "NHibernateExample.Entities.*")]
```

You could add this to the standard AssemblyInfo.cs file in your project, but it might be a better idea to put it into its own file, such as AspectInfo.cs. Now every single class that's in the NHibernateExample.Entities namespace will have the NHEntity scalar constraint applied to it at runtime. Create a Book class in the NHibernate-Example.Entities namespace, as shown in this listing, but don't make one of the members virtual.

> **Listing 8.10   An NHibernate entity with a nonvirtual property**

```
namespace NHibernateExample.Entities {
    public class Book {
        public virtual Guid Id { get; set; }
        public string Name { get; set; }              ⟵  Whoops, I forgot
        public virtual string Publisher { get; set; }      virtual. AGAIN.
        public virtual decimal Price { get; set; }
    }
}
```

When I try to compile, I'll get an informative error message like the one shown in figure 8.7 that gives me a chance to fix the code before executing the program.

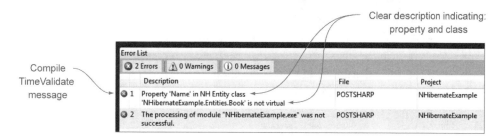

Figure 8.7   Result of NHEntity scalar constraint

Attribute multicasting isn't limited to architectural constraints and can be useful with normal PostSharp aspects to maximize reuse as it minimizes repetition. And unlike architectural constaints, attribute multicasting is a feature that's available in the free Express edition.

8.3   *Multicasting*

In chapter 1, I defined a pointcut as the "where" of an aspect. Think of a pointcut as a sentence describing where an aspect could be placed (I described it by adding extra arrows to a flowchart, shown in figure 8.8 and repeated from chapter 1).

They can be simple, as "before every method in a class", or they can be complex, as "before every method in a class in the namespace `MyServices` except for private methods and method `DeleteName`".

Up until now, the examples in this book have had simple and narrow pointcuts: a member or two, or possibly a whole class. So to keep it simple, I put a couple of attributes in the code and call it a day. In reality, many aspects will have much broader pointcuts, and using attributes on every single class or method can be another form of scattered boilerplate (albeit less intrusive and less tangled). If you have a lot of code on which to use aspects, or the code changes often, I recommened you don't keep using attributes over and over.

This is where the PostSharp attribute multicasting feature helps (some other AOP tools have a feature called dynamic pointcuts, which is similar). We can apply PostSharp aspects at three levels:

- At the individual method/location level (most of the examples in the rest of the book)
- At the class level (will be applied to all members in the class)
- At the assembly level (will be applied to multiple classes/members in the assembly)

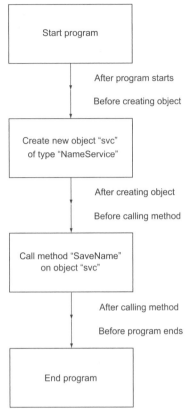

Figure 8.8 Pointcuts on a low-level flowchart

You've already seen plenty of examples of the first level. Putting attributes on individual properties or methods gives you maximum control and flexibility over where aspects are applied. For the next section, let's start at the class level and work our way up to the assembly level.

8.3.1 *At the class level*

If you write a `LocationInterceptionAspect` and apply it at the class level, by default it will intercept all of the locations in that class.

If you write a method aspect (`OnMethodBoundaryAspect` or `LocationInterception-Aspect`) and apply it at the class level, by default it will be applied to all of the methods in that class. This approach would be equivalent to using the attribute four times, once on each method (see figure 8.9).

Multicasting at the class level

```
[LogAspect]
public class MyClass {
   public MyClass() { }
   public void Method1() { }
   public void Method2() { Method3(); }
   private void Method3() { }
}
```

Equivalent usage without multicasting

```
public class MyClass {
    [LogAspect]
    public MyClass() { }
    [LogAspect]
    public void Method1() { }
    [LogAspect]
    public void Method2() { Method3(); }
    [LogAspect]
    private void Method3() { }
}
```

Figure 8.9   Multicasting at the class level

When using an aspect as an attribute, you'll have a lot of configuration options available for multicasting in the attribute's constructor. These are all covered in the Post-Sharp documentation, but here are a few notable examples:

- AttributeExclude—Selectively exclude methods from receiving a multicasted attribute
- AspectPriority—Define what order the aspects are applied (in C#, attribute order isn't inherently deterministic)
- AttributeTargetElements—Choose what type of targets the aspect is applied to

To demonstrate, let's write the LogAspect class, which will only report on which method(s) the aspect is being applied to. Once we have this aspect, we can change the configuration options and see what happens. I'll use a Console project to keep it simple:

```
[Serializable]
public class LogAspect : OnMethodBoundaryAspect {
    public override void OnEntry(MethodExecutionArgs args) {
        Console.WriteLine("Aspect was applied to {0}",
            args.Method.Name);
    }
}

class Program {
    static void Main(string[] args) {
        var m = new MyClass();
        m.Method1();
        m.Method2();
    }
}
```

Apply this aspect as shown in figure 8.10 and execute the program. You should see that the aspect is being applied to the constructor and Method1/2/3.

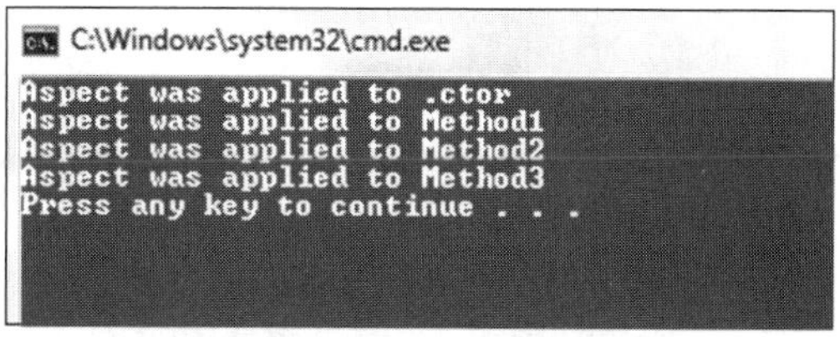

Figure 8.10   Aspect applied to the constructor and three methods

Let's suppose that I want the aspect to be applied to everything in the class, except for `Method3`. I'd use the `AttributeExclude` setting, as in this listing.

Listing 8.11 Excluding a member with `AttributeExclude`

```
[LogAspect]
public class MyClass {
    public MyClass() { }
    public void Method1() { }
    public void Method2() {
        Method3();
    }
    [LogAspect(AttributeExclude = true)]        Exclude this method
    private void Method3() { }                  from the multicast
}
```

Compile and run, and—as you can see in figure 8.11—Method3 has not had the aspect applied to it.

Using multiple aspects can be a common scenario. The order the aspects are applied can be important. You may want to use an aspect for caching and an aspect for security on the same class, for instance. In the

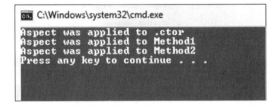

Figure 8.11   No aspect applied to `Method3`

next listing, I demonstrate how to create another aspect and use it on `MyClass`.

Listing 8.12 `AspectPriority` for ordering

```
[Serializable]
public class AnotherAspect : OnMethodBoundaryAspect {
    public override void OnEntry(MethodExecutionArgs args) {
        Console.WriteLine("Another Aspect was applied to {0}",
            args.Method.Name);
    }
}

[LogAspect(AspectPriority = 1)]                    LogAspect has
[AnotherAspect(AspectPriority = 2)]                highest priority
 public class MyClass {
    public MyClass() { }                           AnotherAspect has
    public void Method1() { }                      lower priority than
    public void Method2() {                        LogAspect
        Method3();
    }
    private void Method3() { }
}
```

When you use the C# compiler, you don't have any guarantee that the attributes will be applied in the order that you specify them (I mentioned this in chapter 2). To enforce the order, you can use the `AspectPriority` setting, as shown in figure 8.10.

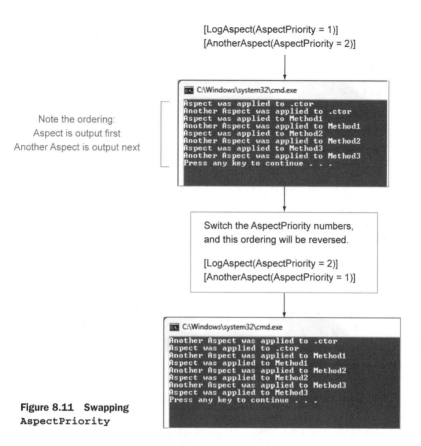

Figure 8.11 Swapping AspectPriority

LogAspect has a higher priority than AnotherAspect, so it will be applied first. If I swap those numbers, AnotherAspect would be applied first instead.

With AttributeTargetElements, you can indicate in more detail to which elements to multicast. This setting (see the following listing) uses the MulticastTargets enumeration, which includes choices such as Method, InstanceContructor, and StaticConstructor. If I choose InstanceConstructor, the aspect is applied only to constructor(s).

Listing 8.13 AttributeTargetElements to target only the instance constructor

```
[LogAspect(AttributeTargetElements =
    MulticastTargets.InstanceConstructor)]        ◁──┐ Target only the
public class MyClass {                                │ instance constructor
    public MyClass() { }
    public MyClass(int x) { }
    public void Method1() { }
    public void Method2() {
        Method3();
    }
    private void Method3() { }
}
```

With multicasting at the class level, you get a sensible default (apply to everything) and flexible configuration, down to the individual member if you need it. You can use these same configuration options when multicasting at the assembly level.

8.3.2   *At the assembly level*

Earlier in this chapter, you saw a sneak peek on how to use attribute multicasting at the assembly level. We set up PostSharp to apply the NHEntity scalar constraint attribute to every class in a certain namespace:

```
[assembly: NHEntity(AttributeTargetTypes =
    "NHibernateExample.Entities.*")]
```

Although that wasn't an aspect, because aspects and constraints are both attributes, they both can be multicasted.

Let's start with the basics. To apply an aspect to an entire assembly, use the syntax [assembly: MyAspect]. This syntax would apply the aspect to every valid target in the entire assembly.

To narrow it down, use the PostSharp configuration options in the attribute constructor. You have the same options available to you at the assembly level as at the class level. But at the assembly level, the AttributeTargetTypes setting becomes much more useful, because you can use it to apply an aspect to multiple classes and/or namespaces.

In the NHEntity example, I set the target to be a namespace with a wildcard (NHibernateExample.Entities*). In addition to that wildcard (the *), you can use regular expressions or exact names of classes.

You can use wildcards for any part of a namespace or type hierarchy. If I had multiple Entities namespaces (Sales.Entities and Support.Entities, for instance), I could also use a wildcard for the first part of the namespace:

```
[assembly: MyAspect(AttributeTargetTypes = "*.Entities.*")]
```

Using regular expressions can be helpful when you want to use conventions to determine where aspects are applied. If I establish a convention that every class that accesses the database is named with Repository at the end (InvoiceRepository, TerritoryRepository, and so on) and I want to apply transactional aspects to every repository class, I can use regex to do that:

```
[assembly: TransactionAspect(AttributeTargetTypes
    = "regex:.*Repository$")]
```

Don't abuse regular expressions—keep them simple. Use clear and sensible conventions, and be certain that expressions won't pick up any targets that they aren't supposed to. If a regular expression gets much more complex than this example, you may want to rethink your architecture/organization.

You can also multicast to individual members that have a certain name by using the AttributeTargetMembers configuration. The same rules apply: you can use an exact name, wildcards, or regular expressions.

If I want to apply a logging aspect to all methods that contain Delete in the name, I could do so with `AttributeTargetMembers`:

```
[assembly: LogAspect(AttributeTargetMembers="*Delete*")]
```

If your architecture contains a good structure with the use of namespaces and/or judicious use of conventional naming, you'll have total control over where aspects are applied through the use of these assembly-level aspects. With all the configuration options, you can also define some complex pointcuts if necessary.

The benefits to using assembly-level attributes to help define pointcuts are that you don't need to clutter your code by using attributes everywhere. Additionally, you have all of your pointcuts defined in one convenient file (such as AspectInfo.cs), which makes it easier to see where aspects are being used.

8.4 Summary

In this chapter, we dived into PostSharp's architectural functionality. Castle Dynamic-Proxy and other runtime AOP tools have some clear benefits that PostSharp (and comparable compile-time AOP frameworks) can't match. But when it comes to raw power, PostSharp is hard to match.

In the past three chapters, I've highlighted the key differences between the two approaches to AOP using the two leading tools in .NET. They're both amazing frameworks, and comparing and contrasting them helps illuminate the underlying concept of AOP and the significant trade-offs between approaches.

In this chapter, I briefly touched on the idea of multiple aspects being applied to the same code. We used an `AspectPriority` to determine the order of application. In the next chapter, we'll get back to looking at both tools, and I'll show how you'd do this with DynamicProxy, as well as a potentially more robust and less ambiguous way to do it with PostSharp.

Aspect composition: example and execution

As you continue to use AOP, you'll want to apply multiple aspects to the same pieces of code, and this chapter covers how to compose aspects together in a predictable way. If you're new to AOP, it's best to start small until you get the hang of it. Introduce a simple aspect (like logging) to your project and see how it goes. For me, it went well, so I wanted to start creating more aspects to handle more cross-cutting concerns. At some point, though, I'll run into overlap in the code that aspects get applied to. In chapter 2, we wrote aspects for multiple cross-cutting concerns, all on the same piece of code, repeated here in this listing.

Listing 9.1 Multiple aspects on the same method

```
[DefensiveProgramming]                    ⊲┐  Four aspects, all applied
[ExceptionAspect]                            to the same method
[LoggingAspect]
[TransactionManagement]
public void Accrue(RentalAgreement agreement) {
                                           ⊲── Omitted

}
```

I briefly mentioned that ordering was a concern, because the order that C# attributes are applied to code is non deterministic (that is, the order you put attributes on code isn't necessarily maintained by the C# compiler).

The goal for this chapter is to create two projects that demonstrate the composition of multiple, complex aspects that keep each individual component loosely coupled (and testable). First, we'll look at how Castle DynamicProxy works with an IoC tool like StructureMap to apply aspects in the appropriate order. Then we'll look at how PostSharp handles aspect composition by configuring aspect roles and aspect dependencies when using attributes. Finally, we'll put together a project with real-world aspects to demonstrate and compare the two approaches. This project will use either PostSharp or DynamicProxy, but we'll build it in such a way as to maximize reuse between the two.

9.1 Using multiple aspects

In some cases, it may not be critical which order the aspects get applied. Consider a method that has both a logging aspect and a background threading aspect applied to it. Table 9.1 shows that logging and threading aspects can be executed in either order without problem. In the second case, logging is performed on a separate thread, but it is still performed successfully.

Table 9.1 Ordering of aspects

Executed first	Executed second	Result
Logging aspect	Background threading aspect	First, the log is written to. Then, the threading aspect takes over and runs the method on a new thread.
Background threading aspect	Logging aspect	The method is first run on a new thread. Writing to the log takes place on the background thread, but still writes to log successfully.

In both cases, the code is still functional no matter what order is applied (assuming the logger can run on any thread). But the order often does matter. A classic example of this is two common cross-cutting concerns used together on a single method: security and caching. A caching aspect will return whatever value has already been cached, instead of executing the method. A security aspect will determine if the method's

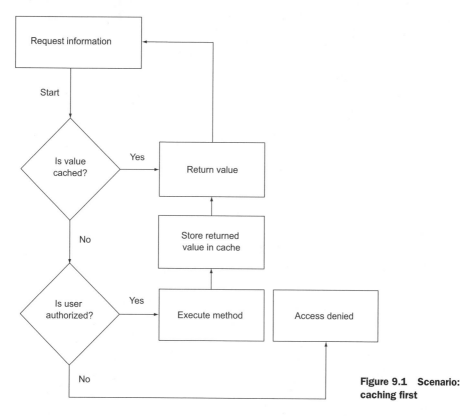

Figure 9.1 Scenario: caching first

results are allowed to be viewed by the current user (or perhaps perform security trimming on the results, filtering out what the current user is allowed to see). With security and caching together, it's possible for access to be allowed or denied, and it's possible for a cached value to be found (hit) or not found (miss). Let's examine the possible scenarios shown in figure 9.1, which assumes that caching is executed first.

You can trace a valid path through figure 9.1, where a (cached) result gets returned without authorization. This is obviously not desirable; authorization should always be performed first, as figure 9.2 illustrates.

In the second scenario (figure 9.2), there's no way for a value to be returned without authorization being performed. If a method needs to be secure and cached, then we need to be sure that those aspects run in the correct order. Let's start by looking at the basics of how to compose aspects with PostSharp (you've already seen a little bit of this with `AspectPriority` in the previous chapter). After that, we'll look at how to do it with Castle DynamicProxy, and then we'll be ready to look at the real-world example.

9.2   *Aspect roles with PostSharp*

In the previous chapter, one of the configuration options for PostSharp aspects was `AspectPriority`. `AspectPriority` is just a simple number that specifies the order in which aspect attributes are applied. An attribute with a priority of 1 is applied before

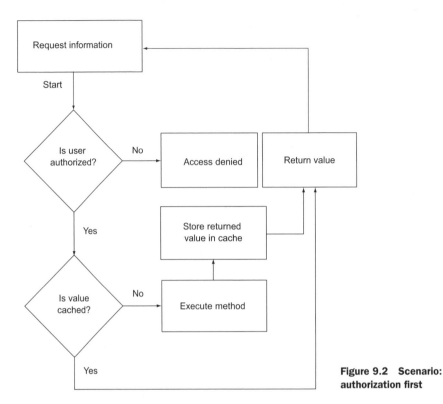

Figure 9.2   Scenario: authorization first

an aspect of priority 2, and so on. In this piece of code, `AnotherAspect` will be executed first, followed by `LogAspect`.

```
[LogAspect(AspectPriority = 2)]
[AnotherAspect(AspectPriority = 1)]
```

This is a feature that works with all licenses of PostSharp, including the free Express edition. In many cases, a simple aspect priority may be adequate. Using priority numbers may be tricky to refactor at times. If you're old enough to remember writing BASIC with line numbers, then you may have faced similar problems, and thus the reason that `AspectPriority` numbers, like BASIC line numbers, should be spread out (10,20,30 instead of 1,2,3).

If you have more complex dependencies, then a simple ordinal priority may not be enough. A better solution would be to define aspect roles and dependencies, instead of using plain numbers. This is a feature that is limited to the paid commercial license of PostSharp, but it is a feature that allows you to compose aspects in a more robust and clear way, so that the aspects work together how you expect them to.

In this section we're going to use PostSharp aspect roles to compose aspects, and make them execute in the order we want them to.

9.2.1 PostSharp aspect roles

When you create an aspect, you can specify what role that aspect provides by using the ProvideAspectRole attribute. If I create a caching aspect, then I could specify that it is an aspect that provides the caching role.

Listing 9.2 Specifying an aspect role

```
[Serializable]
[ProvideAspectRole(
    StandardRoles.Caching)]
public class CachingAttribute : OnMethodBoundaryAspect {

}
```

ProvideAspectRole attribute

A StandardRoles value for caching

The StandardRoles class provides a variety of common cross-cutting concern roles that you can use to configure ProvideAspectRole. Examples are Caching, Security, Threading, Validation, Tracing, and many more.

When I place a ProvideAspectRole attribute on my aspect, I'm giving PostSharp some information about what job this aspect does—what category it falls in. When PostSharp's post compiler runs, it will know that CachingAttribute is a caching aspect. I can even define multiple aspects that all have a role of StandardRoles.Caching.

Note that StandardRoles is not an enumeration. Each of those members (Caching, Security, and so on), are simply strings. Therefore, you can create your own custom aspect roles by simply using strings.

```
[Serializable]
[ProvideAspectRole("MyCustomRole")]
public class CachingAttribute : OnMethodBoundaryAspect {

}
```

The aspect role is "MyCustomRole"

Once your aspects have aspect roles, you can start to define in what order aspects get applied.

9.2.2 Role dependencies

Once you have defined roles for each aspect, you can define dependencies. However, the dependencies are not between aspects, but between roles. For example, we could say "apply security aspect(s) before applying caching aspect(s)." We wouldn't say "apply AuthorizationAttribute before CachingAttribute."

In PostSharp, this is done via another attribute you can put on your aspects called AspectRoleDependency. Here's an example of making sure that a security aspect always executes before caching aspects.

Listing 9.3 Specifying aspect role dependency

Position, in this case Auth runs before

```
[AspectRoleDependency(
    AspectDependencyAction.Order,
    AspectDependencyPosition.Before,
```

Type of action, in this case a strict ordering

```
        StandardRoles.Caching)]
public class AuthorizationAttribute : OnMethodBoundaryAspect
{

}
```

**The relative role,
in this case it's
Caching**

When PostSharp starts modifying code, it will now understand that the authorization aspect should be executed before any caching aspect code.

There are additional options for specifying the dependencies, and the PostSharp documentation contains more details on all the available options. One example is `AspectDependencyAction`. Instead of `Order`, you could specify `Require`: that this aspect requires another aspect of a certain role also be used. Let's suppose that I define an authorization aspect that requires an aspect in the `StandardRoles.Tracing` role.

Listing 9.4   An aspect that requires another role

```
public class MyClass {
    [Authorization]
    public void MyMethod() { }
}

[Serializable]
[AspectRoleDependency(
    AspectDependencyAction.Require,
    StandardRoles.Tracing)]
public class AuthorizationAttribute : OnMethodBoundaryAspect {

}
```

**Only authorization is
being used on MyMethod**

**Require that another
aspect role is present...**

**...that role
is Tracing.**

The authorization aspect is requiring that an aspect with the `Tracing` role is also being used on the same code. However, in my example, it's not: the authorization attribute is alone. Because of this, when I attempt to build the project, I'll receive a compile-time error message (figure 9.3), similar to the `CompileTimeValidate` functionality we saw in chapter 8.

This can be useful if you have two separate aspects that are required to work together on the same piece of code. Next, let's look at how aspects can be composed with Castle DynamicProxy.

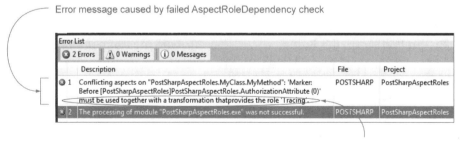

Error message caused by failed AspectRoleDependency check

Tracing aspect must be present, but isn't

Figure 9.3   Failed aspect dependency

9.3 Composing aspects with DynamicProxy

The work of actually applying DynamicProxy aspects is usually handled by an IoC container, as we've seen in previous chapters when I've used StructureMap (with a Proxy-Helper class), and so that's where the work of composing aspects is done.

Castle DynamicProxy is an interception tool that was designed for use with Castle Windsor (an IoC container). However, it exists independently of Windsor and is an excellent AOP framework with a rich set of features on its own. StructureMap is another popular IoC tool for .NET that has its own interception framework.

I prefer Castle DynamicProxy's aspects, but prefer StructureMap to Castle Windsor. I want to get the best of both worlds, so that's why I've used StructureMap and Castle DynamicProxy together in this book (see appendix A for details about other options that are available to you). This is why I wrote the ProxyHelper class in chapter 6 (repeated in the following listing), so that I can more easily use DynamicProxy with StructureMap (or any other IoC container that has functionality similar to Structure-Map's EnrichWithAll).

> **Listing 9.5   ProxyHelper from chapter 6**

```
public class ProxyHelper {
    readonly ProxyGenerator _proxyGenerator;

    public ProxyHelper() {
        _proxyGenerator = new ProxyGenerator();
    }

    public object Proxify<T, K>(object obj) where K: IInterceptor {
        var interceptor = (IInterceptor) ObjectFactory.GetInstance<K>();
        var result = _proxyGenerator
            .CreateInterfaceProxyWithTargetInterface(
            typeof (T), obj, interceptor);
        return result;
    }
}
```

Your preference and familiarity will help you determine which tools to use. For this section, I will continue to use StructureMap as my IoC container, and Castle Dynamic-icProxy as my interception tool.

To accomplish ordering with Castle DynamicProxy and StructureMap, just remember that the classes being generated are being used as decorators: the decorator that is closest to the real object is going to be executed last.

9.3.1 Ordering aspects

I'll start by writing some demonstration aspects and a class that they are to intercept. I plan to have Aspect1 executed first in order, followed by Aspect2, and on to the main implementation in MyClass.

Listing 9.6 A demo class and two demo aspects

```
public interface IMyClass {
    void MyMethod();
}

public class MyClass : IMyClass {
    public void MyMethod() {
        Console.WriteLine("My Method");
    }
}

public class Aspect1 : IInterceptor {
    public void Intercept(IInvocation invocation) {
        Console.WriteLine("Aspect 1");
        invocation.Proceed();
    }
}

public class Aspect2 : IInterceptor {
    public void Intercept(IInvocation invocation) {
        Console.WriteLine("Aspect 2");
        invocation.Proceed();
    }
}
```

> This is the class/interface that the aspects will be applied to.

> This aspect should execute first.

> This aspect should execute second.

To use a single Castle DynamicProxy aspect with StructureMap, I used StructureMap's EnrichAllWith API, as well as `ProxyHelper` (in listing 9.7).

To use multiple aspects, you can use a series of calls to the `ProxyHelper` object inside of a single EnrichAllWith. The `Proxify` method returns an object that's been decorated with a dynamically generated class. You can pass this object to `Proxify` again, to wrap it in another decorator, and so on, as many times as you want.

Because you're continually wrapping, use the aspect you want applied first in the outermost `Proxify` call. The innermost aspect will be called last, followed by the original object, of course.

Listing 9.7 Use of multiple aspects on the same code in StructureMap

```
static void Main(string[] args)
{
    ObjectFactory.Initialize(x => {
        x.Scan(scan => {
                    scan.TheCallingAssembly();
                    scan.WithDefaultConventions();
                });
        var proxyHelper = new ProxyHelper();
        x.For<IMyClass>().EnrichAllWith(r =>
            proxyHelper.Proxify<IMyClass, Aspect1>(
            proxyHelper.Proxify<IMyClass, Aspect2>(r))
        );
    });

    var obj = ObjectFactory.GetInstance<IMyClass>();
    obj.MyMethod();
}
```

> Apply Aspect1 first

> This is the same ProxyHelper as before.

> Apply Aspect2 second

> Ask StructureMap for an implementation

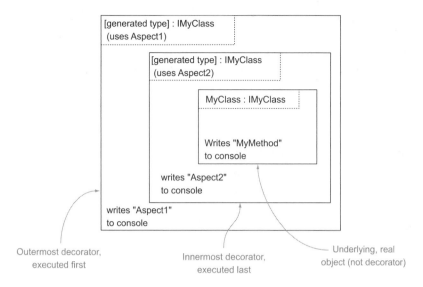

Figure 9.4　A diagram of what gets returned by StructureMap

We start by telling StructureMap to scan the assembly and initialize with the default conventions. That is, if we ask StructureMap for an implementation of `IMyClass`, it will give us an instance of `MyClass`. I'm also telling StructureMap to enrich (decorate) the implementation of `IMyClass` with a dynamic proxy built with the `Aspect2` aspect. That aspect, in turn, is being decorated by a dynamic proxy built with the `Aspect1` aspect. The end result is a decorator that wraps a decorator that wraps the real object, as shown in figure 9.4.

Each of these objects has the same interface (`IMyClass`). The main code calls the outermost decorator's `MyMethod`, which turns around and executes the innermost decorator's `MyMethod`, which finally calls the underlying object's `MyMethod`.

To change the order of the aspects, just change the order in the decoration chain. I could swap `Aspect1` and `Aspect2`, for instance, as in figure 9.5.

To add another aspect, just add another in that decoration chain. If I wanted to add `Aspect3`, and have it be applied first, I would just add another line inside the `EnrichAllWith` (and another closing parenthesis).

```
x.For<IMyClass>().EnrichAllWith(r =>
    proxyHelper.Proxify<IMyClass, Aspect3>(
    proxyHelper.Proxify<IMyClass, Aspect1>(
    proxyHelper.Proxify<IMyClass, Aspect2>(r))
));
```

```
x.For<IMyClass>().EnrichAllWith(r =>           x.For<IMyClass>().EnrichAllWith(r =>
    proxyHelper.Proxify<IMyClass, Aspect1>(        proxyHelper.Proxify<IMyClass, Aspect2>(
    proxyHelper.Proxify<IMyClass, Aspect2>(r))     proxyHelper.Proxify<IMyClass, Aspect1>(r))
);                                             );
```

Figure 9.5　Switching the order of Aspect1 and Aspect2

Keep in mind that this decoration is being applied to only one service (IMyClass). In the last chapter, I talked about how to use PostSharp to multicast attributes. When using a tool like Castle DynamicProxy, you again have to rely on the IoC container to provide for reuse (to use the same aspect on multiple services). I like StructureMap for this because of its flexibility with using conventions. These conventions allow us to multicast the DynamicProxy aspects, so we don't have to specify every individual class to which the aspects should be applied.

9.3.2 *Reducing repetition with custom conventions*

PostSharp's attribute multicasting gave us the ability to specify where to put aspects based on the class name, the namespace, and individual member names.

I could just tell my IoC tool every place I want to use an aspect by using For/Use over and over.

```
ObjectFactory.Initialize(x => {
    x.Scan(scan => {
        scan.TheCallingAssembly();
        scan.WithDefaultConventions();
    });
    var proxyHelper = new ProxyHelper();
    x.For<IMyClassRepository>().EnrichAllWith(
        proxyHelper.Proxify<IMyClassRepository, Aspect1>);
    x.For<IAnotherRepository>().EnrichAllWith(
        proxyHelper.Proxify<IAnotherRepository, Aspect1>);
});
```

Apply Aspect1 to IMyClass-Repository services.

ProxyHelper to help DynamicProxy and StructureMap work together.

...and so on, for every repository service.

Apply Aspect1 to IAnotherRepository services

This would be tedious work, but fortunately we don't have to do it that way. One solution is to define your own convention. StructureMap has a very nice API, allowing you to write any convention you wish. Use of these conventions isn't limited just to AOP, but they happen to be very useful for applying aspects to groups of services. We could, for example, write conventions that examine the class name or namespace.

CLASS NAME CONVENTION

In StructureMap, create a class that implements the IRegistrationConvention interface. I'll create one called RepositoryAspectConvention. This convention will tell StructureMap that any service ending with Repository in its name will also be enriched with two DynamicProxy aspects: Aspect1 and Aspect2.

Listing 9.8   A StructureMap name-based convention for applying aspects

```
public class RepositoryAspectConvention : IRegistrationConvention {

    public void Process(Type type, Registry registry) {

        if (!type.IsInterface)
```

Only match the service interface, so the aspects are only applied once

This is the
Repository
convention
logic

```
                             return;

              var proxyHelper = ObjectFactory.GetInstance<ProxyHelper>();

              if (type.Name.EndsWith("Repository"))
                  registry.For(type)

                      .EnrichWith(o => proxyHelper.Proxify<Aspect2>(type, o))

              .EnrichWith(o => proxyHelper.Proxify<Aspect1>(type, o));

          }

      }
```

This is the Repository convention logic

Aspect2 is the innermost aspect, apply it first

Apply Aspect1 last

You may have noticed that the Proxify signature is different. This is because Type is passed in to Process as a regular parameter and not a generic type parameter, so I had to write an overloaded Proxify method in the ProxyHelper class, but as you can see in this listing it's doing the same thing as before.

Listing 9.9 Added overloaded `Proxify` to `ProxyHelper`

```
public class ProxyHelper {
    readonly ProxyGenerator _proxyGenerator;

    public ProxyHelper() {
        _proxyGenerator = new ProxyGenerator();
    }

    public object Proxify<T, K>(object obj) where K : IInterceptor {
        return Proxify<K>(typeof (T), obj);
    }

    public object Proxify<K>(Type t,
                        object obj) where K : IInterceptor {
        var interceptor = (IInterceptor)ObjectFactory.GetInstance<K>();
        var result =
            _proxyGenerator.CreateInterfaceProxyWithTargetInterface(
            t, obj, interceptor);
        return result;
    }
}
```

Moved the code into the overload

K generic type parameter replaced with Type t parameter

To use the convention, specify it in the assembly scanner portion of Object-Factory.Initialize, as in shown here.

Listing 9.10 Adding a convention to the assembly scanner

```
ObjectFactory.Initialize(x => {
    var proxyHelper = new ProxyHelper();
    x.For<ProxyHelper>().Singleton().Use(proxyHelper);
    x.Scan(scan => {
        scan.TheCallingAssembly();
```

```
        scan.WithDefaultConventions();
        scan.Convention<RepositoryAspectConvention>();
    });
});
```

Convention added to assembly scanner

From this point on, any service with a name that ends with Repository will have Aspect1 and Aspect2 applied to it. Since the class name is a string, you can also use regular expressions just as in PostSharp multicasting, or any other convention you wish to define.

NAMESPACE CONVENTION

For instance, I might want to apply the aspects to a namespace, instead of going by class name.

I could simply change the `Process` method inside of `RepositoryAspectConvention` to look at the namespace, as in this listing.

Listing 9.11   Using a namespace-based convention

```
public void Process(Type type, Registry registry) {
    if (!type.IsInterface)
        return;

    var proxyHelper = ObjectFactory.GetInstance<ProxyHelper>();
    if (type.Namespace == "ConventionDynamicProxyExample.Repositories")
        registry.For(type)
                .EnrichWith(o => proxyHelper.Proxify<Aspect2>(type, o))
                .EnrichWith(o => proxyHelper.Proxify<Aspect1>(type, o));
}
```

Check the namespace instead of class name

Now, any classes in the `ConventionDynamicProxyExample.Repositories` namespace will have Aspect1 and Aspect2 applied to it.

And remember, to change the order the aspects are applied, just change the order of the `EnrichWith` statements.

Now we know how to order aspects with Castle DynamicProxy and with PostSharp. We're prepared to move on to a real-world authorization and caching example.

9.4   *Real-world example: caching and authorization*

For the last real-world example of this book, we're going to focus on two aspects: a caching aspect and an authorization aspect, and we'll be using and applying material from the entire book.

The aspect composition of an authorization aspect and a caching aspect is an example where the ordering is very important. Recall the diagrams earlier in the chapter where I showed that authorization must be executed before caching to prevent an unauthorized user from seeing data that they shouldn't.

In this section, I'll create a program that calls a single service and outputs the results to Console. The service will return the budget for a given account number.

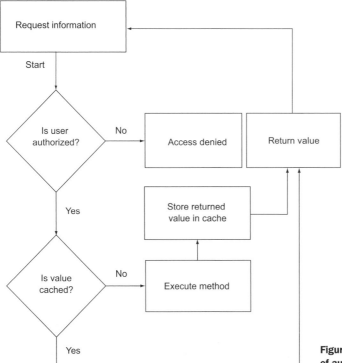

Figure 9.6 The correct ordering of authorization and caching.

Only users in a manager role are allowed to perform this service operation. Since there could be many services and service operations, we'll create a security aspect to lock down access.

The budget figures could come from multiple systems, including 3rd party legacy systems, and getting results from those systems can be quite slow. Caching the operation reduces the load on the legacy machine, improves the speed of the overall user experience, and since budgets don't change very often, caching the results is perfectly acceptable. (Our implementation will be hardcoded and fast, but it's always important to analyze the problem to see if caching is appropriate or not). To handle the caching, we'll use a caching aspect very similar to the one we wrote in chapter 4.

We'll start by building out all of the project that we can without using a specific AOP tool. Then, I'll create the PostSharp implementation, followed by the Castle DynamicProxy implementation. Everything will be reusable between the two examples, save for the aspects themselves.

9.4.1 *Application architecture*

The application will consist of four major areas of functionality: the configuration of dependencies (with IoC), the services, the UI of the program, and the aspects. Figure 9.6 shows the ordering of authorization and caching. Figure 9.7 shows a high-level view of the architecture.

Start by creating a new Console project in Visual Studio.

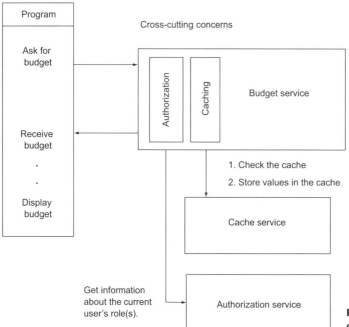

Figure 9.7 A high-level view of the architecture

I want to make the architecture as loosely coupled as possible, no matter which AOP tool is being used. Every class will be built to an interface when appropriate to help make testing in isolation easier. The cross-cutting concern objects as well as the services will be configured and supplied by an IoC tool. I'll again use StructureMap, so let's start by configuring the dependencies.

DEPENDENCY CONFIGURATION

Start by adding StructureMap to the project.

I will stick to the default convention (for example, MyService corresponds to IMy-Service). Since I'm using a Console app, I'll put the StructureMap initialization code right at the start of the Program's Main method as shown here.

Listing 9.12 Configure StructureMap with default conventions

```
static void Main(string[] args) {
    ObjectFactory.Initialize(x => {
        x.Scan(scan => {                                    ⟵  Very minimal initialization
            scan.TheCallingAssembly();                          of the IoC container
            scan.WithDefaultConventions();
        });
    });
```

Note that we're not configuring any aspects here until we switch to Castle Dynamic-Proxy.

SERVICES

There will be three services. These services are very simplified demonstration services, that would in reality contain much more complex code and more methods, that would interact with your database or other specific technologies, depending on the requirements of your software.

Let's start with the budget service (in the following listing), since that is the main functionality of this project. It will have one method to return the budget amount, and I'll make sure to program to an interface.

Listing 9.13 Budget service, interface, and implementation

```
public interface IBudgetService {
    decimal GetBudgetForAccount(string accountNumber);      ◁──── A single method in
}                                                                  this service
public class BudgetService : IBudgetService {
    public decimal GetBudgetForAccount(string accountNumber) {
        var rand = new Random();
        return rand.Next(1000, 5000);       ◁──── Returns a random budget, in
    }                                             reality would query a database
}
```

Since we'll be using caching, let's next define a caching service (listing 9.14). In a real application, this would likely be a wrapper of cache functionality such as ASP.NET's Cache, Windows Azure cache, or some other caching technology. Since this example is demonstrating AOP and not a specific caching technology, I'll make it a static memory cache just as we did in chapter 4. It will only be a wrapper for a static `Dictionary` object, and once again I'll program to an interface.

Listing 9.14 A static caching service

```
public interface ICacheService {
    object this[string cacheKey] { get; set; }       ◁──── String-based indexer to
    bool ContainsKey(string cacheKey);                      get/set cache values
}
                                                     ◁──── Boolean to
                                                           determine if a
                                                           key has been
                                                           cached or not
public class CacheService : ICacheService {
    static readonly Dictionary<string, object> _cache
        = new Dictionary<string, object>();          ◁──── An in-memory
                                                            static Dictionary
    public object this[string cacheKey] {                  acts as a cache
        get { return _cache[cacheKey]; }
        set { _cache[cacheKey] = value; }
    }

    public bool ContainsKey(string cacheKey) {
        return _cache.ContainsKey(cacheKey);
    }
}
```

Finally, since we need role-based authorization, I'll create a `UserRepository` service. A real service would have a lot more functionality, but in our example you only need to get the current user's roles. A real implementation would likely query a database and/ or interact with an authentication framework like ASP.NET Forms Authentication (which we explored back in chapter 1). For this example in the next listing, I'll hard-code it to return `"Manager"`. Later on, you can change this to something else to see what happens when the user is not authorized.

Listing 9.15   User repository

```
public interface IUserRepository {
    List<string> GetRolesForCurrentUser();
}

public class UserRepository : IUserRepository {
    public List<string> GetRolesForCurrentUser() {          With this service, all
        return new List<string> {"Manager"};               users are managers
    }
}
```

I put all of these services into a Services folder in the project (and the `AuthAndCaching.Services` namespace).

CONSOLE UI

The Console UI for this example will be very simple. It will attempt to retrieve the budget for an arbitrary account and output it to the Console. We'll do it twice, since caching is a part of this example.

Listing 9.16   The main UI of the program

```
static void Main(string[] args) {            This is where the IoC
                                             Initialization goes

    var accountNumber = "00112";
    var budgetService = ObjectFactory.GetInstance<IBudgetService>();   ◁—This returns an
                                                                          instance of
    var budget = budgetService.GetBudgetForAccount(accountNumber);      BudgetService
    Console.WriteLine("The budget for account {0} is {1:C}",
        accountNumber, budget);

    var budgetAgain = budgetService.GetBudgetForAccount(accountNumber);  ◁—
    Console.WriteLine("The budget for account {0} is {1:C}",
        accountNumber, budgetAgain);            If caching is working, I would expect the same
                                                value to be returned, even though a random
}                                               number generator is used in BudgetService
```

I'll also add in a `try`/`catch` just in case authorization fails, as shown here.

Listing 9.17   The main UI prepared for exception

```
static void Main(string[] args) {
                                     ◁— Initialization code here

    var accountNumber = "00112";
    var budgetService = ObjectFactory.GetInstance<IBudgetService>();
```

Wrapping budget service usage in try

```
try {
    var budget = budgetService.GetBudgetForAccount(accountNumber);
    Console.WriteLine("The budget for account {0} is {1:C}",
        accountNumber, budget);


    var budgetAgain = budgetService
                        .GetBudgetForAccount(accountNumber);
    Console.WriteLine("The budget for account {0} is {1:C}",
        accountNumber, budgetAgain);
}
catch (Exception ex) {
    Console.WriteLine("Unable to retrive budget. Error: {0}",
        ex.Message);
}
}
```

catch will handle unauthorized access attempts

Now, if authorization is working and an unauthorized user tries to run this program, then they will only see an exception message (an Access Denied error, probably).

CONCERNS

Recall in chapter 6 when I showed you how to write thin aspects (like in figure 9.7). The aspect delegates as much logic as it can to another object (let's call it a concern object, because it handles the cross-cutting concern).

I'm going to do that for this real-world example for two reasons:

1 It makes it possible for us to write a project that is loosely coupled to the AOP framework. Not only does this give us the benefit of easier long-term maintainence, but it also allows us to more easily write unit tests.

2 Second, it makes it possible for me to switch from using PostSharp (in section 9.4.2) to using Castle DynamicProxy (in section 9.4.3) with minimal changes.

The first concern we'll write is for caching. This concern will be built to an interface, and it will use the caching service from listing 9.14. I want two methods on this concern's interface: one for OnEntry and OnSuccess.

NOTE I've chosen to use the same naming convention that PostSharp uses, but you can name these whatever you want. See listing 9.18.

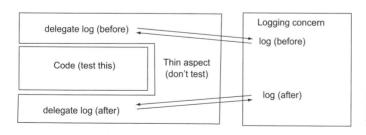

Figure 9.8 The thin logging aspect, repeated from chapter 6

Listing 9.18 Caching concern interface and constructor

```
public interface ICachingConcern {
    void OnEntry(IMethodContextAdapter methodContext);
    void OnSuccess(IMethodContextAdapter methodContext);
}

public class CachingConcern : ICachingConcern {
    readonly ICacheService _cache;

    public CachingConcern(ICacheService cache) {
        _cache = cache;
    }
}
```

Executed before the method

Executed after the method succeeds

An injected cache service object

OnEntry and OnSuccess implementations here

The OnEntry method in listing 9.19 will be called before the method is executed. It will also be responsible for building the cache key, checking the cache, setting the return value (if necessary), and determining if the method should be aborted (not executed) or not. I'll use the simple "ToString" cache key building strategy here, which you could replace with other strategies as discussed in chapter 4.

Listing 9.19 OnEntry of the caching concern

```
public void OnEntry(IMethodContextAdapter methodContext) {
    var cacheKey = BuildCacheKey(methodContext);
    if (!_cache.ContainsKey(cacheKey)) {
        Console.WriteLine("[Cache] MISS for {0}", cacheKey);
        methodContext.Tag = cacheKey;
        return;
    }
    Console.WriteLine("[Cache] HIT for {0}", cacheKey);
    methodContext.ReturnValue = _cache[cacheKey];
    methodContext.AbortMethod();
}

string BuildCacheKey(IMethodContextAdapter methodContext) {
    var key = methodContext.MethodName;
    foreach (var argument in methodContext.Arguments)
        key += "_" + argument.ToString();
    return key;
}
```

Put the key in a tag so it can be used in OnSuccess later

Don't allow the method to be called

Since the value is cached, return it

This is the simple ToString key building method

Note that at this point, we still have not added any AOP libraries to the project. We have yet to take any dependencies.

You may have also noticed the IMethodContextAdapter interface, the details of which are in the following listing. This interface is responsible for giving us information about the method, its arguments, and so on.

Listing 9.20 Adapter interface to get method context

```
public interface IMethodContextAdapter {
    object Tag { get; set; }
```

```
    object ReturnValue { get; set; }
    string MethodName { get; }
    object[] Arguments { get; }
    void AbortMethod();
}
```

You'll see in the next sections that we'll use the adapter pattern to allow our concern objects to stay independent of a specific framework, as well as keep the concern objects easily testable. These adapters will wrap the APIs that we've seen in previous chapters (for example, `MethodExecutionArgs` and `IInvocation`) and make them conform to the `IMethodContextAdapter` interface.

The `OnSuccess` method (shown in the following listing) will be called after the method has been executed. This will only occur if the method has not been aborted, so this is where the return value gets cached.

Listing 9.21 OnSuccess of the caching concern

```
public void OnSuccess(IMethodContextAdapter methodContext) {        Pull the key
                                                                     back out of the
    var cacheKey = (string)methodContext.Tag;                  ◁──   Tag property

    Console.WriteLine("[Cache] storing value for {0}", cacheKey);

    _cache[cacheKey] = methodContext.ReturnValue;  ◁──  Store the return value
                                                        with the cache service
  }
```

The authorization concern (the second concern) will be constructed similarly. It will have a dependency on `IUserRepository`, and it will need an `OnEntry` method in the interface as shown here.

Listing 9.22 Authorization concern interface and constructor

```
public interface IAuthorizationConcern {                            ◁──  Will be
    void OnEntry(IMethodContextAdapter methodContext, string role);       executed
}                                                                         before the
                                                                          method
public class AuthorizationConcern : IAuthorizationConcern {
    readonly IUserRepository _user;                       ◁──  User repository
                                                               object injected
    public AuthorizationConcern(IUserRepository user) {        from the
        _user = user;                                          constructor
    }

                      ◁───  The OnEntry implemenation goes here

}
```

The `OnEntry` code will run before the method is executed. It will use the service to determine if the current user is allowed to access the method. If they are, then the concern will return without doing anything else. If they aren't, then the concern will keep the method from executing, and perform whatever action should occur when unauthorized access is attempted. In my example in the next listing, I'm going to throw an exception with an "Access denied" exception, but you could instead return a 0, null, empty string, and so on, if appropriate.

Listing 9.23 `OnEntry` of the authorization concern

```
public void OnEntry(IMethodContextAdapter methodContext, string role) {
    Console.WriteLine("[Auth] Checking if user is in {0} role", role);
    if (UserIsInRole(role)) {
        Console.WriteLine("[Auth] User IS authorized");        User is authorized,
        return;                                                return to normal
    }                                                          execution
    Console.WriteLine("[Auth] User is NOT authorized");
    UnauthorizedAccess();                                      User is not authorized,
}                                                              take action

bool UserIsInRole(string role) {
    var roles = _user.GetRolesForCurrentUser();               Use service to get
    return roles.Contains(role);                              current user's roles
}

void UnauthorizedAccess() {
    throw new UnauthorizedAccessException("Access denied.");
}                                                     Throw an exception
                                                      (or take other action)
```

Though the pattern is similar, note that the `AuthorizationConcern` has the `role` parameter to deal with. This role must be passed in from the aspect, in addition to the method context object.

Now we have everything we need in place except for the aspects themselves. Let's start with PostSharp.

9.4.2 *PostSharp*

I'll create a caching aspect called `CachedAttribute`. It will inherit from PostSharp's `OnMethodBoundaryAspect` base class.

In keeping with the thin aspect strategy, this aspect (next listing) will mostly be delegating its work to an `ICachingConcern` object. I'll make that object a private member of the aspect, and I'll populate it in the `RuntimeInitialize` method.

Listing 9.24 PostSharp caching aspect

```
[Serializable]
public class CachedAttribute : OnMethodBoundaryAspect {
    [NonSerialized]                              Since the caching concern won't be
    ICachingConcern _cacheConcern;               referenced until runtime, there's no
                                                 sense serializing it at compile time.

    public override void RuntimeInitialize(MethodBase method) {
        _cacheConcern = ObjectFactory.GetInstance<ICachingConcern>();
    }
```

Get the concern when the aspect is initialized at runtime

```
public override void OnEntry(MethodExecutionArgs args) {
    IMethodContextAdapter methodContext
        = new PsharpMethodContextAdapter(args);
    _cacheConcern.OnEntry(methodContext);
}

public override void OnSuccess(MethodExecutionArgs args) {
    IMethodContextAdapter methodContext
        = new PsharpMethodContextAdapter(args);
    _cacheConcern.OnSuccess(methodContext);
}
}
```

Use a PostSharp implementation of the adapter

Delegate everything in OnEntry to the caching concern

Delegate everything in OnSucess to the caching concern

In listing 9.25 I'm using an implementation of IMethodContextAdapter for PostSharp called PsharpMethodContextAdapter. This is a class that wraps the MethodExecution-Args functionality that we need (note that it does not wrap everything, so you could consider this class a façade as well as an adapter).

Listing 9.25   PostSharp method context adapter

```
public class PsharpMethodContextAdapter : IMethodContextAdapter {
    readonly MethodExecutionArgs _args;

    public PsharpMethodContextAdapter(MethodExecutionArgs args) {
        _args = args;
    }

    public string MethodName { get { return _args.Method.Name; } }

    public object Tag {
        get { return _args.MethodExecutionTag; }
        set { _args.MethodExecutionTag = value; }
    }

    public object[] Arguments {
        get { return _args.Arguments.ToArray(); }
    }

    public object ReturnValue {
        get { return _args.ReturnValue; }
        set { _args.ReturnValue = value; }
    }

    public void AbortMethod() {
        _args.FlowBehavior = FlowBehavior.Return;
    }
}
```

This adapter is wrapping a PostSharp API object

Wrapping the method name

Wrapping the execution tag

Wrapping the arguments

Wrapping the return value property

Wrapping the flow behavior

Other than create an adapter object, the only other thing that this aspect does is delegate to the concern's `OnEntry` and `OnSuccess` methods. This is what a thin aspect should look like: just the bare minimum.

The aspect is now complete, so put an attribute on `GetBudgetForAccount` to tell PostSharp that this method should be cached.

```
[Cached]
public decimal GetBudgetForAccount(string accountNumber) {
    var rand = new Random();
    return rand.Next(1000, 5000);
}
```

If you run the program now, you should see that the cache aspect is being executed. There should be a cache miss, followed by a cache hit, just like figure 9.8.

Cache miss: the cache
    is empty at first.

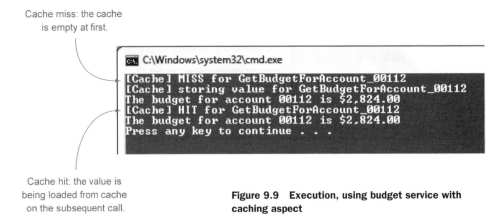

Cache hit: the value is
being loaded from cache
on the subsequent call.

Figure 9.9   Execution, using budget service with caching aspect

Right now, there is no checking to see if the user is in a role that's authorized to view the budget data. So the next step is to write an authorization aspect. I'll create an `AuthorizedAttribute` class, also inheriting from `OnMethodBoundaryAspect`. This aspect will have an explicit constructor that allows us to specify which role is allowed to access a method. That role will be stored as a private member. This aspect (in the following listing) will also be a thin aspect, so it will lean on an `IAuthorizationConcern` object (initialized at runtime) for most of its functionality.

> **Listing 9.26   PostSharp authorization aspect**

```
[Serializable]
public class AuthorizedAttribute : OnMethodBoundaryAspect {
    [NonSerialized]                                          Storing role as
    IAuthorizationConcern _authConcern;                      a member of
    readonly string _role;                                   the aspect

    public AuthorizedAttribute(string role) {
        _role = role;
    }
```

```
public override void RuntimeInitialize(MethodBase method) {
    _authConcern =
        ObjectFactory.GetInstance<IAuthorizationConcern>();
}
```
Again, getting the concern from a service locator

```
public override void OnEntry(MethodExecutionArgs args) {
    var methodContext = new PsharpMethodContextAdapter(args);
    _authConcern.OnEntry(methodContext, _role);
  }
}
```
Again, delegating everything to the concern, with the method context adapter

As before, `OnEntry` is creating an adapter instance, and delegating everything else to the concern.

Put an attribute on `GetBudgetForAccount` and specify the `"Manager"` role with an attribute constructor.

```
[Cached]
[Authorized("Manager")]
public decimal GetBudgetForAccount(string accountNumber) {
    var rand = new Random();
    return rand.Next(1000, 5000);
}
```

Execute the program. Since we didn't specify any aspect roles or aspect priority, one possible outcome could be figure 9.10.

> **NOTE** This is a *possible* outcome: the order of C# attributes is not guaranteed by the compiler one way or the other.

Check cache; not found.

Check authorization; found.

Check cache; found.

NOT checking authorization ?

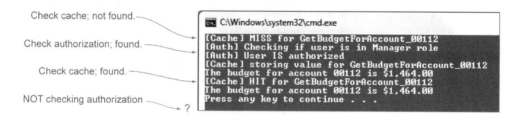

```
C:\Windows\system32\cmd.exe
[Cache] MISS for GetBudgetForAccount_00112
[Auth] Checking if user is in Manager role
[Auth] User IS authorized
[Cache] storing value for GetBudgetForAccount_00112
The budget for account 00112 is $1,464.00
[Cache] HIT for GetBudgetForAccount_00112
The budget for account 00112 is $1,464.00
Press any key to continue . . .
```

Figure 9.10 Execution again, with caching and authorization aspects, undefined composition

There's a problem here. On the second attempt, *there was no authorization being performed.* Caching is running first, and results are being returned without even checking authorization. To compose these aspects properly, we have to define an aspect role for `CachedAttribute` and define an `AspectRoleDependency` for `AuthorizedAttribute`, as in this listing.

Listing 9.27 Aspect composition of caching and authorization

```
[Serializable]
[AspectRoleDependency(                          This aspect must be
    AspectDependencyAction.Order,               applied in order, before
    AspectDependencyPosition.Before,            caching aspects.
    StandardRoles.Caching)]
public class AuthorizedAttribute : OnMethodBoundaryAspect {
                                                     <—— (omitted)

}
[Serializable]                                   This aspect is a
[ProvideAspectRole(StandardRoles.Caching)]       caching aspect.
public class CachedAttribute : OnMethodBoundaryAspect {
                                                     <—— (omitted)

}
```

And now when you execute the program, authorization is performed both times, as seen in figure 9.11. In this particular case, you could also use `AspectPriority` setting and achieve the same result.

```
[Cached(AspectPriority = 20)]
[Authorized("Manager", AspectPriority = 10)]
public decimal GetBudgetForAccount(string accountNumber) {
    var rand = new Random();
    return rand.Next(1000, 5000);
}
```

So now we have the complete architecture defined. At this point, you could add more methods to the budget service interface, and more services, while keeping the cross cutting concern logic in separate, testable classes.

And because of this architecture, we easily switch over to Castle DynamicProxy.

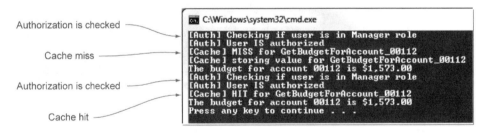

Figure 9.11 Execution, with authorization and caching composed correctly

9.4.3 *Castle DynamicProxy*

To do the same thing with Castle DynamicProxy, we only need to write two more thin aspects and one adapter class. Instead of using attributes, we'll use the IoC configuration to specify where the dynamic proxies will be used.

WRITE TWO NEW ASPECTS

The caching aspect will look similar to the PostSharp aspect. I'll call it Cached-Interceptor, and it will implement DynamicProxy's IInterceptor interface. I can use plain constructor injection on this class to get an ICachingConcern instance.

```
public class CachedInterceptor : IInterceptor {
    readonly ICachingConcern _cacheConcern;

    public CachedInterceptor(ICachingConcern cacheConcern) {    ◁─┐ Caching service
        _cacheConcern = cacheConcern;                                supplied with
    }                                                                dependency
                                                                     injection
                        ◁─── Implementation of IInterceptor here
}
```

Because this is an interception aspect and not a boundary aspect, the Intercept method in the next listing contains code that's a combination of the code in OnEntry and OnSuccess in the previous section.

Listing 9.28 DynamicProxy caching aspect Intercept code

```
public void Intercept(IInvocation invocation) {

        var methodContext = new CdpMethodContextAdapter(invocation);    ◁─┐ Using a
                                                                            Castle-
        _cacheConcern.OnEntry(methodContext);                               specific
Call                                                                        adapter
OnEntry      if (!methodContext.Proceed)         ◁─┐ If it's not okay to proceed,  object
first                                                return immediately
                return;                             without calling Proceed.

        invocation.Proceed();

        _cacheConcern.OnSuccess(methodContext);    ◁─── Call OnSuccess afterwards

}
```

I have to create that new adapter class, but this time it will wrap an IInvocation object.

Listing 9.29 Castle DynamicProxy method context adapter

```
public class CdpMethodContextAdapter : IMethodContextAdapter {
    readonly IInvocation _invocation;


    public CdpMethodContextAdapter(IInvocation invocation) {
        _invocation = invocation;
        Proceed = true;                    ◁─── Proceeding will occur by default
    }


    public bool Proceed { get; private set; }    ◁─┐ Proceed is not a member of
                                                      IMethodContextAdapter, so it's
                                                      specific to this implementation.
```

Interceptors have no need of a tag, so I'm using an autoproperty to simulate one. ┌─▷

```
public object Tag { get; set; }

public object ReturnValue {                          ◁─┐ Wrap the return
    get { return _invocation.ReturnValue; }             │ value property
    set { _invocation.ReturnValue = value; }
}

public string MethodName {                           ◁─┐ Wrap the
    get { return _invocation.Method.Name; }             │ method name
}

public object[] Arguments {                          ◁─┐ Wrap the
    get { return _invocation.Arguments; }               │ argument
}

public void AbortMethod() {                          ◁─┐ Aborting the method means
    Proceed = false;                                    │ that invocation.Proceed()
}                                                       │ shouldn't be called.
}
```

Similarly, I will create an `AuthorizedInterceptor` class, as shown next. This will also use constructor injection to get an `IAuthorizationConcern` instance, but it will also have a string parameter to specify the role (for example, `"Manager"`).

Listing 9.30 Constructor and members of the `Authorization` interceptor

```
public class AuthorizedInterceptor : IInterceptor {
    readonly IAuthorizationConcern _authConcern;
    readonly string _role;

    public AuthorizedInterceptor(
            IAuthorizationConcern authConcern, string role) {      ◁─┐
        _authConcern = authConcern;                    The concern and the role will be
                                                       resolved by the IoC container.
        _role = role;
    }
}
```

The `Intercept` body (listing 9.31) will be similar to the cache interceptor. Notice that the role is being passed as a second parameter to `OnEntry`. I did not make role a member of the method context adapter, since it's not method context, but it is information that the concern needs.

Listing 9.31 Authorization Intercept code

```
public void Intercept(IInvocation invocation) {
    var methodContext = new CdpMethodContextAdapter(invocation);
    _authConcern.OnEntry(methodContext, _role);        ◁─┐ Delegate everything to
    if (methodContext.Proceed)                            │ the concern object
        invocation.Proceed();        ◁─┐ Proceed is true
}                                       │ by default
```

REMOVE POSTSHARP ATTRIBUTES

If you're following along and using the same project files, the next thing you should do is make sure to remove the Cached and Authorized attributes from GetBudgetFor-Account.

```
public decimal GetBudgetForAccount(string accountNumber) {
    var rand = new Random();
    return rand.Next(1000, 5000);
}
```

Otherwise, you'll end up with authorization and caching being executed twice.

CHANGE IOC CONFIGURATION

With PostSharp, the IoC container was only used to initialize the services. With Castle DynamicProxy, we have to lean on it to apply the aspects as well.

Start with the same ObjectFactory.Initialize code as before. Now we need to tell StructureMap two things: (a) how to configure the authorized aspect for the "Manager" role, and (b) which aspects to use on BudgetService.

Once again, I'll be making use of the ProxyHelper to make StructureMap and Castle DynamicProxy get along. I'm going to add a new Proxify overload (in listing 9.32) that can work with named instances. In StructureMap, you can give mappings an arbitrary name, and if we want to use the authorization aspect for multiple roles (for example, Manager, Administrator, Editor, and so on), we'll need to do this. The only difference is that it takes an additional string parameter and uses GetNamedInstance instead of GetInstance.

> **Listing 9.32   Another Proxify overload in ProxyHelper**

```
public object Proxify<T, K>(
              string name, object obj) where K : IInterceptor {
    var interceptor =
          (IInterceptor)ObjectFactory.GetNamedInstance<K>(name);      ◁──┐
    var result = _proxyGenerator
                  .CreateInterfaceProxyWithTargetInterface(
                      typeof(T), obj, interceptor);          **Using**
    return result;                                    **GetNamedInstance is**
}                                                     **the only difference**
```

Once that's in place, we need to configure a named instance of Authorized-Interceptor that uses "Manager" as the role. Since the role is passed in to the constructor, we'll need to use StructureMap's ability to inline constructor dependencies, as shown in the next listing.

Listing 9.33   Name a mapping for `Manager` authorization

```
ObjectFactory.Initialize(x => {
    x.Scan(scan => {                              Same default
        scan.TheCallingAssembly();                conventions
        scan.WithDefaultConventions();
    });
                                                  Configure
    x.ForConcreteType<AuthorizedInterceptor>()    AuthorizedInterceptor...
        .Configure.Ctor<string>("role").Is("Manager")    ...to have it's constructor
        .Named("ManagerAuth");                            role parameter injected
                                                          with "Manager".
});
```

...and name this setup "ManagerAuth" → `.Named("ManagerAuth");`

From this point on, if I specify that the `"ManagerAuth"` named instance is used, then `AuthorizedInterceptor`'s role parameter will be `"Manager"`. I could create other named instances for other roles as well.

Finally, I'll just enrich the `IBudgetService` as we've done in previous chapters, this time using the new `Proxify` overload to handle the authorization aspect.

Take careful note of the order of the enrich statements in the following listing: caching needs to be the innermost aspect. This way, it is applied first, and we ensure that caching will be executed after authorization.

Listing 9.34   Complete IoC initialization

```
ObjectFactory.Initialize(x => {
    x.Scan(scan => {                              Same default
        scan.TheCallingAssembly();                conventions
        scan.WithDefaultConventions();
    });
                                                  Same named
    x.ForConcreteType<AuthorizedInterceptor>()    instance setup
        .Configure.Ctor<string>("role").Is("Manager")
        .Named("ManagerAuth");
                                                  When a budget
    var proxyHelper = new ProxyHelper();          service is
    x.For<IBudgetService>()                       requested...
        .EnrichAllWith(
            proxyHelper.Proxify<IBudgetService, CachedInterceptor>)
        .EnrichAllWith(o =>
            proxyHelper.Proxify<IBudgetService, AuthorizedInterceptor>
                            ("ManagerAuth", o));   I'm using the ManagerAuth
});                                                named instance.
```

Use a proxy helper → `var proxyHelper = new ProxyHelper();`

..use the new Proxify overload to help enrich.

Run the program, and you'll see the Console output (figure 9.12) is the same that we saw with PostSharp (figure 9.11).

Both projects are able to handle multiple complex aspects and complex dependencies while remaining testable and loosely coupled (the Castle DynamicProxy version is easier to test, of course, as we covered in chapter 6).

Authorization is checked

Cache miss

Authorization is checked

Cache hit

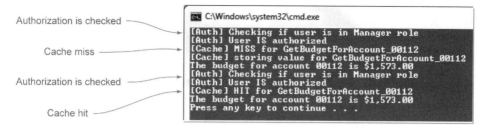

Figure 9.12   Execution with Auth and Cache aspects, using Castle DynamicProxy

9.5   *Summary*

Ordering is often important, and both runtime and compile-time AOP tools give you the ability to specify ordering. Runtime AOP will often rely on the IoC container to specify ordering (as well as for reuse). With PostSharp, using attributes alone in C# is not deterministic, so you have to specify the ordering through the PostSharp API. You can use a simple `AspectPriority` or the more robust aspect roles configuration options.

I've taken you through my personal journey, using the tools that I know the best and that I feel comfortable with. I like Castle DynamicProxy when writing basic aspects, provided I have the ability to intercept all the necessary objects via my IoC tool of choice (which is usually StructureMap). When the situation calls for more power, features, and flexibility, I like to use PostSharp as a compile-time AOP tool. Using a combination of the two in the same project is absolutely feasible, given their strengths and weaknesses.

I've explored AOP techniques and tools in this book, but there's so much more to explore in *your* personal journey. Use the tools and techniques that you like, that you feel comfortable with, and that enable you to write high-quality code.

appendix A
Ecosystem of
.NET AOP tools

The majority of this book focuses on two major general-purpose AOP tools for .NET: PostSharp and Castle DynamicProxy. I often paired Castle DynamicProxy with StructureMap, which is an IoC container. I also touched briefly on more specific-purpose tools, including NotifyPropertyWeaver, ASP.NET MVC ActionFilters, and ASP.NET HttpModules.

These are the tools I am most familiar and comfortable with, and that's why I chose them as the canvas on which to write about AOP. However, there are many tools in the .NET space that also allow you to write and use aspects. My intention is that this book will teach you how to use PostSharp and Castle DynamicProxy in-depth and help you explore the breadth of other tools.

This appendix is a crash course on tools that fit into two categories:

- *Compile-time AOP tools.* Like PostSharp, these tools make themselves part of the build process and modify the compiled CIL to perform weaving.
- *Runtime AOP tools.* Like Castle DynamicProxy, these tools generate decorators at runtime using Reflection, and they are usually closely related to an IoC tool (such as Castle Windsor).

For each tool, I'll give a very simple example of how to use it, much like the "Hello, World" aspect from chapter 1. My goal is to show you that even though the APIs change and features vary, the essentials of AOP are present in each tool. The intention of this appendix isn't to be an exhaustive list of every tool. Inclusion in this appendix does not mean that I endorse the tool; exclusion does not mean that I reject the tool.

I haven't used every tool to the same extent that I've used PostSharp and Castle DynamicProxy. Look at this appendix as the first step in a journey to find the tool or combination of tools that's right for you.

A.1   Compile-time AOP tools

A compile-time AOP tool uses a postcompiler to analyze the CIL created by the C#
compiler. These tools then make changes by directly manipulating the CIL. In this section, we'll examine some of the tools that belong to this family.

A.1.1   PostSharp

PostSharp is the tool I've spent the most time on in this book, so there's no need to say
much more about it here.

The stable release when most of this book was written was PostSharp 2.1, but Post-
Sharp 3 is now officially released. The focus of PostSharp 3 is to start putting more
emphasis on design pattern automation, which basically means that PostSharp will
emphasize prewritten aspects that are ready to be applied to your code. PostSharp
Ultimate is a major part of that: it has a collection of aspects that are ready to use in
your project. (They do require a commercial license of PostSharp to use.)

Although design pattern automation becomes the focus of the PostSharp product,
the ability to write your own aspects is still a major part of the product, and I don't
believe the need to write your own custom aspects will ever go away.

A.1.2   LinFu

LinFu is a library that contains many features, including dependency injection, mix-
ins, and AOP capabilities. LinFu is unique because it provides compile-time AOP capability as well as runtime AOP capability. So it's a "hybrid" AOP tool.

LinFu can be added from NuGet (`Install-Package LinFu.Core`). In the following listing I've created a familiar aspect example that writes to `Console` before and
after a method.

Listing A.1   Simple LinFu example

```
class Program {
    static void Main(string[] args) {
        var obj = new MyClass();

        var modifiableType = obj as IModifiableType;        ◁──┐  LinFu modifies a
                                                                │  class so that it
        if (modifiableType != null)                            │  implements this
            modifiableType.MethodBodyReplacementProvider       ┘  interface.
                = new SimpleMethodReplacementProvider(
                    new SampleInterceptor());         ◁──┐  A method body
        obj.DoStuff();                                    │  replacement uses
    }                                                     │  an interception
}                                                         ┘  aspect.

public class MyClass {
    public void DoStuff() {
        Console.WriteLine("Do stuff!");
    }
```

```
}
public class SampleInterceptor : IInterceptor {        ⊲──┐ Same name as Castle
    public object Intercept(IInvocationInfo info) {    ⊲──  DynamicProxy
        var methodName = info.TargetMethod.Name;           Same name as Castle
        Console.WriteLine("Before '{0}'", methodName);     DynamicProxy
        var result = info.TargetMethod
                          .Invoke(info.Target, info.Arguments);  ⊲──┐ There is no
        Console.WriteLine("After '{0}'", methodName);              Proceed; use a full
                                                                   Reflection Invoke.
        return result;
    }
}
```

Like Castle DynamicProxy, LinFu is meant to work with an IoC container (such as the LinFu IoC container).

Additionally, you have to make changes to your project file so that an MSBuild task runs the LinFu postcompiler after normal compilation. This listing shows an example of how that might look.

Listing A.2 Modifying project file to add `PostWeaveTask`

```
<PropertyGroup>
  <PostWeaveTaskLocation>
      $(MSBuildProjectDirectory)\$(OutputPath)..\..\..\
          packages\LinFu.Core.2.3.0.41559\lib\net35\LinFu.Core.dll    ⊲──
  </PostWeaveTaskLocation>
</PropertyGroup>                                          The DLL file where
<UsingTask TaskName="PostWeaveTask"                       the PostWeaveTask
          AssemblyFile="$(PostWeaveTaskLocation)" />          is located.
<Target Name="AfterBuild">
  <PostWeaveTask
      TargetFile="$(MSBuildProjectDirectory)\
                      $(OutputPath)$(MSBuildProjectName).dll"    ⊲──
      InterceptAllExceptions="false"
      InterceptAllFields="false"                       The DLL that the
      InterceptAllNewInstances="false"                 PostWeaveTask will
      InterceptAllMethodCalls="false"                       modify
      InterceptAllMethodBodies="true" />    ⊲──  Only intercept method
</Target>                                          bodies in this example.
```

Name the task for MSBuild ⊳

Once that `AfterBuild` task is in place, running the program should give you a `Console` output such as this:

```
C:\Windows\system32\cmd.exe
Before DoStuff
Do stuff!
After DoStuff
Press any key to continue . . .
```

On the plus side, LinFu is free and open source and available on GitHub. However, LinFu's documentation is somewhat limited. There is example code in blog posts and the GitHub repository. The LinFu project has a lot of potential, but at the time of this writing, according to GitHub, the LinFu source code hasn't been updated in a year, and there are outstanding issues from almost a year ago that have not been addressed.

But because it is an open source project, it's definitely worth checking out if you are interested in learning more about the details of postcompile weaving. LinFu appears to use both Mono.Cecil and Microsoft.Cci, both of which are briefly discussed later in this appendix.

A.1.3   SheepAspect

SheepAspect is inspired by AspectJ for Java. It is something of a newcomer to AOP in .NET. It's an open source project that has appeared within the last year and has made positive strides in the area of features and documentation in a short time.

With SheepAspect, you define everything together in a single class, including pointcut and advice. A pointcut is defined by creating an empty method which will have one or more attributes that specify the pointcut. Another method is defined that contains the advice. This method is tied to the pointcut via another attribute.

Add SheepAspect to a new `Console` project with NuGet (`Install-Package SheepAspect`). The NuGet installation will automatically make changes to your project so that the postweaving task will run. For the next listing I've written what should be a familiar example at this point: a very basic aspect that writes to `Console` before and after a method.

Listing A.3   Simple SheepAspect example

```
class Program {
    static void Main(string[] args) {
        var obj = new MyClass();
        obj.DoStuff();
    }
}
public class MyClass {
    public void DoStuff() {
        Console.WriteLine("Do stuff!");
    }
}
[Aspect]
public class MyAspect {
    [SelectMethods("Public & InType: 'SheepAspectExample.MyClass'")]
    public void MyPointcut() {}
```

This pointcut specified public member methods of MyClass.

Attribute that indicates this class is an aspect.

An empty method names the pointcut

Use the pointcut method name for an Around advice

```
[Around("MyPointcut")]
public void MyAdvice(MethodJointPoint jp) {
    Console.WriteLine("Before {0}", jp.Method.Name);
    jp.Execute();
    Console.WriteLine("After {0}", jp.Method.Name);
}
}
```

MethodJointPoint contains method context information

The console output of that program is what you would probably expect:

```
C:\Windows\system32\cmd.exe
Before DoStuff
Do stuff!
After DoStuff
Press any key to continue . . .
```

In the `SelectMethod` attribute, the string argument consists of SAQL, the SheepAop Query Language. This is the most intriguing feature of SheepAspect, because it gives you a lot of options and control in defining pointcuts.

This tool is very promising, and if it keeps up the rate of development and documentation, it is definitely a tool to keep an eye on. It's currently classified as an alpha release.

SheepAspect uses the Mono.Cecil library to perform CIL manipulation, which is one of several CIL manipulation tools available.

A.1.4   Fody

Fody is a compile-time tool that is more general purpose, but it warrants including in this appendix. Fody isn't referred to as an AOP tool; instead it's called an extensible tool for weaving .NET assemblies. That certainly includes the ability to write aspects or at least aspect-like functionality. Fody's strength lies with its extensibility and its flexibility.

Like PostSharp Ultimate's ready-made aspects, Fody takes a modular approach to introducing functionality. Along with the core Fody framework, you also install one (or more) add-ins, that provide functionality through CIL manipulation. There are 25 add-ins with functionality, much the same as what we've covered in this book, including `PropertyChanged` (for `INotifyPropertyChanged`), `Virtuosity` (changes all members to virtual, which could be helpful with NHibernate or other tools that rely on Castle DynamicProxy), and `NullGuard` (defensive programming).

For more general-purpose AOP, you can also use a plugin like `MethodDecorator`, which gives you a way to write method boundary aspects. Install with NuGet (`Install-Package MethodDecorator.Fody`). The NuGet install will modify your project and add a few files to it, and you'll be ready to go.

Listing A.4   Simple MethodDecorator example

```
namespace FodyExample {
    class Program {
        static void Main(string[] args) {
            var obj = new MyClass();
            obj.DoStuff();
        }
    }

    public class MyClass {
        [Interceptor]
        public void DoStuff() {
            Console.WriteLine("Do stuff!");
        }
    }
}

public interface IMethodDecorator {
    void OnEntry(MethodBase method);
    void OnExit(MethodBase method);
    void OnException(MethodBase method, Exception exception);
}

[AttributeUsage(AttributeTargets.Method | AttributeTargets.Constructor)]
public class InterceptorAttribute : Attribute, IMethodDecorator {
    public void OnEntry(MethodBase method) {
        Console.WriteLine("Before {0}", method.Name);
    }

    public void OnExit(MethodBase method) {
        Console.WriteLine("After {0}", method.Name);
    }

    public void OnException(MethodBase method, Exception exception) { }
}
```

> **An attribute is applied, just like PostSharp.**

> **Pay careful attention to namespace usage.**

> **By convention, this is the interface you need to write.**

Additionally, there are other plugins that aren't strictly AOP-related, but they are useful bits of functionality that can make coding easier. An add-in called Scalpel removes tests from an assembly, which could be useful when building deployment packages. Another add-in called Stamp automatically adds git information to an assembly's AssemblyInformationVersion. This flexibility that Fody brings allows you to accomplish a variety of tasks outside of the normal realm of AOP.

Of course, Fody's extensibility means that you can write your own add-ins. Writing these plugins can be more difficult than writing aspects, because you often have to use Mono.Cecil, work with CIL op codes, and make sure that the resulting assembly is valid (with a tool like PEVerify).

Fody is an open source project that is being actively maintained, and is principally authored by Simon Cropp (who also created the NotifyPropertyWeaver tool that was mentioned in chapter 5). Like NotifyPropertyWeaver, Fody tends to rely on convention over configuration, which works well when the conventions are clear. Although this tool is less than a year old, it is still quite impressive, well documented, and definitely worth exploring.

A.1.5 *CIL manipulation tools*

If you want to write your own CIL-manipulating AOP framework, then you might consider using one of the following existing CIL manipulation libraries. Use of these libraries requires a thorough knowledge of CIL; they are for very advanced development. Additionally, documentation is often scant, and there are few practical examples available.

MONO.CECIL

Cecil is part of the Mono project, which is an open source implementation of the .NET framework. Cecil allows you to examine and modify .NET assemblies. It is free, and has been used by a few open-source AOP frameworks (including SheepAspect).

POSTSHARP SDK

The main PostSharp library is called PostSharp.dll, which is what we used throughout this book. This is a library that contains base classes and other API elements that you need to build and use aspects.

Another library, PostSharp.Sdk.dll, is essentially the internal API that the PostSharp tool uses to perform the CIL manipulation necessary to apply aspects. This library is not supported and not documented (publicly). It is available only because a very small number of PostSharp users need it, and have the necessary expertise in CIL to use it.

MICROSOFT CCI

The Microsoft Common Compiler Infrastructure (CCI) is a set of tools from Microsoft that provide you with the ability to analyze and modify .NET assemblies. These projects are available on CodePlex, but the documentation hasn't been updated in about two years (at the time of writing this book). Other metaprogramming/compiler-related projects such as Phoenix and Roslyn have also been created by Microsoft, but these are tangentially related to AOP.

One last note about CIL manipulation in general: its functionality is not limited to AOP and can be used for other tasks. For instance, NCover, a test coverage tool for .NET, uses CIL manipulation to do its instrumentation.

A.2 *Runtime AOP tools*

Runtime AOP tools create decorator/proxy classes dynamically at runtime. These classes are built by examining the signature of classes/interfaces along with an interception aspect that you've written, then generate a decorator class. Typically, these tools are part of IoC containers, as such containers allow you to use these generated classes transparently.

My goal in this appendix isn't to comprehensively document and explore these IoC tools, but to show a basic demonstration of their interception capabilities. If you want to learn more about IoC, Dependency Inversion, and DI, I recommend picking up *Dependency Injection in .NET* by Mark Seeman (Manning, 2011).

A.2.1 Castle Windsor/DynamicProxy

Castle DynamicProxy is the name of the AOP tool that was originally created to work with Castle Windsor (an IoC tool). Castle is a project with a collection of frameworks and tools for building enterprise applications in .NET. I've shown you several examples throughout the book of Castle DynamicProxy with StructureMap. The next listing shows how you might use it with Castle Windsor (which isn't remarkably different from using it with StructureMap, except that there is no need for a `ProxyHelper` class). The listing is a Console application; I've installed Castle Windsor with NuGet (`Install-Package Castle.Windsor`), which will install Castle.Core automatically.

Listing A.5 A basic Castle Windsor and DynamicProxy example

```
class Program {
    static void Main(string[] args) {
        var container = new WindsorContainer();          ◁── Create a Windsor container
        container.Register(Component.For<MyInterceptor>()
                    .Register(Component.For<IMyClass>()
                    .ImplementedBy<MyClass>()             ◁── Register the service class
                    .Interceptors<MyInterceptor>()));     ◁
        var obj = container.Resolve<IMyClass>();                Specify the interceptor
        obj.DoStuff();                                          for the service class
    }
}
public interface IMyClass {
    void DoStuff();
}
public class MyClass : IMyClass {
    public void DoStuff() {
        Console.WriteLine("Stuff");
    }
}
public class MyInterceptor : IInterceptor {               ◁── Standard Castle
    public void Intercept(IInvocation invocation) {            DynamicProxy interceptor
        Console.WriteLine("Before {0}", invocation.Method.Name);   aspect
        invocation.Proceed();
        Console.WriteLine("Before {0}", invocation.Method.Name);
    }
}
```

Register the aspect

The entire Castle project umbrella—including Windsor, DynamicProxy, and Mono-Rail—has been one of the cornerstones of open source tools and frameworks for .NET since 2004. It is a popular and widely used set of tools, with a very active support and development community.

A.2.2 StructureMap

I used StructureMap throughout this book, and its EnrichWith functionality combined with Castle DynamicProxy has been covered. It's certainly possible to use other AOP tools as well. But StructureMap does not contain any AOP capabilities itself. To quote the StructureMap documentation: "StructureMap will never include its own Aspect Oriented Programming model (the world does not need a new one)."

However, StructureMap does have its own interception capability. Its unique approach to interception is worth discussing in this appendix. StructureMap intercepts the object itself, instead of generating a decorator class, and allows you to manipulate the object. You do this by implementing the InstanceInterceptor interface, as shown in the next listing. This interface contains one method—Process—that receives the object as an argument, and returns the object, giving you a chance to manipulate, examine, or wrap the object.

Listing A.6 StructureMap interception

```
class Program {
    static void Main(string[] args) {
        ObjectFactory.Initialize(x => {
            x.Scan(scan => {
                    scan.TheCallingAssembly();
                    scan.WithDefaultConventions();
                });
            x.For<IMyClass>().InterceptWith(new MyInterceptor());    ◁⎯⎯  InterceptWith used in initialization
        });

        var obj = ObjectFactory.GetInstance<IMyClass>();
        obj.DoStuff();
    }
}
public class MyInterceptor : InstanceInterceptor {   ◁⎯  Interceptor implements InstanceInterceptor.
    public object Process(object target, IContext context) {
        Console.WriteLine("Intercepting {0}", target.GetType().Name);   ◁⎯  Write a message to console about the instance's Type.
        return target;   ◁⎯  Return the object unchanged
    }
}
public interface IMyClass {
    void DoStuff();
}

public class MyClass : IMyClass {
    public void DoStuff() {
        Console.WriteLine("Do stuff!");
    }
}
```

The console output is different than the other example in this appendix, because it is intercepting an object instead of method call(s):

```
C:\Windows\system32\cmd.exe
Intercepting MyClass
Do stuff!
Press any key to continue . . .
```

You could also use Castle DynamicProxy within an `InstanceInterceptor` as an alternative to using a `ProxyHelper` class. I've found that it takes roughly the same amount of effort, depending on how heavy your usage of aspects is, whether custom conventions are being used, and so on.

A.2.3   *Unity*

The Unity Interception Extension (installed with NuGet with `Install-Package Unity.Interception`) is a component that is an extension of Unity (also known as the Unity Application Block). This component gives AOP interception capabilities to the core Unity functionality. Unity is an IoC container created by Microsoft with an emphasis on configurability and extension for building enterprise software. With Unity, aspects implement the `IInterceptionBehavior` interface. This interface has an `Invoke` method that is analogous to Castle DynamicProxy's `Intercept` method.

There are two other members of this interface. `GetRequiredInterfaces` returns a list of interfaces that you want the dynamically created proxy object to implement (`INotifyPropertyChanged`, for instance, would be a good candidate for this). `WillExecute` is for optimization: if it returns false, then the interceptor will be skipped. The aspect in this listing does not use these capabilities.

Listing A.7   Unity interception example

```
class Program {
    static void Main(string[] args) {
        var container = new UnityContainer()           // Interception is an
            .AddNewExtension<Interception>()            // extension, and
            .RegisterType<IMyClass, MyClass>(          // must be explicitly
                new Interceptor<InterfaceInterceptor>(),  // added
                new InterceptionBehavior<MyAspect>());    // Use interface
                                                          // interception, so
        var obj = container.Resolve<IMyClass>();          // virtual members
        obj.DoStuff();                                    // are not required
    }
}                                                    // Specify the aspect to use

public class MyAspect : IInterceptionBehavior {
    public IMethodReturn Invoke(
                IMethodInvocation input,
                GetNextInterceptionBehaviorDelegate getNext) {
        Console.WriteLine("Before {0}", input.MethodBase.Name);
        var returnValue = getNext().Invoke(input, getNext);
        Console.WriteLine("After {0}", input.MethodBase.Name);
```

```
            return returnValue;
        }

        public IEnumerable<Type> GetRequiredInterfaces() {      No
            return Type.EmptyTypes;                             interfaces
        }                                                       are added

        public bool WillExecute { get { return true; } }      This aspect
    }                                                          will always
    public interface IMyClass {                                execute.
        void DoStuff();
    }

    public class MyClass : IMyClass {
        public void DoStuff() {
            Console.WriteLine("Do stuff!");
        }
    }
```

The output, once again to `Console`, is the same as other examples in this appendix:

The Unity framework is both open source and backed by Microsoft, and thus it is widely used. It is still under active development, with a .NET 4.5 preview available at the time of writing.

A.2.4 *Spring.NET*

Spring.NET is a framework based on the popular Spring framework for Java. It contains a number of features for building enterprise applications (much like Castle Windsor), including Spring.Core (DI) and Spring.Aop (runtime AOP). Spring.NET tends to use XML for configuration of everything, so that's what I'm going to use in this appendix, but Spring.CodeConfig allows you to configure in C# instead of XML if you wish.

Install Spring's AOP functionality with NuGet (`Install-Package Spring.Aop`). This listing shows an aspect that implements the `IMethodInterceptor` interface, which just has one member: `Invoke`.

Listing A.8   Spring.NET example

```
class Program {                                          Context is
    static void Main(string[] args) {                    configured
        var context = ContextRegistry.GetContext();      by XML
        var obj = (IMyClass)context.GetObject("MyClass");
```

```
            obj.DoStuff();
        }
    }

    public class MyAspect : IMethodInterceptor {
        public object Invoke(IMethodInvocation invocation) {
            Console.WriteLine("Before {0}", invocation.Method.Name);
            object returnValue = invocation.Proceed();
            Console.WriteLine("After {0}", invocation.Method.Name);
            return returnValue;
        }
    }

    public interface IMyClass {
        void DoStuff();
    }

    public class MyClass : IMyClass {
        public void DoStuff() {
            Console.WriteLine("Do stuff!");
        }
    }
```

> **Aspect implements IMethodInterceptor interface**

> **IMethodInvocation contains method context information**

In a Console project, the Spring configuration will be in app.config, as in the next listing. In an ASP.NET project, it would be in Web.config instead.

Listing A.9 Spring.NET configuration

```xml
<configuration>
  <configSections>
    <sectionGroup name="spring">
      <section name="context"
        type="Spring.Context.Support.ContextHandler, Spring.Core"/>
      <section name="objects"
        type="Spring.Context.Support.DefaultSectionHandler,
                                        Spring.Core" />
    </sectionGroup>
  </configSections>
  <spring>
    <context>
      <resource uri="config://spring/objects"/>
    </context>
    <objects xmlns="http://www.springframework.net">
      <object id="myAspect" type="SpringNetExample.MyAspect"/>
      <object id="MyClass"
              type="Spring.Aop.Framework.ProxyFactoryObject">
        <property name="target">
          <object id="MyClassTarget"
                  type="SpringNetExample.MyClass"/>
        </property>
        <property name="interceptorNames">
          <list>
            <value>myAspect</value>
          </list>
        </property>
      </object>
```

> **Basic Spring configuration**

> **Define an aspect**

> **Define a dynamic proxy object**

> **The target of the proxy**

> **The aspect used in the proxy**

```
      </objects>
   </spring>
</configuration>
```

Besides interception aspects, Spring.NET has boundary aspects (`IMethodBefore-Advice`, `IAfterReturningAdvice`, and `IThrowsAdvice`). Beyond the simple mapping in this configuration, Spring.NET also has more complex configuration options, including regular expressions and dynamic pointcuts (akin to attribute multicasting as seen with PostSharp in chapter 8).

appendix B
NuGet basics

Because I use NuGet for all the demos and examples in this book, I thought it would be a good idea to go over the basics of NuGet for those who aren't familiar with it. NuGet is a tool that has fundamentally changed the way I install, update, and use third-party libraries when writing .NET projects. It's become one of those "how did I ever get anything done without it?" tools.

In this appendix I'll show you how to install NuGet (if you are using Visual Studio 2012, then you already have it installed). Then I'll show you how to use it to install packages, then how package restore works. I'm not going to attempt to document every feature of NuGet—just enough to get by in this book. Comprehensive NuGet documentation (including how to build your own packages and how to run private NuGet servers) is available at NuGet.org.

B.1 *Introduction to NuGet*

NuGet is an open source package manager for .NET that used to be known as NuPack. NuGet was created by a team at Microsoft and was contributed to the Outercurve Foundation. It has become the de facto package manager tool for .NET and is currently integrated with Visual Studio 2012.

B.1.1   Installing NuGet

If you don't already have NuGet, there are just a few easy steps to install it. First, you are required to have PowerShell installed. If you are running Windows 7 or later, you already have it, otherwise you'll need to manually install PowerShell. Second, go to NuGet.org and click the Install NuGet button to download the VSIX (Visual Studio extension) file, as shown in figure B.1. Open that file, and you will be taken through the installation process. Administrator access is required.

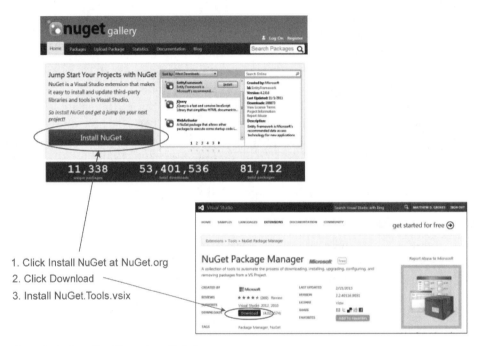

1. Click Install NuGet at NuGet.org
2. Click Download
3. Install NuGet.Tools.vsix

Figure B.1   Installing Nuget from NuGet.org

Alternatively, you can install it right from Visual Studio's extension manager (Tools -> Extension Manager), as in figure B.2. Again, administrator access is required.

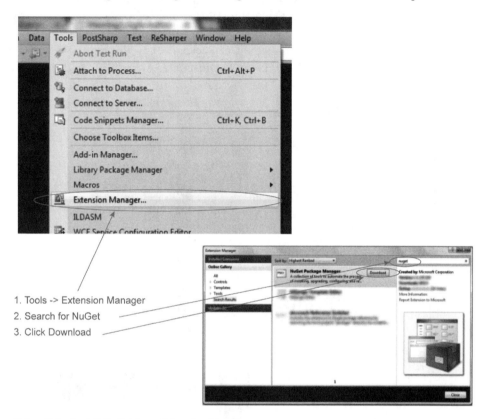

1. Tools -> Extension Manager
2. Search for NuGet
3. Click Download

Figure B.2   Install NuGet from Extension Manager

B.1.2   *Installing packages with NuGet UI*

There are two primary ways to install NuGet packages while in Visual Studio: you can use the NuGet UI, or you can type commands at the NuGet Package Manager Console.

To use the NuGet UI as show in figure B.3, right-click a project's References in the Solution Explorer. Click Manage NuGet Packages. Use the search box to search for keywords or a specific package name. For instance, you could search for NHibernate or for ORM. Once you've found the package you want, click the Install button.

Figure B.3   Installing a package with the NuGet UI

If the package you are installing has dependencies on other packages, NuGet will also install those. For instance, the Fluent NHibernate package has a dependency on NHibernate, so if I install Fluent NHibernate, it will check to make sure that NHibernate is already installed, and install it if it's not.

You can also see a list of packages that you've already installed and update/uninstall them. Packages are installed to a Packages folder that NuGet creates. NuGet also creates repositories.config and packages.config files that tell your project where to find the dependencies (as well as how to restore them, as you'll see later).

B.1.3 *Install packages with Package Manager Console*

Once NuGet is installed, you will have a new window available in Visual Studio called the Package Manager Console. To show this window, click View -> Other Windows -> Package Manager Console. As in figure B.4, you will then see a PowerShell window with a PM> prompt where you can type in commands.

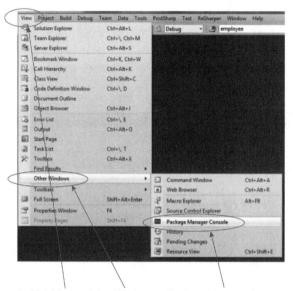

1. Click View -> Other Windows -> Package Manager Console

2. Window with PM> prompt appears

Figure B.4   Opening the Package Manager Console

At this command prompt, you can get a list of commands by typing get-Help NuGet. To install a package, use the Install-Package command, with the name of the package. If you aren't sure of the spelling, you can use the Tab key to get intellisense. For instance, if I type Install-Package PostS then press Tab, I'll see a list of suggestions, starting with PostSharp.

Once a package installs, you should see a message like the following:

```
PM> Install-Package jQuery
Successfully installed 'jQuery 1.9.1'.
Successfully added 'jQuery 1.9.1' to HelloWorld.
```

After that, another PM> prompt will appear for further commands.

B.2   *NuGet package restore*

NuGet has a very convenient feature called package restore that allows you to restore a package from a NuGet repository automatically. If the actual DLL and associated files of a package are not checked into source control, for instance, NuGet will notice that the files are missing and attempt to restore them when you try to compile.

B.2.1   *Solution Explorer*

By default, Visual Studio 2010's Solution Explorer only lists the solution if there are multiple projects in the solution. To change that behavior so that it always shows the solution, go to Tools -> Options -> Projects and Solutions -> General, and check the Always show solution box, as in figure B.5.

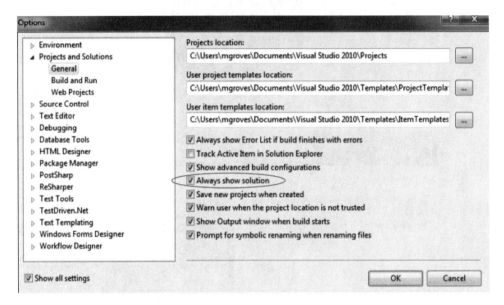

Figure B.5   Always show solution in Visual Studio

Once you do this, then you can more easily access the solution settings in Solution Explorer.

B.2.2   *Enabling package restore*

Now that you have the solution showing, right-click the solution in Solution Explorer and click Enable NuGet package restore (as in figure B.6). This will add a .nuget folder to your solution that contains NuGet.Config, NuGet.exe, and NuGet.targets.

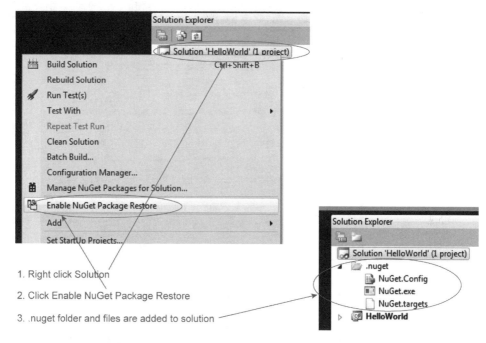

Figure B.6 Enabling package restore feature

At this point, NuGet package restore is now enabled for your solution. I have enabled it on all the source code samples available for this book. Therefore, the .nuget folder is in source control (GitHub), but not the packages themselves.

B.2.3 *What package restore does*

Try this: install a package in your project using NuGet, then enable NuGet Package Restore, close Visual Studio, and then delete the package from the packages folder. When you open the solution in Visual Studio again and try to compile, you will get an error, because the package files that your project depends on have been deleted.

NuGet Package restore can fix this problem. In Visual Studio, go to Tools -> Options -> Package Manager and check Allow NuGet to download missing packages during build (as in figure B.7). This does exactly what it sounds like. When you try to compile, NuGet will notice that a package is missing and attempt to download the missing package files. Once NuGet is finished restoring the package, the build process will continue as normal.

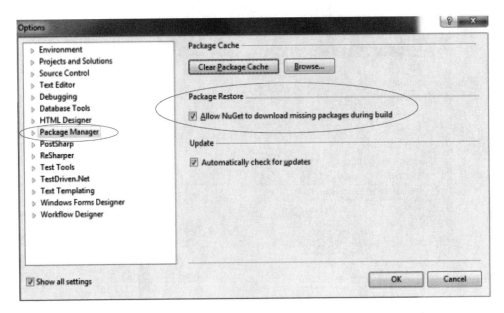

Figure B.7 Enabling downloading of missing packages

This step allows you to commit everything except the package binaries to source control. Binaries can be very large, and keeping them in source control can make using a distributed version control system more difficult. The source code samples for this book, for instance, would be several hundred megabytes bigger. Using NuGet's package restore with the samples is like lazy loading the packages: you don't actually need them until you start compiling.

index